VCP-Cloud
Official Cert Guide

VMware Press is the official publisher of VMware books and training materials, which provide guidance on the critical topics facing today's technology professionals and students. Enterprises, as well as small- and medium-sized organizations, adopt virtualization as a more agile way of scaling IT to meet business needs. VMware Press provides proven, technically accurate information that will help them meet their goals for customizing, building, and maintaining their virtual environment.

With books, certification and study guides, video training, and learning tools produced by world-class architects and IT experts, VMware Press helps IT professionals master a diverse range of topics on virtualization and cloud computing. It is the official source of reference materials for preparing for the VMware Certified Professional Examination.

VMware Press is also pleased to have localization partners that can publish its products into more than 42 languages, including Chinese (Simplified), Chinese (Traditional), French, German, Greek, Hindi, Japanese, Korean, Polish, Russian, and Spanish.

For more information about VMware Press, visit **vmwarepress.com**.

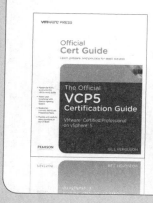

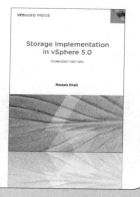

VCP-Cloud
Official Cert Guide

Tom Ralph
Nathan Raper

vmware® PRESS

Upper Saddle River, NJ • Boston • Indianapolis • San Francisco
New York • Toronto • Montreal • London • Munich • Paris • Madrid
Capetown • Sydney • Tokyo • Singapore • Mexico City

VCP-Cloud Official Cert Guide

Warning and Disclaimer

Corporate and Government Sales

VMware Press offers excellent discounts on this book when ordered in quantity for bulk purchases or special sales, which may include electronic versions and/or custom covers and content particular to your business, training goals, marketing focus, and branding interests. For more information, please contact

U.S. Corporate and Government Sales
(800) 382-3419
corpsales@pearsontechgroup.com

For sales outside the United States, please contact:
International Sales
international@pearsoned.com

ASSOCIATE PUBLISHER
David Dusthimer

ACQUISITIONS EDITOR
Joan Murray

VMWARE PRESS PROGRAM MANAGERS
Erik Ullanderson
Anand Sundaram

DEVELOPMENT EDITOR
Ellie Bru

MANAGING EDITOR
Sandra Schroeder

SENIOR PROJECT EDITOR
Tonya Simpson

COPY EDITOR
Megan Wade-Taxter

INDEXER
WordWise Publishing Services

PROOFREADER
Anne Goebel

COORDINATOR
Vanessa Evans

BOOK DESIGNER
Chuti Prasertsith

COMPOSITION
TnT Design, Inc.

Contents at a Glance

Table of Contents

About the Authors

Tom Ralph is a senior cloud services architect at VMware. He is a senior member of VMware Global Services organization and has worked for VMware for more than 2 years. Prior to joining VMware, he worked for Catholic Health Initiatives in Denver, Colorado.

He is certified as a VMware Certified Design Expert (VCDX 3, 4, and 5), VMware Certified Advanced Professional (4 and 5)-DCD, VCP (3, 4, and 5), VCP5-Cloud, CISSP, CCSK, MCSE: Messaging, MCITP: Enterprise, and ITIL Foundations.

When VMware started to build a cloud team to deliver vCloud, he was one of the first members to be recruited from outside of VMware. Tom has become an expert in this field and delivered several vCloud seminars and troubleshooting workshops at various VMware public events in the United States and around the world.

Tom lives in Colorado with his wife and daughters and can be found on Twitter at @tomralph.

Nathan Raper is a highly skilled IT professional with 15 years of experience designing, engineering, administering, and supporting physical and virtual infrastructures. He has worked as both a customer and a consultant, participating in all phases of engagement–sales, design, engineering, implementation, training, and support. An early believer in VMware solutions, Nate began server consolidations on the VMware ESX Server 1.5 platform and earned his first VMware certification (VCP2 #306) in early 2004. Following tours with customers and a VMware/EMC/Cisco partner, Nate now works for the VMware Global Center of Excellence (CoE) with several of his VCDX peers.

Nate lives in Colorado with his extraordinarily patient wife and his three adorable children. You can find him on Twitter at @nateraper and on LinkedIn at www.linkedin.com/pub/nathan-raper/8/934/b41/.

Dedication

This book is dedicated to our wives. Crystal and Joelle, thank you so much for standing by us and supporting us during this incredibly arduous process. This book was more work than we anticipated and required many late nights and long weekends to complete. We couldn't have done it without your support. THANK YOU!

Acknowledgments

First, thank you to Joan Murray, who tried to explain the amount of work a book is to complete and for giving us the chance to write this book. I am very grateful that we met and chatted at VMworld in San Francisco. Thank you to Ellie Bru, who supported shuffling chapters back and forth and the logistics of getting this book edited. Joan and Ellie, thank you both for supporting a couple of new authors who didn't quite know what they were doing at times.

We would also like to thank our technical editors, Jon Hall, Todd Simmons, and Matt Vandenbeld. Being a technical editor is not an easy job, and we thank you for your expertise and timely reviews of the material.

Thank you to Anees Iqbal, who allowed Tom to take time off to complete the book, and to Jim de la Pena and the rest of Nate's team at MSN, who understood why he couldn't use nights and weekends to supplement the requirements of his day job.

Finally, we would like to acknowledge all those family and friends who prayed for the completion of this book, so that we could return to seeing them on the weekends.

It takes more than we realized to take a book from idea to completion, and without all of your input, advice, and expertise, this book would still be something that we "wanted to do." You all have certainly made it possible.

Thank you,

Tom and Nate

About the Reviewers

Jon Hall is currently a senior technical certification developer with VMware. In 2005, Jon joined VMware as an instructor, teaching classes on VMware technologies across the globe. Three years later, Jon joined the certification team. While continuing to teach, Jon began developing exams and worked to grow VMware's certification program to cover VMware's cloud, end-user computing, and network virtualization technologies. Jon is a VMware Certified Instructor (VCI) and a VMware Certified Advanced Professional in multiple disciplines.

Todd Simmons is currently a consultant at Training Revolution and spends the majority of his time on contract assignments for VCE, EMC, and VMware. Todd began his technology career in 1997 as a Microsoft Exchange administrator for Renaissance Worldwide, Inc. In 1998, Todd began teaching night classes as a Microsoft Certified Trainer for Boston University. In 2003, he was hired by Collective Technologies in Austin, Texas as a senior consultant and then as the practice technical manager for the Active Directory and Exchange Professional Services Team. There, he performed large-seat Exchange migrations and VMware implementations and authored several Professional Services. Since 2007, Todd has been working on contract for EMC Engineering. He has authored and coauthored multiple instructor-led courses and delivered training for VCE partners and employees. Todd maintains several industry certifications including, but not limited to, VMware Certified Professional – Cloud, VCI, VCP2, VCP3, VCP4, VCP5, VCAP-DCA, VCAP-DCD, Microsoft Certified Trainer, Microsoft Certified Systems Engineer (Messaging), Cisco Data Center Support for UC Specialist, and EMC Proven Professional CLARiiON Expert.

Matt Vandenbeld is a technical architect with Long View Systems in Calgary, Alberta, Canada, specializing in delivering cloud and virtualization on converged infrastructure. Matt was an early VMware virtualization adopter and has been very passionate about it ever since. He currently works with all size clients, from SMB to enterprise, designing and implementing virtualization and cloud solutions. Matt, or "Cloudmatt," is also active in the VMware community; he maintains a blog at www.cloudmatt.com, blogs for trainsignal.com, participates in many vBrownBag sessions, and is usually involved in various discussions on Twitter. Along with his VCDX, Matt holds numerous industry certifications, including certifications from Cisco, NetApp, Red Hat, and others. Matt is an active member of the VCDX community as well as demonstrating the skills the certification highlights.

We Want to Hear from You!

As the reader of this book, *you* are our most important critic and commentator. We value your opinion and want to know what we're doing right, what we could do better, what areas you'd like to see us publish in, and any other words of wisdom you're willing to pass our way.

We welcome your comments. You can email or write us directly to let us know what you did or didn't like about this book—as well as what we can do to make our books better.

Please note that we cannot help you with technical problems related to the topic of this book.

When you write, please be sure to include this book's title and author as well as your name, email address, and phone number. We will carefully review your comments and share them with the author and editors who worked on the book.

Email: VMwarePress@vmware.com

Mail: VMware Press
         ATTN: Reader Feedback
         800 East 96th Street
         Indianapolis, IN 46240 USA

Reader Services

Visit our website and register this book at www.informit.com/title/9780789750273 for convenient access to any updates, downloads, or errata that might be available for this book.

Introduction

The value of certification in the IT industry cannot be overstated. Love them or hate them, certifications and their associated exams are required if you want to prove your knowledge and excel in IT. For individuals that love to learn and challenge themselves, certification exams can become somewhat of an addiction. For those that hate them, these exams are tedious and annoying—but necessary nonetheless.

Employers look for candidates with experience, but they also expect potential employees to have proven their experience and knowledge by obtaining certifications. And if you work for a VMware (or other manufacturer) partner, you will be required to pass many certification exams for your employer. VMware vSphere is technology that is widely used in data centers throughout the world, and the VMware Certified Professional (VCP) certification is considered by many to be required for consideration by a potential employer.

The VCP certification has evolved over the past decade from being a niche offering mostly for VMware partners to being one of the most popular and desired vendor certifications in the IT industry. As VMware and their products have grown and expanded, so too have the certifications which they offer, including basic (VCP), advanced (VCAP), and expert (VCDX) level certifications. VMware now offers certifications in core vSphere data center virtualization, Horizon View desktop virtualization, and cloud infrastructure. This book covers the entry-level exam for the Cloud Infrastructure path, VCP-Cloud.

The VCP-Cloud certification is emerging as an up-and-coming offering from VMware. It is a certification that expands on core VMware vSphere knowledge to include vCloud Director, vCloud Connector, vCloud Networking and Security, and vCenter Chargeback concepts. If you are currently working with VMware's vSphere product line, then you understand that the transition to the VMware software-defined data center (SDDC) will include vCloud Director, and in that transition this certification will be valuable for you. We expect that the VCP certification will either be replaced by VCP-Cloud or will incorporate core vCloud knowledge in the near future as VMware moves away from core virtualization to SDDCs.

Whether you are just starting out in the IT field, are new to VMware certification, or are moving into the data center space, the VCP5-Cloud certification will give you a solid foundation in virtual environments and emerging technologies such as vCloud Director. IT veterans and new VMware administrators alike will benefit from this book and gain the knowledge necessary to achieve VCP-Cloud certification.

Who Should Read This Book?

This book is for anyone who wants to learn about VMware vCloud Director and associated technologies, and is written especially for those that plan on taking the VCP–VMware Infrastructure as a Service (IaaS) exam. We wrote this book to augment your skills and knowledge of VMware vSphere with vCloud Director and its associated products and to fill any knowledge gaps in preparation for your VCP-IaaS exam.

This book is aimed particularly at administrators who hold the VCP-DCV certification. The core VCP certification was rebranded in 2013 as VMware Certified Professional – Data Center Virtualization (VCP-DCV) and is required to schedule the VCP-IaaS exam. Passing both exams earns you the VCP-Cloud certification. For those who do not hold the VCP-DCV certification, this book should be supplemented with *The Official VCP5 Certification Guide* by Bill Ferguson to prepare you for the VCP-Cloud exam.

Goals and Methods

Our goal in writing this book is to help you prepare for the VCP-IaaS or VCP-Cloud exam. It is intended to be a basic, 100-level introduction to the concepts of vCloud Director and its accompanying technologies. It is *not* intended to be an exhaustive treatise or deep-dive design guide on these subjects. As such, you might find detail lacking in certain areas or find that you wish to learn more. In such cases, we encourage you to review the full product documentation and the vCloud Architecture Toolkit, as well as seek out blog posts and information from the community.

While writing this book, we adhered to the current IaaS and VCP-Cloud blueprints from VMware, which can be found at the following locations:

- **IaaS Exam:** http://mylearn.vmware.com/register.cfm?course=136589
- **VCP-Cloud Exam:** http://mylearn.vmware.com/register.cfm?course=159512

Please check the blueprints often, as they are updated regularly and some aspects might change.

We did not write linearly to the blueprint. By that, we mean that you will not find that this book goes objective-by-objective and chapter-by-chapter through the published exam blueprint. Instead, we tried to approach the exam topics in a way that made sense from an administrator's point of view. All the exam objectives are covered in this book, however, and we point out the covered objectives at the beginning of each chapter. We suggest that you read this book cover to cover as we feel that we have laid it out in a way that makes the most sense. When you have read the entire book and are ready to study for the exam, read through the blueprint objective-by-objective and refer to the corresponding sections of this book.

How to Use This Book

This book consists of 10 chapters, detailed below. As mentioned earlier, we have written this book from a vCloud administrator's point of view rather than following the exam objectives in order.

The chapters of the book cover the following topics:

- **Chapter 1, "Introduction to the vCloud Suite Certifications"**—This chapter introduces the reader to the levels of VMware certification and the specific exams available in the vCloud certification track. Specific exam details as well as preparation hints are provided.

- **Chapter 2, "Install and Configure vCloud"**—This chapter details the process for installing vCloud Director and vShield Manager. It also provides the theory behind the operations and offers some troubleshooting information.

- **Chapter 3, "Administer vCloud Users, Roles, and Privileges"**—This chapter details the differences between roles and privileges and the principles of role-based access controls. It details the different roles available in vCloud Director, provides instructions on creating custom roles, and explains integration with LDAP.

- **Chapter 4, "Configure and Administer Chargeback"**—This chapter covers the vCenter Chargeback Manager product, introducing the concept of chargeback and why it is needed in a cloud environment. From there, we explore Chargeback permissions and roles, cost elements, billing policies, and modeling, and conclude with a discussion on reporting in vCenter Chargeback Manager.

- **Chapter 5, "vCloud Connector"**—This chapter provides details on the vCloud Connector product, including identification and functionality of the different components. Installation and usage of vCloud Connector are covered and troubleshooting information is provided.

- **Chapter 6, "Configure and Administer vCloud Networking"**—This chapter covers one of the more difficult ideas of vCloud Director: networking. It covers how and when to create the different types of vCloud networks and network pools and the requirements for each, as well as VXLAN and the various types of network services that can be created in vCloud Director.

- **Chapter 7, "Configure and Administer vCloud Organizations"**—This chapter covers the creation and modification of vCloud Director organizations, the logical container for each cloud tenant.

- **Chapter 8, "Allocate and Manage vCloud Resources"**—This chapter details how to create and administer provider and organization virtual data centers. In addition, you learn the different resource allocation models, catalogs, and vApps and vApp templates.

- **Chapter 9, "Monitor a vCloud Implementation"**—This chapter provides information on gathering logs and viewing resource utilization in vCloud Director. Specific instruction is provided on monitoring provider and organization virtual datacenters (vDCs) and the different types of networks, as well as viewing and searching for tasks and events. The chapter concludes with information on troubleshooting vCenter Chargeback Manager.

- **Chapter 10, "What Do I Do Now?"**—This chapter answers the question, "What now?" You learn specific exam details and logistical information, such as how to register and what to expect on the day of the exam.

- **Appendix A, "Answers to the 'Do I Know This Already?' Quizzes and Review Questions"**—This appendix provides the answers to the "Do I Know This Already?" quizzes that you will find at the beginning of each chapter, as well as the "Review Questions" sections found at the end of each chapter.

- **Appendix B, "vCenter to vCloud Resource Table"**—This appendix provides a table mapping resources in vCloud Director to objects in vCenter, along with a description of each.

- **Appendix C, "Configuring vSphere for vCloud Director"**—This appendix provides information on the vSphere resources and components necessary to install vCloud Director. It briefly covers vSphere licensing, vCenter Server configuration, vSphere host and cluster requirements, and networking and storage elements.

Book Content Updates

Because VMware occasionally updates exam topics without notice, VMware Press might post additional preparatory content on the web page associated with this book at www.pearsonitcertification.com/title/9780789751652. It is a good idea to check the website a couple of weeks before taking your exam, to review any updated content that might be posted online. We also recommend that you periodically check back to this page on the Pearson IT Certification website to view any errata or supporting book files that might be available.

Pearson IT Certification Practice Test Engine and Questions on the DVD

The DVD in the back of this book includes the Pearson IT Certification Practice Test engine—software that displays and grades a set of exam-realistic multiple-choice questions. Using the Pearson IT Certification Practice Test engine, you can either study by going through the questions in Study Mode or take a simulated exam that mimics real exam conditions.

The installation process requires two major steps: installing the software, and then activating the exam. The DVD in the back of this book has a recent copy of the Pearson IT Certification Practice Test engine. The practice exam—the database of exam questions—is not on the DVD.

NOTE The cardboard DVD case in the back of this book includes the DVD and a piece of paper. The paper lists the activation code for the practice exam associated with this book. *Do not lose the activation code*. On the opposite side of the paper from the activation code is a unique, one-time-use coupon code for the purchase of the Premium Edition eBook and Practice Test.

Install the Software from the DVD

The Pearson IT Certification Practice Test is a Windows-only desktop application. You can run it on a Mac using a Windows virtual machine, but it was built specifically for the PC platform. The minimum system requirements are as follows:

- Windows XP (SP3), Windows Vista (SP2), or Windows 7
- Microsoft .NET Framework 4.0 Client
- Microsoft SQL Server Compact 4.0
- Pentium class 1GHz processor (or equivalent)
- 512MB RAM
- 650MB disc space plus 50MB for each downloaded practice exam

The software installation process is pretty routine as compared with other software installation processes. If you have already installed the Pearson IT Certification Practice Test software from another Pearson product, there is no need for you to reinstall the software. Just launch the software on your desktop and proceed to activate the practice exam from this book by using the activation code included in the DVD sleeve.

The following steps outline the installation process:

Step 1. Insert the DVD into your PC.

Step 2. The software that automatically runs is the Pearson software to access and use all DVD-based features, including the exam engine and the DVD-only appendixes. From the main menu, click the **Install the Exam Engine** option.

Step 3. Respond to window prompts as with any typical software installation process.

The installation process gives you the option to activate your exam with the activation code supplied on the paper in the DVD sleeve. This process requires that you establish a Pearson website login. You need this login to activate the exam, so please do register when prompted. If you already have a Pearson website login, there is no need to register again. Just use your existing login.

Activate and Download the Practice Exam

After installing the exam engine, you should then activate the exam associated with this book (if you did not do so during the installation process) as follows:

Step 1. Start the Pearson IT Certification Practice Test software from the Windows **Start** menu or from your desktop shortcut icon.

Step 2. To activate and download the exam associated with this book, from the My Products or Tools tab, click the **Activate** button.

Step 3. At the next screen, enter the activation key from the paper inside the cardboard DVD holder in the back of the book. When entered, click the **Activate** button.

Step 4. The activation process downloads the practice exam. Click **Next**, and then click **Finish.**

When the activation process completes, the My Products tab should list your new exam. If you do not see the exam, make sure you have opened the My Products tab on the menu. At this point, the software and practice exam are ready to use. Simply select the exam and click the **Open Exam** button.

To update a particular exam you have already activated and downloaded, open the Tools tab and click the **Update Products** button. Updating your exams will ensure you have the latest changes and updates to the exam data.

If you want to check for updates to the Pearson Cert Practice Test exam engine software, open the Tools tab and click the **Update Application** button. This will ensure you are running the latest version of the software engine.

Activating Other Exams

The exam software installation process, and the registration process, only has to happen once. Then, for each new exam, only a few steps are required. For instance, if you buy another new Pearson IT Certification Cert Guide or VMware Press Official Cert Guide, extract the activation code from the DVD sleeve in the back of that book; you do not even need the DVD at this point. From there, all you have to do is start the exam engine (if not still up and running), and perform steps 2 through 4 from the previous list.

Premium Edition

In addition to the free practice exam provided on the DVD, you can purchase two additional exams with expanded functionality directly from Pearson IT Certification. The Premium Edition eBook and Practice Test for this title contains TWO full additional practice exams and an eBook (in both PDF and ePub format). In addition, the Premium Edition title has remediation for each question to the specific part of the eBook that relates to that question.

If you have purchased the print version of this title, you can purchase the Premium Edition at a deep discount. A coupon code in the DVD sleeve contains a one-time-use code and instructions for where you can purchase the Premium Edition.

To view the Premium Edition product page, go to www.pearsonitcertification.com/title/9780133480818.

This chapter covers the following subjects:

- **VMware Certification Overview**—The available certification tracks and the exams common to each track

- **vCloud Suite Certifications**—The specific exams available in the vCloud suite of certifications and information on each exam

- **Preparing for vCloud Certifications**—What you should do to prepare for the exams

This chapter does not cover any specific objectives of the VCP-Cloud or VCP-IaaS exams. Instead, we provide general information and guidance on preparing for the vCloud certifications.

CHAPTER 1

Introduction to the vCloud Suite Certifications

Congratulations! Whether you're new to information technology certifications, just starting down the VMware certification path, or a seasoned VMware certification veteran, this book is your first step on the vCloud Suite certification path. This book is specifically designed to help you study for either the VMware Infrastructure as a Service (IaaS) exam VCPVCD510 or the IaaS objectives of the VCP-Cloud exam VCPC510. This book covers the entire set of objectives of the IaaS exam, which are also Objectives 8–15 of the VCP-Cloud exam. Objectives 1–7 of the VCP-Cloud exam are covered in *The Official VCP5 Certification Guide* by Bill Ferguson.

This first chapter orients you to the overall VMware certification tracks and then takes you deeper into the certifications available in the vCloud certification track. The benefits of all VMware certifications include

- Recognition of your technical knowledge and skills
- Official transcripts
- Use of the certification's official logo
- Access to the certification-specific portal and logo merchandise store
- Invitations to beta exams and classes
- Discounted admission to VMware events
- Greater opportunities for career advancement

Foundation Topics

VMware Certification Overview

VMware has offered the VMware Certified Professional (VCP) exam since the early 2000s and expanded their offerings a few years ago to include the VMware Certified Advanced Professional (VCAP) and VMware Certified Design Expert (VCDX) certifications. Even more recently, VMware has increased the certification tracks to include End User Computing (EUC)—also known as "Desktop"—and Cloud certifications and has renamed the core virtualization track Data Center Virtualization (DCV). This means that anyone with the legacy "VCP" certification is now considered a VMware Certified Professional – Data Center Virtualization (VCP-DCV).

What is common to each track is that a progressive certification path takes the candidate from VCP to VCAP to VCDX. What's involved with each step on the path?

VCP – VMware Certified Professional

This level of certification demonstrates a foundation of knowledge for each of the tracks (DCV, Desktop, and Cloud). Most people begin with the DCV track, but that isn't necessary. Regardless of the initial path, an approved instructor-led course is required.

NOTE   You must attend a VMware-approved instructor-led course to achieve your first VCP certification. You can take an exam without the course, but you will not achieve VCP status without attending a course. Fortunately, this needs to be done only once for any track and not once for each track. Because the core vSphere product is central to all certification tracks, a good strategy for all candidates, regardless of your chosen certification track(s), is to attend the "VMware vSphere: Install, Configure, Manage [V5.x]" course at a VMware Authorized Training Center. If you are seeking certification in the Cloud or Desktop tracks, you could alternatively (or additionally) attend the foundation class for your chosen track—either "VMware vCloud Director: Install, Configure, Manage [v5.x]" or "VMware View: Install, Configure, and Manage [v5.x]".

VCAP – VMware Certified Advanced Professional

This is (as the title indicates) an advanced certification and is intended for candidates with extensive product experience. There are two VCAP exams within each track: an administration exam and a design exam. The administration exam tests the candidate for mastery of administration in the associated track—DCV, Desktop/EUC, and Cloud. You must be able to quickly configure and troubleshoot all aspects of the chosen track. The design exam, on the other hand, probes your knowledge for design and architecture experience. The design exams generally prove more difficult to study for than the administration exams because they require more hands-on design and architecture experience versus the ability to study and simulate administration tasks.

VCDX – VMware Certified Design Expert

At the time of writing, there are just over 100 certified design experts in the world. The authors of this book happen to be two of them. VCDX is the current pinnacle of VMware certification. This is an expert-level certification and requires that the candidate first obtain VCP and then pass both the VCAP administration and design certifications for the chosen track. After these requirements are met, the candidate must submit a qualifying design for review by current VCDX holders. If the design is considered to be of high enough quality and meets the published criteria for the chosen track, the candidate is invited to defend his design and the choices therein in front of a panel of VCDX holders—a daunting task! In addition to defending the submitted design, the candidate participates in both a mock design and a trouble-shooting scenario. The troubleshooting and mock design scenarios are fictitious and are intended to evaluate the candidate's thought processes and methodologies, not his ability to arrive at an answer.

The vCloud Suite Certifications

The certifications related to the vCloud Suite are as follows:

- VCP-Cloud
- VCAP-CIA (Cloud Infrastructure Administration)
- VCAP-CID (Cloud Infrastructure Design)
- VCDX-Cloud

Let's explore each certification in more detail.

VCP-Cloud

The VCP-Cloud certification is the foundation-level certification for the vCloud suite of products. It is designed to allow administrators, engineers, and architects of vCloud infrastructures to demonstrate a fundamental level of knowledge of not only the core vSphere product, but also vCloud Director, vCloud Connector, vCenter Chargeback, and vCloud Networking and Security (formerly known as vShield).

There are two possible paths to obtain the VCP-Cloud certification. One is for cur-rent VCP5-DCV holders; one is for those who hold an older or alternative VCP certification or who are new to VMware certifications.

Current VCP5-DCV holders need only pass the VCP-IaaS, VCAP-CIA, or VCAP-CID exam to obtain VCP-Cloud certification. This book examines all the topics of the VCP-IaaS exam, so if you already hold the VCP5-DCV certification, studying the topics in this book will help you pass the exam. VMware also recommends that you attend the official, instructor-led "VMware vCloud Director: Install, Configure, Man-age [v5.1]" course, but it is not required. VMware also recommends the "VMware vCenter Chargeback Manager Fundamentals [V2.5]" course, which is available as a free, self-paced online course after you log in to your mylearn.vmware.com account.

The VCP-IaaS exam VCPVCD510 contains 85 questions, along with a pre-exam survey of 8 questions. The passing score is 300 on a scale of 100–500, and candidates have 90 minutes to complete the exam and another 15 minutes to complete the pre-exam survey. Candidates taking the exam in a country where English is not the primary language automatically have an additional 30 minutes to complete it.

For full details, please reference the official IaaS exam blueprint at http://mylearn.vmware.com/register.cfm?course=136589.

Candidates seeking VCP-Cloud certification who do not hold the VCP5-DCV certification must attend a qualifying VMware course. There are a couple of options here. You could take a qualifying course for VCP5-DCV, pass the VCP5-DCV exam (and obtain VCP5-DCV certification), and then pass the VCP-IaaS exam (as noted previously). Alternatively, you could take the "VMware vCloud Director: Install, Configure, Manage [v5.1]" course and pass the VCP-Cloud exam VCPC510. The VCP-Cloud exam tests principles from both the VCP5-DCV and VCP-IaaS exams and is therefore a much longer exam than either individual exam.

The VCP-Cloud exam contains 135 questions. The passing score is 300 on a scale of 100–500, and candidates have 120 minutes to complete the exam. The exam is currently offered only in English and is administered through Pearson VUE.

For full details, please reference the official VCP-Cloud exam blueprint at http://mylearn.vmware.com/register.cfm?course=159512. Table 1-1 serves to help you determine which course and exam you should take.

Table 1-1   Who Should Take the IaaS and VCP-Cloud Exams

If You Are...	Training Courses	Exam	Certification
Currently VCP5-DCV Certified	Recommended: VMware vCloud Director: Install, Configure, Manage [v5.1] vCenter Chargeback Fundamentals	Pass the IaaS Exam	VCP-Cloud
Just starting with VMware cloud technologies or Currently VCP4-DCV Certified	Required: VMware vCloud Director: Install, Configure, Manage [v5.1] or VMware vCloud: Deploy and Manage the VMware Cloud [v1.5]	Pass the VCP-Cloud Exam	VCP-Cloud

1. VCP5 and VCP4 have been renamed VCP5-DCV (VMware Certified Professional 5 – Data Center Virtualization) and VCP4-DCV (VMware Certified Professional 4 – Data Center Virtualization), respectively. Certification requirements are subject to change and might not be retroactive to previous versions. Please regularly check vmware.com/certification for updates.

VCAP-CIA (Cloud Infrastructure Administration)

The VCAP-CIA exam VCIA510 expands on the concepts tested in the VCP-Cloud and VCP-IaaS exams, probing deeper into your knowledge of vCloud infrastructures and your ability to install, configure, and maintain complex vCloud environments. You are not required to take any specific course for this certification (other than those required by any prerequisite certifications), but you must be authorized by VMware to take the exam. Authorization includes verifying that you hold one of the following certifications:

- VCP-Cloud
- VCP5-DCV
- VCP5-DT (Desktop)

The VCAP-CIA exam is a live lab exam consisting of approximately 32 activities. If you have taken any of the other VCAP administration exams, then this exam experience will be familiar to you. Candidates connect to a management workstation that has several tools installed, including vSphere client, PuTTY client, and web browser, similar to what an administrator of a vCloud infrastructure would have access to. Candidates are then expected to be able to perform activities related to installing, configuring, and maintaining a vCloud environment. There's no guessing at the answer here. You either know how to do what is requested or you don't!

The ability to troubleshoot is important with this exam. The vCloud environment that you will be presented with will contain some configurations that are incorrect or incomplete. Some activities will depend on you having successfully completed tasks in prior questions, and although product documentation is generally made available for VCAP exams, don't expect to have much time to look up answers. This is definitely an exam where you need to know exactly what you are doing and how to complete specific tasks.

For full details, please reference the official VCAP-CIA exam blueprint located at http://mylearn.vmware.com/register.cfm?course=167496.

NOTE Candidates who pass the VCAP-CIA exam will also earn the VCP-Cloud certification if they have not already done so.

VCAP-CID (Cloud Infrastructure Design)

The VCAP-CID exam VCID510 tests your ability to design public, private, hybrid, single-tenant, and multitenant VMware vCloud infrastructures. Like the VCAP-CIA

exam, there is no specific course requirement to take the exam (other than those required by any prerequisite certifications), but candidates must hold one of the following certifications:

- VCP5-DCV

- VCP-Cloud

- VCAP5-DCA (Data Center Administration)

- VCAP5-DCD (Data Center Design)

- VCDX5-DCV

Also like the VCAP-CIA exam, passing the VCAP-CID exam earns you the VCP-
Cloud certification if you do not already hold that certification.

This exam tests for the ability to design to specific customer requirements around
manageability, availability, scalability, recoverability, and performance. It consists
of 115 multiple-choice, drag-and-drop, and extended design questions where you
will be expected to use an in-exam design tool to design solutions based on customer
requirements. The exam has six of these design items, and they take significantly
longer to complete than the others. Candidates should understand the differences
between conceptual, logical, and physical designs and be able to complete the requirements for each type of design. A mastery of vCloud design principles and
methodologies is encouraged prior to attempting this exam.

NOTE   Candidates who pass the VCAP-CID exam will also earn the VCP-Cloud
certification if they have not already done so.

VCDX-Cloud

As noted previously, VCDX is the pinnacle of VMware certifications. There isn't a
VCDX-Cloud exam; instead, the candidate follows a two-step process.

First, the candidate must submit a multidocument, production-ready design and
implementation set based on an actual customer installation. The design submission
includes documentation of customer requirements and business drivers, as well as
the architectural drawings, elevation plans, installation and configuration guides, run
books, and any other documentation necessary to support a successful implementation. Consider this the documentation set deliverables that you would turn over to a
client following a consulting engagement. The design documentation set is submitted along with an application and an associated fee.

Following submission, the design is then reviewed by an existing VCDX-Cloud certified individual for completeness, accuracy, and quality against an unpublished rubric.

If the submission meets the requirements, the candidate is invited to the second step of VCDX certification—the defense. During the defense, the candidate is given the opportunity to briefly present her design and then defend her design choices and answer questions raised by the panelists. The panelists are a group of veteran VCDX holders who have been through the process themselves. In addition to presenting and defending her design, the candidate undergoes an oral troubleshooting exercise and a mock design exercise in which panelists act as potential customers.

For further information on the VCDX process and preparation information, please see *VCDX Boot Camp: Preparing for the VCDX Panel Defense* by John Arrasjid, Ben Lin, and Mostafa Khalil.

Preparing for vCloud Certifications

Preparing for any of the certifications in the vCloud track is similar to any of the other tracks—practice, practice, practice. None of these are easy exams, and they get progressively more difficult.

VMware maintains information about each exam at the following location: http://mylearn.vmware.com/portals/certification.

Each exam has its own specific page with the following information:

- Certification roadmap and requirements
- Suggested training courses
- Exam blueprints
- Practice exam (VCP)
- Interactive exam simulation (VCAP)

The exam certification blueprints and the practice exams are two particularly useful resources. The blueprint outlines the necessary knowledge and study resources, and the practice exam provides questions similar to what you can expect on the exam.

The contents of this book are intended to prepare the VCP5-DCV holder for the VCP-IaaS exam. If you do not hold the VCP5-DCV certification and need to take the VCP-Cloud exam, this book plus *The Official VCP5 Certification Guide* by Bill Ferguson will help you to prepare for that exam. See Chapter 10, "What Do I Do Now?" for specific details on preparing for the VCP-IaaS and VCP-Cloud exams.

This chapter covers the following subjects:

- **Preparing to Install vCloud Director**—This section covers preparation required to install vCloud Director.

- **Installing vCloud Director**—This section covers the installation of vCloud Director.

- **Installing and Configuring vShield Manager**—This section covers the deployment and connection of vShield Manager.

- **Final Configuration of vCloud Director**—This section covers the configuration of vCloud Director for system administration.

This chapter covers a portion of the VCP-Cloud Exam Objective 8.1, VCP-Cloud Exam Objective 8.3, VCP-IaaS Exam Objective 1.1, and VCP-IaaS Exam Objective 1.3.

CHAPTER 2

Install and Configure vCloud

The vCloud Suite of products from VMware offers a great deal of agility and flexibility in the way a cloud is consumed, but before you can consume cloud resources, you must install the suite correctly. In this chapter, we focus on installing vCloud Director and vShield Manager. We also cover why things are being done and how to troubleshoot problems when they arise.

"Do I Know This Already?" Quiz

The "Do I Know This Already?" quiz enables you to assess whether you should read this entire chapter or simply jump to the "Exam Preparation Tasks" section for review. If you are in doubt, read the entire chapter. Table 2-1 outlines the major headings in this chapter and the corresponding "Do I Know This Already?" quiz questions. You can find the answers in Appendix A, "Answers to the 'Do I Know This Already?' Quizzes and Review Questions."

Table 2-1 "Do I Know This Already?" Foundation Topics Section-to-Question Mapping

Foundations Topics Section	Questions Covered in This Section
Preparing to Install vCloud Director	1, 2, 4, 5
Installing vCloud Director	3
Installing and Configuring vShield Manager	7
Configuring vCloud Director	6, 8

1. What is the command switch to generate a certificate for 365 days?

   a. length 365

   b. days 365

   c. validity 365

   d. certificate 365

2. Which database types are supported by vCloud Director 5.x? (Choose two.)

   a. Microsoft SQL Server

   b. Oracle

   c. DB2

   d. Postgres

3. Which version(s) of Microsoft Server requires a separate SysPrep package? (Choose all that apply.)

   a. Windows Server 2008

   b. Windows Server 2003

   c. Windows Server 2000

   d. Windows Server 2012

4. How much memory is required for vCloud Director?

   a. 1GB

   b. 2GB

   c. 4GB

   d. 8GB

5. vCloud Director can be installed on which operating system?

   a. Red Hat

   b. Windows 2008 R2

   c. Windows 2008 SP2

   d. Oracle Linux

6. Before configuring vCloud Director, which software must be installed to continue? (Choose two.)

   a. vShield Manager

   b. vCenter Chargeback Server

   c. vCenter

   d. vSphere

7. vShield Manager is installed by?

    a. OVF

    b. Windows Installable file

    c. Red Hat RPM

    d. SLES package installer

8. Which log would you look at to identify problems with your vCloud Director cell starting?

    a. /opt/vmware/vcloud-director/logs/cell.log

    b. /var/log/messages

    c. /opt/vmware/vcloud-director/logs/requests.log

    d. /opt/vmware/vcloud-director/logs/vcloud.debug.log

Foundation Topics

Preparing to Install vCloud Director

vCloud Director Server is the center of any vCloud Suite installation. Not only is it responsible for the creation of virtual machines and networks, but it is also responsible for the access to those machines and their corresponding workloads.

vCloud Director allows for installation on multiple servers, called *cells*. The ability to deploy multiple cells allows for highly available and/or load-balanced vCloud Director solutions. We discuss the requirements of vCloud Director cells in the section "Configuring vCloud Director for Multiple Cells."

This first section focuses on the proper installation and configuration of vCloud Director. We discuss the requirements to install vCloud Director on Red Hat Enterprise Linux (RHEL), the creation of certificates, and proper database configuration.

The RHEL server should be configured with at least 2GB of RAM and 1GB of free hard drive space, though it is highly recommended to provide additional memory and storage for optimal performance.

Requirements for RHEL Server Installation

To install vCloud Director on a RHEL server, several packages are required and must be preinstalled. The supported Server Operating systems for vCloud Director are

- Red Hat Enterprise Linux 5 (64 bit), Update 4
- Red Hat Enterprise Linux 5 (64 bit), Update 5
- Red Hat Enterprise Linux 5 (64 bit), Update 6
- Red Hat Enterprise Linux 5 (64 bit), Update 8
- Red Hat Enterprise Linux 6 (64 bit), Update 1
- Red Hat Enterprise Linux 6 (64 bit), Update 2
- Red Hat Enterprise Linux 6 (64 bit), Update 3

The required software packages for a vCloud Director installation are shown in the following list.

NOTE   To install the required packages, after connecting to the RedHat Network (RHN), you can use the yum install command, as shown here:

```
yum install alsa-lib
```

alsa-lib	intiscripts	libZau	net-tools
bash	krb5-libs	libXdmcp	pciutils
chkconfig	libgcc	libXext	procps
coreutils	libICE	libXi	redhat-lsb
findutils	libSM	libXt	sed
glibc	libstdc	libXtst	tar
grep	libX11	module-init-tools	which

vCloud Director also requires 1GB of RAM, though 2GB is recommended, and 950MB of disk space to properly install.

After you have ensured that the server meets these requirements, it is time to install the vCloud Director server.

Configuring vCloud Director for Multiple Cells

vCloud Director can utilize multiple cells (multiple servers in a single vCloud instance) for load balancing and high availability. The use of multiple cells requires a couple of items. The first item is a load balancer that is compatible with persistent secure sockets layer (SSL) sessions; the second item is a network file system (NFS) export that is mounted on all cell servers.

vCloud Director cells elect a vCenter proxy for each vCenter that is attached to vCloud Director. This proxy server will execute all tasks and events related to that vCenter. The proxy service is not without a resource cost. To compensate for this cost, your vCloud deployment should contain one more cloud cell than managed vCenter servers (n+1). This recommendation allows for a failure of a single cloud cell, while still maintaining the one-to-one cloud cell to vCenter server ratio.

Load Balancer Requirements

vCloud Director supports the use of load balancers to enable high availability and performance when accessing the vCloud cell servers, as shown in Figure 2-1.

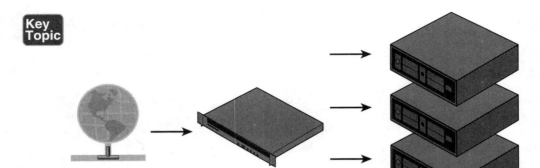

Figure 2-1   Load Balancer Example

To use a load balancer with vCloud Director, the load balancer must support sticky SSL sessions, which are sometimes referred to as *persistent* sessions. vCloud Director does not support SSL offloading or non-SSL connections to the vCloud cell servers.

NFS Transfer Export

The NFS transfer share keeps the vCloud Director cells in sync. It is also utilized for transferring vApps between vCenter servers, as a staging area for importing vApps and media files, and for exporting vApps. When sizing the transfer share, it should be large enough to support the export of your largest vApp. In practice, a 1TB transfer share has proven to be adequately sized for most environments.

NOTE   If you are installing only a single vCloud Director cell server, an NFS transfer share is not required. You will need to increase the size of the RHEL server to accommodate items that would normally be stored on the NFS transport.

If you are not going to load balance your vCloud Director cells, you can skip this step during the installation. The proper way to set up the transfer share is this:

NOTE   You should make sure that the RHEL firewall is disabled or configured to allow for NFS connections.

Activity 2-1: Configuring NFS Export

1. You will need to create the directory structure for the NFS transfer share. Execute this on all the vCloud Director cells, as shown in Figure 2-2.

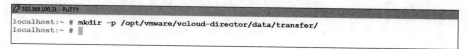

```
192.168.100.31 - PuTTY
localhost:~ # mkdir -p /opt/vmware/vcloud-director/data/transfer/
localhost:~ #
```

Figure 2-2 Creating the NFS Mount Directory

2. Next, you need to mount the NFS export to the directory you just created, as shown in Figure 2-3.

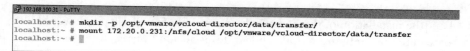

```
192.168.100.31 - PuTTY
localhost:~ # mkdir -p /opt/vmware/vcloud-director/data/transfer/
localhost:~ # mount 172.20.0.231:/nfs/cloud /opt/vmware/vcloud-director/data/transfer
localhost:~ #
```

Figure 2-3 Mounting an NFS Export

3. Finally, add the NFS export to the fstab file. This will cause the transfer directory to be automatically mounted on each reboot. Your fstab file should look similar to the one shown in Figure 2-4.

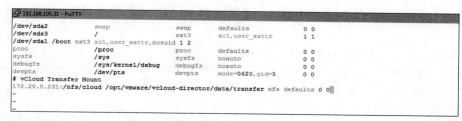

```
192.168.100.31 - PuTTY
/dev/sda2            swap            swap     defaults       0 0
/dev/sda3            /               ext3     acl,user_xattr 1 1
/dev/sda1 /boot ext3 acl,user_xattr,nosuid 1 2
proc                 /proc           proc     defaults       0 0
sysfs                /sys            sysfs    noauto         0 0
debugfs              /sys/kernel/debug debugfs noauto        0 0
devpts               /dev/pts        devpts   mode=0620,gid=5 0 0
# vCloud Transfer Mount
172.20.0.231:/nfs/cloud /opt/vmware/vcloud-director/data/transfer nfs defaults 0 0
~
~
~
```

Figure 2-4 Adding NFS Mount to fstab

Now that the NFS transfer is mounted in the proper directory structure, it is time to install the vCloud Director binary.

Activity 2-2: Installing vCloud Director

1. Locate the vCloud Director installation file. After you have acquired the latest vmware-vcloud-director.bin file, copy it to the server.

NOTE The vCloud Director file can be downloaded from my.vmware.com. To copy a file to the cell server, use WinSCP or similar technologies.

2. Execute the installation file as shown in Figure 2-5.

> **NOTE** You must be logged in as root or an account with the ability to utilize sudo to execute the installation and configuration commands.

```
root@vcd-book~
[root@vcd-book ~]# sh vmware-vcloud-director-5.1.1-868405.bin
```

Figure 2-5   vCloud Installation File

3. After the installation of the downloaded binary file, it will ask if you would like to execute the configure scripts. Unless this is an additional cell server for an existing cluster, select **No**. We cover the remaining requirements in the latter part of this chapter.

Certificate Creation

The next step is to create a Java Certificate store where the certificates for vCloud Director's webpage and console proxy service will be kept.

> **NOTE** After the certificate keystore is created, it contains both the public and private keys for your vCloud Director certificates. The password chosen for the file should be complex, and the file should be kept off the server in a secure location to minimize the risk of someone stealing your certificates.

If your organization has a root certificate authority, you will need to create a certificate signing request. If not, a self-signed certificate can be created. You will also need to create a signing request if you intend to have a third party, such as Verisign, sign your certificate. A self-signed certificate will provide the same level of data encryption as a signed certificate, but it will not be marked as trusted and might produce a warning of "unsigned certificate" when an administrator logs in.

To create your certificate signing request, you must use the keystore tool that came with the vCloud Director installation. Other versions might be incompatible with vCloud Director. The default installation path for vCloud Director is

/opt/vmware/vcloud-director

The keystore tool is located here:

/opt/vmware/vcloud-director/jre/bin/keytool

To create your certificates, follow the steps outlined in Activity 2-3.

Activity 2-3: Creating Certificate Keystore

1. First, create the certificate keystore:

   keytool -keystore certificates.ks -storetype JCEKS -storepass *password* **-genkey -keyalg RSA -alias http**

   This will generate a certificate that is valid for 90 days. To increase the length of time this certificate can be valid, add -validity days to the creation command.

2. Answer the questions that are presented. The first question asking for a first and last name is actually asking for the fully qualified domain name (FQDN) of the vCloud Director server.

3. Next, create a certificate for the console proxy service similar to Figure 2-6.

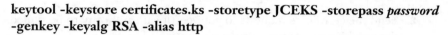

```
localhost:~ # /opt/vmware/vcloud-director/jre/bin/keytool -keystore certificate.ks -storetype JCEKS
-storepass password -genkey -keyalg RSA -alias consoleproxy
What is your first and last name?
  [Unknown]:   consoleproxy.thevsg.local
What is the name of your organizational unit?
  [Unknown]:   IT
What is the name of your organization?
  [Unknown]:   TheVSG
What is the name of your City or Locality?
  [Unknown]:   Denver
What is the name of your State or Province?
  [Unknown]:   CO
What is the two-letter country code for this unit?
  [Unknown]:   US
Is CN=consoleproxy.thevsg.local, OU=IT, O=TheVSG, L=Denver, ST=CO, C=US correct?
  [no]:  yes

Enter key password for <consoleproxy>
        (RETURN if same as keystore password):
localhost:~ #
```

Figure 2-6   Keystore Creation Answers

keytool -keystore certificates.ks -storetype JCEKS -storepass *password* **-genkey -keyalg RSA -alias consoleproxy**

This will generate a certificate that is valid for 90 days; to increase this, add the option described in Step 1.

If you are going to use a signed certificate, follow the procedures outlined in Activity 2-4; if not, you can skip to Step 5.

Activity 2-4: Creating Signed Certificates

1. Export the certificate signing request for both the http certificate and the consoleproxy certificate:

   keytool -keystore certificates.ks -storetype JCKES -storepass *password* **-certreq -alias http -file http.csr**

   keytool -keystore certificates.ks -storetype JCKES -storepass *password* **-certreq -alias consoleproxy -file consoleproxy.csr**

2. Send the certificate requests to your certificate authority to be signed. After they are signed, continue to the next step.

3. When the certificates are received, they typically come with the root certificate and any intermediate certificates that are required to validate the certificate chain. The root and intermediate certificates will need to be imported into the keystore prior to the signed certificates:

   keytool -storetype JCEKS -storepass *password* **-keystore certificates.ks -import -alias root -file root.cer**

   keytool -storetype JCEKS -storepass *password* **-keystore certificates.ks -import -alias intermediate -file intermediate.cer**

4. Now you can import the signed certificates:

   keytool -storetype JCEKS -storepass *password* **-keystore certificates.ks -import -alias http -file http.cer**

   keytool -storetype JCEKS -storepass *password* **-keystore certificates.ks -import -alias consoleproxy -file consoleproxy.cer**

5. Verify that the certificates imported properly to the keystore, as shown in Figure 2-7.

   keytool -storetype JCEKS -storepass *password* **-keystore certificates.ks -list**

```
tore certificate.ks -list

Keystore type: JCEKS
Keystore provider: SunJCE

Your keystore contains 3 entries

consoleproxy, Jan 25, 2013, PrivateKeyEntry,
Certificate fingerprint (MD5): DD:9D:4A:EA:E0:09:1B:E7:FF:22:94:67:7E:A0:EC:3D
root, Jan 25, 2013, trustedCertEntry,
Certificate fingerprint (MD5): 8A:AF:BC:BA:C1:2E:5D:9F:70:41:3D:69:01:3C:A1:6F
http, Jan 25, 2013, PrivateKeyEntry,
Certificate fingerprint (MD5): 51:24:93:3C:70:5B:8A:10:1B:76:9A:B4:34:48:29:CA
localhost:~ #
```

Figure 2-7   Listing Imported Certificates

Additional options that can be specified in the keytool process are

- **keysize**—This will affect the size of the key that is generated (that is, 2048, 1024, and so on).

- **validity**—This will affect the length of time that the certificate generated will be valid for in days.

Configuring the vCloud Director Database Server

vCloud Director can be installed to Microsoft SQL Server or Oracle Database server. There are many ways to optimize and configure database servers, but we cover only the necessities to get vCloud Director installed properly.

Regardless of the chosen database platform, vCloud Director cannot share the same schema as another VMware product.

When determining the availability requirements for the solution, consider that nearly all configuration information is contained in the vCloud Director database. Without this database, your vCloud Suite will be offline.

Although there are many ways to configure and optimize database servers, we cover only the base requirements for a vCloud Director installation.

Oracle Database

The recommendation from VMware on the sizing of an Oracle database server is 16GB of RAM, 100GB of hard drive space, and 4 CPUs. For complete Oracle DB preparation tasks, please refer to: http://kb.vmware.com/kb/1025768.

NOTE   The Oracle server should be configured to allow for more than 75 concurrent connections to the database per cell server, plus 50 for the Oracle server itself.

SQL Server

Sizing recommendations for a Microsoft SQL Server are 16GB RAM, 100GB hard drive space, and 4 CPUs.

NOTE To set the proper snapshot creations for the database on a Microsoft SQL Server, the following script should be run against the vCloud Director database:

```
USE [vCloud_Database_Name]
GO
ALTER DATABASE [vCloud_Database_Name] SET SINGLE_USER WITH ROLLBACK
    IMMEDIATE;
ALTER DATABASE [vCloud_Database_Name] SET ALLOW_SNAPSHOT_ISOLATION
    ON;
ALTER DATABASE [vCloud_Database_Name] SET READ_COMMITTED_SNAPSHOT ON
    WITH NO_WAIT;
ALTER DATABASE [vCloud_Database_Name] SET MULTI_USER;
GO
```

For complete SQL Database preparation tasks, please refer to http://kb.vmware.com/kb/2034540.

Installing vCloud Director

Now that you have all the requirements for vCloud Director configured and ready for installation, it is time to actually install vCloud Director on your first server or cell.

Activity 2-5: Installing vCloud Director

1. After the installation binary is located on the vCloud Director cell, execute the binary, as shown in Figure 2-8.

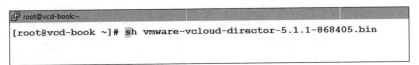

Figure 2-8   Binary Execution of vCloud Director Installation

2. After the Red Hat Package Manager (RPM) package has expanded and is installed, decline to run the configuration wizard because this will be completed in a later step. Your installation should look similar to the one in Figure 2-9.

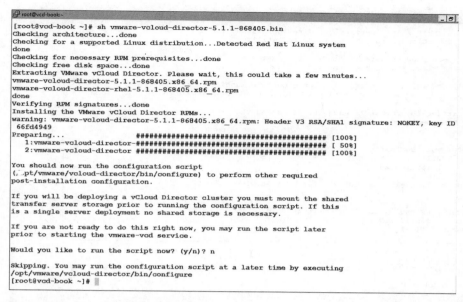

```
root@vcd-book:~
[root@vcd-book ~]# sh vmware-vcloud-director-5.1.1-868405.bin
Checking architecture...done
Checking for a supported Linux distribution...Detected Red Hat Linux system
done
Checking for necessary RPM prerequisites...done
Checking free disk space...done
Extracting VMware vCloud Director. Please wait, this could take a few minutes...
vmware-vcloud-director-5.1.1-868405.x86_64.rpm
vmware-vcloud-director-rhel-5.1.1-868405.x86_64.rpm
done
Verifying RPM signatures...done
Installing the VMware vCloud Director RPMs...
warning: vmware-vcloud-director-5.1.1-868405.x86_64.rpm: Header V3 RSA/SHA1 signature: NOKEY, key ID
  66fd4949
Preparing...             ########################################### [100%]
   1:vmware-vcloud-director-########################################### [ 50%]
   2:vmware-vcloud-director ########################################### [100%]

You should now run the configuration script
(/opt/vmware/vcloud-director/bin/configure) to perform other required
post-installation configuration.

If you will be deploying a vCloud Director cluster you must mount the shared
transfer server storage prior to running the configuration script. If this
is a single server deployment no shared storage is necessary.

If you are not ready to do this right now, you may run the script later
prior to starting the vmware-vcd service.

Would you like to run the script now? (y/n)? n

Skipping. You may run the configuration script at a later time by executing
/opt/vmware/vcloud-director/bin/configure
[root@vcd-book ~]#
```

Figure 2-9   Post vCloud Installation

3. After you have completed the certificate creation and the database server configuration in the previous section, you can proceed with the configure process. To start the process, run the command in Figure 2-10.

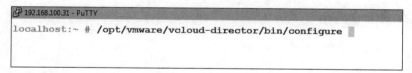

```
192.168.100.31 - PuTTY
localhost:~ # /opt/vmware/vcloud-director/bin/configure
```

Figure 2-10   Starting the vCloud Director Configuration Process

4. Select the proper IP address binding for the HTTP service and the console proxy service, as shown in Figure 2-11.

5. Next, the full path of your certificate store is required along with the password that you chose to secure it with, as shown in Figure 2-12.

6. If you are going to log system events to a syslog server, specify that IP address now.

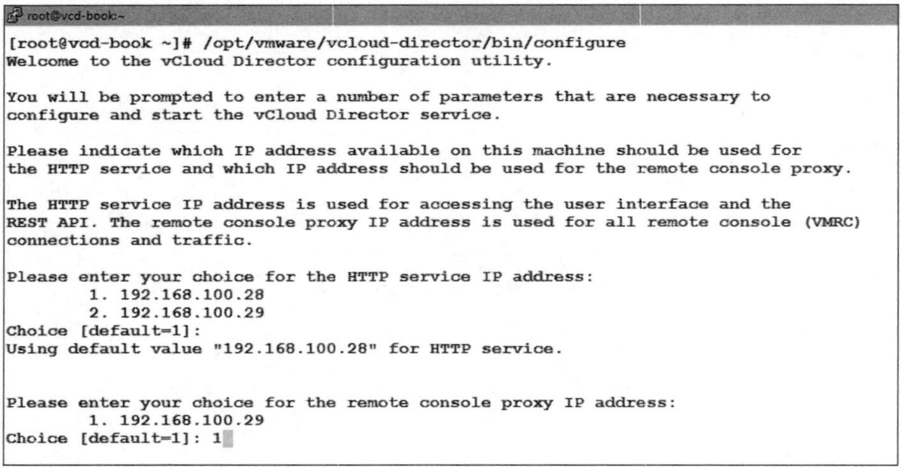

```
root@vcd-book:~
[root@vcd-book ~]# /opt/vmware/vcloud-director/bin/configure
Welcome to the vCloud Director configuration utility.

You will be prompted to enter a number of parameters that are necessary to
configure and start the vCloud Director service.

Please indicate which IP address available on this machine should be used for
the HTTP service and which IP address should be used for the remote console proxy.

The HTTP service IP address is used for accessing the user interface and the
REST API. The remote console proxy IP address is used for all remote console (VMRC)
connections and traffic.

Please enter your choice for the HTTP service IP address:
        1. 192.168.100.28
        2. 192.168.100.29
Choice [default=1]:
Using default value "192.168.100.28" for HTTP service.


Please enter your choice for the remote console proxy IP address:
        1. 192.168.100.29
Choice [default=1]: 1
```

Figure 2-11 IP Address Selection

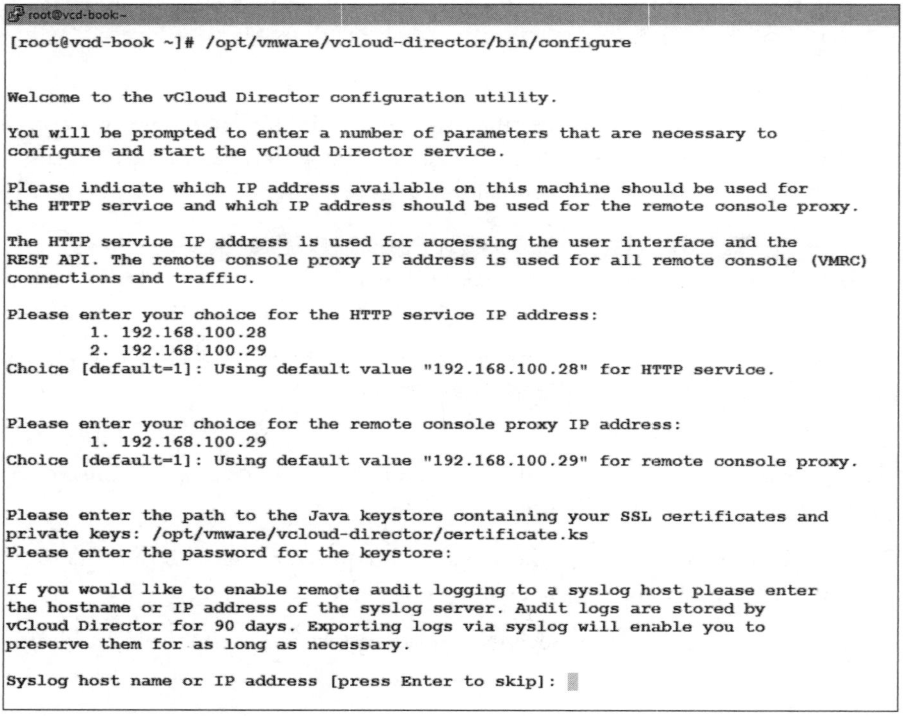

```
root@vcd-book:~
[root@vcd-book ~]# /opt/vmware/vcloud-director/bin/configure

Welcome to the vCloud Director configuration utility.

You will be prompted to enter a number of parameters that are necessary to
configure and start the vCloud Director service.

Please indicate which IP address available on this machine should be used for
the HTTP service and which IP address should be used for the remote console proxy.

The HTTP service IP address is used for accessing the user interface and the
REST API. The remote console proxy IP address is used for all remote console (VMRC)
connections and traffic.

Please enter your choice for the HTTP service IP address:
        1. 192.168.100.28
        2. 192.168.100.29
Choice [default=1]: Using default value "192.168.100.28" for HTTP service.


Please enter your choice for the remote console proxy IP address:
        1. 192.168.100.29
Choice [default=1]: Using default value "192.168.100.29" for remote console proxy.


Please enter the path to the Java keystore containing your SSL certificates and
private keys: /opt/vmware/vcloud-director/certificate.ks
Please enter the password for the keystore:

If you would like to enable remote audit logging to a syslog host please enter
the hostname or IP address of the syslog server. Audit logs are stored by
vCloud Director for 90 days. Exporting logs via syslog will enable you to
preserve them for as long as necessary.

Syslog host name or IP address [press Enter to skip]:
```

Figure 2-12 Certificate Path

7. You will now need to enter your database connection details, as demonstrated in Figure 2-13.

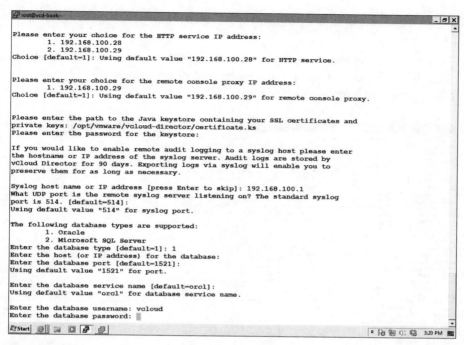

Figure 2-13   Database Connections

8. If everything is correct, allow the configure process to start the vCloud Director service. Your installation will look like Figure 2-14 if everything went fine.

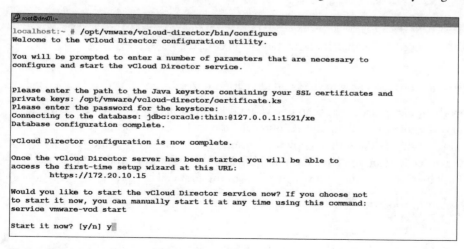

Figure 2-14   Completing the vCloud Configuration

If there are errors, resolve them and rerun the configuration command from Step 1.

9. To verify whether the vCloud Director cell started properly, you can check the cell.log file located in /opt/vmware/vcloud-director/logs/cell.log. A successful boot will look similar to Figure 2-15.

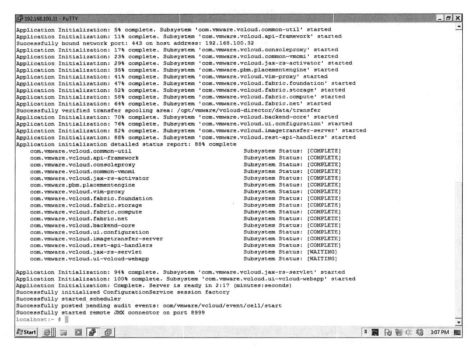

Figure 2-15 Successful Startup of vCloud Director in cell.log

Congratulations, you now have installed vCloud Director on your first vCloud cell.

If you are going to use more than one vCloud Director in a load-balanced configuration or require more than one vCloud cell, you will need to complete Activity 2-1 and Activity 2-2, and then copy the keystore from Activity 2-3 and Activity 2-4 to the new cell. After you have mounted the NFS transfer store and installed the vCloud binaries, copy the following files from the first cell server:

- global.properties
- certificates.ks

The copying of these files will allow for an easier installation of the remaining cell servers.

After you have completed installing vCloud on all planned cell servers, you need to deploy and configure vShield Manager.

Installing and Configuring vShield Manager

A requirement for vCloud Director to be configured with vCenter is a single vShield Manager. vShield Manager and vCenter can be configured only in a one-to-one configuration. This means for every vCenter that vCloud Director will manage there must be one vShield Manager deployed and registered to that vCenter.

vCloud Director will use vShield Manager to manage most of the network configuration in a cloud instance. This includes VXLAN and Edge device deployments. vShield Manager is also responsible for the configuration of the Edge devices and their monitoring.

This section covers the deployment of the vShield Manager appliance as well as the configuration of VXLAN to enable vCloud Director to utilize VXLAN as a network pool. We cover network pools and the usage of network pools in Chapter 6, "Configure and Administer vCloud Networking."

The first step in the deployment of vShield Manager is obtaining the files for deployment. The vShield Manager appliance is downloadable from VMware as an OVA file. An OVA is a compressed file that contains an OVF and several VMDK files. After you have obtained the file, proceed to deploy it to vCenter.

NOTE   VMware installation files can be downloaded from my.vmware.com.

Activity 2-6: Deploying vShield Manager

1. Open the vSphere client and connect to the vCenter where this vShield Manager will be deployed. Then select **File > Deploy OVF Template**. Then select the vShield Manager Appliance that was downloaded, as shown in Figure 2-16.

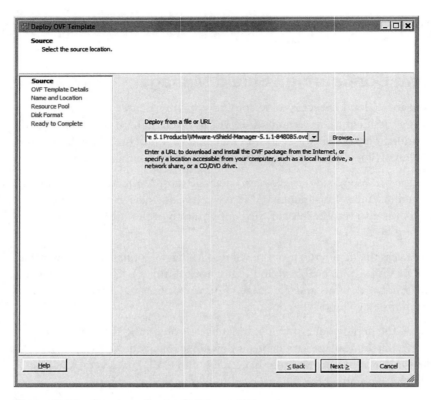

Figure 2-16　Opening vCenter OVF Import Wizard

　　2. Select the name and location of where you want to deploy this vShield Man-
　　　　ager appliance, similar to Figure 2-17.

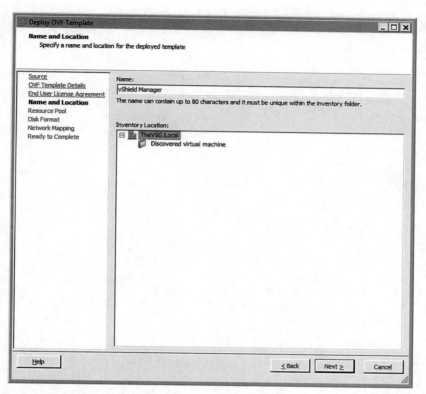

Figure 2-17   Selecting the OVF for vShield Manager

   3. Select the storage device and the disk format that will be used to deploy the
      vShield Manager Appliance. Thick is the preferred disk option, but thin will
      work if space is a constraint.

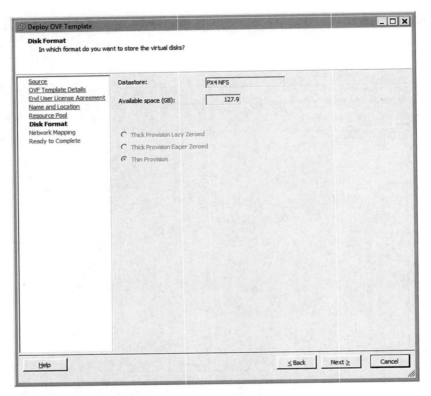

Figure 2-18   Disk Format Selection for vShield Manager

4. Select the network where the vShield Manager will be bound. This network will need to be capable of accessing the vCenter server and the vCloud Director cells, as shown in Figure 2-19.

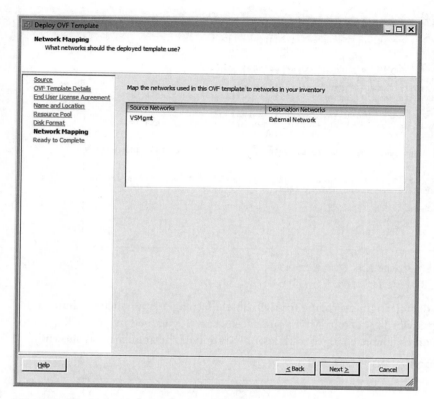

Figure 2-19   Network Selection for vShield Manager

If you have security requirements for a firewall or access control list (ACL) between the vShield Manager, vCenter, and vCloud Director, you can refer to VMware KB article 2034339.

Now that you have the appliance deployed, it is time to power it on and configure the IP settings of the appliance. You will need an IP address, subnet, and default gateway, as well as DNS servers and a hostname for the appliance. We configure them in the next section.

Activity 2-7: Configuring vShield Manager

1. After the vShield Manager appliance has completed booting, launch the console to it in vSphere Client. If vShield Manager started properly, you will see a login screen similar to the one in Figure 2-20.

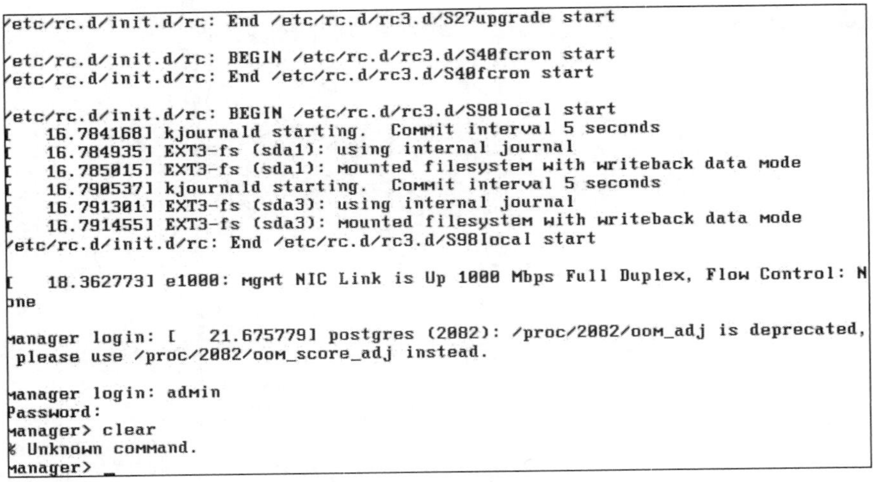

```
/etc/rc.d/init.d/rc: End /etc/rc.d/rc3.d/S27upgrade start

/etc/rc.d/init.d/rc: BEGIN /etc/rc.d/rc3.d/S40fcron start
/etc/rc.d/init.d/rc: End /etc/rc.d/rc3.d/S40fcron start

/etc/rc.d/init.d/rc: BEGIN /etc/rc.d/rc3.d/S98local start
[   16.784168] kjournald starting.  Commit interval 5 seconds
[   16.784935] EXT3-fs (sda1): using internal journal
[   16.785015] EXT3-fs (sda1): mounted filesystem with writeback data mode
[   16.790537] kjournald starting.  Commit interval 5 seconds
[   16.791301] EXT3-fs (sda3): using internal journal
[   16.791455] EXT3-fs (sda3): mounted filesystem with writeback data mode
/etc/rc.d/init.d/rc: End /etc/rc.d/rc3.d/S98local start

[   18.362773] e1000: Mgmt NIC Link is Up 1000 Mbps Full Duplex, Flow Control: N
one

Manager login: [   21.675779] postgres (2002): /proc/2002/oom_adj is deprecated,
 please use /proc/2002/oom_score_adj instead.

Manager login: admin
Password:
Manager> clear
% Unknown command.
Manager>
```

Figure 2-20   vShield Manager Start Complete

2. The default login username for the vShield Manager Appliance is admin and the password is default. After you have successfully logged in, you will need to type **en** to enable changes to the configuration of the appliance, as shown in Figure 2-21.

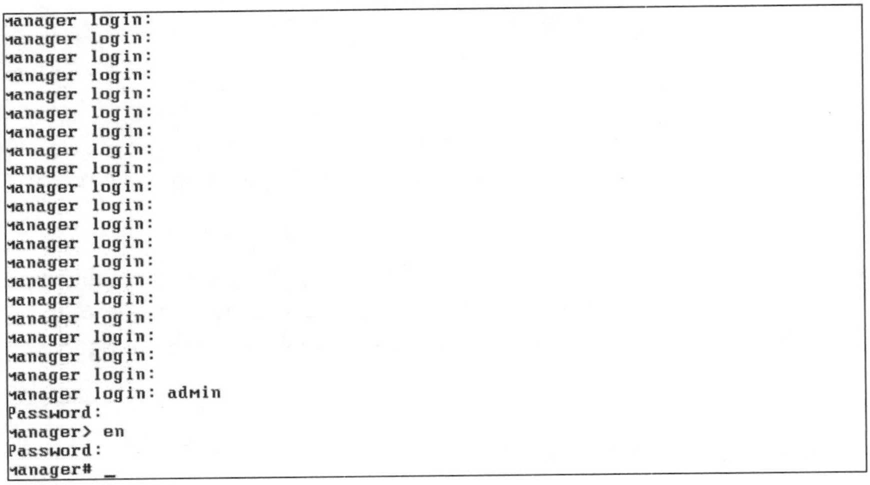

```
Manager login:
Manager login:
Manager login:
Manager login:
Manager login:
Manager login:
Manager login:
Manager login:
Manager login:
Manager login:
Manager login:
Manager login:
Manager login:
Manager login:
Manager login:
Manager login:
Manager login:
Manager login:
Manager login:
Manager login:
Manager login:
Manager login: admin
Password:
Manager> en
Password:
Manager#
```

Figure 2-21   vShield Shield Login

3. Next, you configure the IP settings for the vShield Appliance. To start this process, type **setup**. You will then be prompted for all the relevant IP information, similar to Figure 2-22.

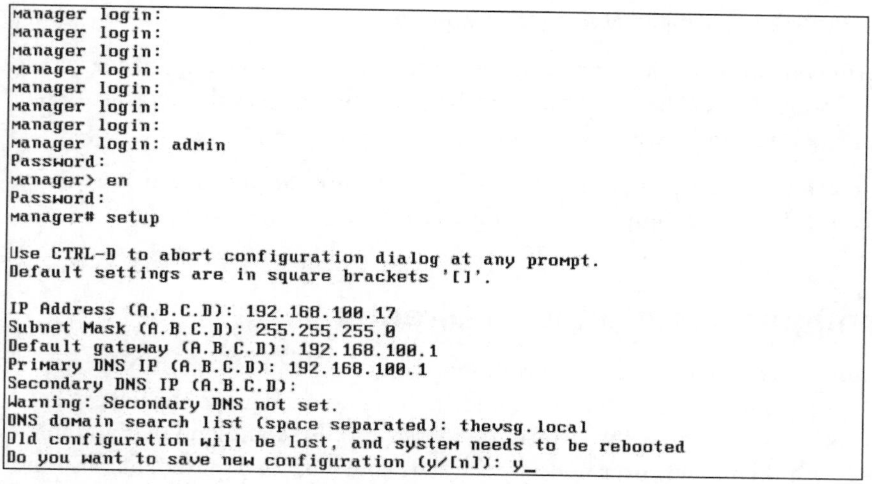

```
Manager login:
Manager login:
Manager login:
Manager login:
Manager login:
Manager login:
Manager login:
Manager login: admin
Password:
Manager> en
Password:
Manager# setup

Use CTRL-D to abort configuration dialog at any prompt.
Default settings are in square brackets '[]'.

IP Address (A.B.C.D): 192.168.100.17
Subnet Mask (A.B.C.D): 255.255.255.0
Default gateway (A.B.C.D): 192.168.100.1
Primary DNS IP (A.B.C.D): 192.168.100.1
Secondary DNS IP (A.B.C.D):
Warning: Secondary DNS not set.
DNS domain search list (space separated): thevsg.local
Old configuration will be lost, and system needs to be rebooted
Do you want to save new configuration (y/[n]): y_
```

Figure 2-22 vShield Manager Configuring IP Settings

After you have completed entering the IP information, the vShield Appliance will ask you to log out. You can accomplish this by typing **exit** and pressing Enter until you see the login prompt. After you have logged out, you can close the Console connection to the server. The remaining configuration steps will be performed through the appliance's webpage.

License Options for vShield (vCloud Network and Security)

vCloud Network Security comes in two license versions, Standard and Advanced. The Advanced version includes the capability to configure high availability (HA) for the Edge devices, a load balancer, and data security. We cover the configuration of HA and the load balancer in Chapter 6.

vShield Manager retrieves the license information from vCenter after it has been registered to the vCenter Server. Prior to registering vShield Manager to vCenter, you should ensure that the vCloud Network Security licenses are properly applied.

To verify whether the license is registered properly, open the vSphere Client and navigate to the license section under Administration > Licenses. Verify that you have a vCloud Network Security Standard, vCloud Network Security Advanced, or vCloud Suite license file registered.

After you have verified that the license key is properly applied, you will need to register your vShield Manager appliance to the vCenter server. Keep in mind that this is a one-to-one relationship: one vCenter per one vShield Manager and vice versa.

Activity 2-8: Registering vShield Manager to vCenter

1. Open your web browser and navigate to the vShield Manager appliance via https://ipaddress. The login to this web page is the same as the console username (admin) and password (default).

2. You will need to type in the FQDN of your vCenter Server as well as a service account that has administrator privileges to the vCenter Server.

Final Configuration of vCloud Director

At this point, it is time to finalize the configuration of vCloud Director. Next, we will define our first administrator in vCloud, an installation ID, and the license key. If this is your first time actually performing these steps, I recommend that you follow along with them. We cover not only the steps and what is required, but also the reason behind performing these actions.

To get started, open a web browser and navigate to the FQDN of the vCloud Cell. This will test your certificates, your DNS resolution, and the basic health of your vCloud installation. On your first connection to the cell server, you will be presented with a prompt, similar to Figure 2-23, to create an administrative user as well as a password for this user.

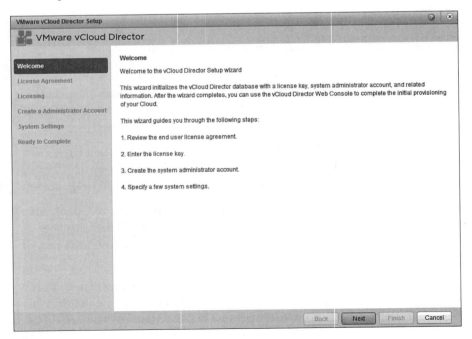

Figure 2-23 First Configuration Wizard for vCloud Director

After you have accepted the End User License Agreement (EULA) from VMware and entered your license key for vCloud Suite, you will create an administrator account for vCloud. We cover the importance of email addresses for administrative users in Chapter 9, "Monitor a vCloud Implementation."

NOTE   With vCloud Director, any user that is defined or created at the system level (that is, not in an Organization) has full administrative control through the vCloud Director user interface (UI). There is no read-only role or definable permissions that can be set for a user at the system level.

NOTE   The vCloud Director Installation ID should not be in conflict with any other vCloud Director installation in your datacenter. This field is much like the vCenter installation ID—it is responsible for a field in the MAC address when a virtual machine (VM) is created. This field is not changeable after it has been set without reinstalling vCloud Director. The cloud installation shown in Figure 2-24 is 95.

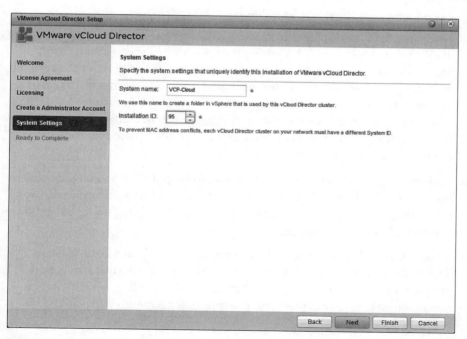

Figure 2-24   Cloud Installation ID

vCloud Director System Settings

vCloud Director has several settings that are considered global by nature, meaning they will affect every organization on the instance. They are as follows:

- Extensibility
- Roles
- Public URLs
- Logging

There are also settings that organizations can opt out of, including the LDAP and SMTP settings. It is important to understand the implications that the settings will have on your cloud installation. We cover roles and their settings in Chapter 3, "Administer vCloud Users, Roles, and Privileges." The remaining settings are covered in this section.

General

The following is a brief description of the settings found on the General settings page of the Administration tab in the System console of vCloud Director:

- **LDAP Synchronization**—vCloud Director automatically synchronizes Group and User information from the LDAP servers. This aids in speeding up the login times for users. This setting does not affect a user account that has been disabled. When a user attempts to log in to vCloud Director, the account is verified as being valid and as having a valid password. Setting this value too high could allow a user who had access to vCloud Director through an LDAP group, that has since been removed from that group, to continue to have access until this synchronization has taken place. If this is a security concern, you can turn this setting down to 1 hour.

- **Activity Log**—This one specifies how long to keep the log and how much of the log to show in the UI. To conserve database space and performance, these values should be kept as low as possible, while using a syslog server to capture and retain long-term information.

- **Networking**—Syslog servers can be configured here for network devices. This will set a default syslog setting on all vShield Edge devices that are deployed via vCloud Director. There is also an option to allow overlapping external networks if your deployment contains other methods (not VLANs) for isolating networks.

NOTE The IP Address Release Timeout setting makes vCloud Director consider an IP address still in use even after the vApp has been powered off or deleted until the timeout value is reached. Setting this value too high will prevent IP addresses from being released and can cause the IP allocation pool to run out of addresses in the event of a high churn of vApps. The purpose of this setting is to let ARP tables, firewall rules, and other processes clear before reassigning the IP to a new vApp.

- **Provider Locale**—This is where you change the language of the vCloud Director deployment.

- **Timeouts**—Idle Session Timeout is the amount of time a user session can be idle without activity. Maximum Session Timeout is the amount of time that a session can remain active, even if in use. Exceeding the timeout value will force a user to reauthenticate to vCloud Director even if he is actively using the application.

  The Host Refresh Frequency setting defines how often vCloud Director will check to see if the host is still alive. When added to the amount of time defined by the Host Hung Timeout setting, it enables a host to be offline for 330 seconds (using default values) before vCloud Director considers the host inaccessible. This should be taken into consideration when configuring the vCenter HA host detection timeout settings; these settings should be equal.

  With vCloud Director 5.x, you can configure an upload quarantine timeout. This setting should be used if you need to verify and check uploads before they are made usable by vCloud Director.

- **Certificates**—Much like we created a certificate store in the first part of this chapter, you can combine the trust certificate authority (CA) certificates in a JCEKS file and then upload that store to vCloud Director. This will enable vCloud Director to verify the vCenter, vShield Manager, and vSphere Single Sign On (SSO) service instances, as well as encrypt their traffic.

- **Miscellaneous**—Your Cloud Installation ID is located here and is viewable for troubleshooting purposes. After it is set during the installation process, it is not changeable. You can also allow vCloud Director to provide default names for vApps. These names will be in the format of

  vApp_<username>_#

NOTE   If you are logged in to the System organization, your username inside the organization will be defined as a system. Even though you can create a vApp in an organization while logged in to the System Organization, you must share that vApp to your users before logging in to the Organization to consume that vApp.

NOTE   You can verify how you are logged in to vCloud by looking at the upper-right corner of the vCloud Director UI. As a system user, it will indicate System Administrator; as an organization user, it will state your role in that organization.

Email

This is the section where you will define the SMTP server for the vCloud Instance. The organizations will use this SMTP server unless a specific one is defined for the organization. We cover this in Chapter 7, "Configure and Administer vCloud Organizations." In the event you have multiple vCloud Director installations, you can define the prefix of emails coming from vCloud Director to reflect the name of the vCloud Director instance. System alerts are defined here, as well as to which email address those alerts are sent.

LDAP

The system LDAP server can be configured here. It enables you to define system administrators from LDAP as well as the default LDAP instance for organizations.

vCloud Director supports Windows Active Directory using Simple SSL or Kerberos and Linux LDAP using Simple SSL or Kerberos authentication methods. If your installation of LDAP utilizes a different schema from the default schema for active directory, you can modify the attributes for users and groups in the next section.

We cover LDAP and the settings for LDAP in depth in Chapter 3.

Password Policy

The lockout settings configured in this section of the UI apply only to locally defined users in vCloud Director; they will not cause LDAP or SAML accounts to be locked out. vCloud Director relies on the underlying authentication mechanism to perform that action.

Branding

Branding of your vCloud Director installation occurs here, and you are able to change multiple values for the vCloud installation. This includes the title of the vCloud instance, which will affect email alerts that are sent to users, as well as log entries. The logo file is also changeable, though after it is changed, the original logo file is overwritten. VMware publishes a UI customization and theming guide for vCloud Director. This can be found on the VMware website.

The links that some of the URLs refer to in vCloud Director can also be customized, including

- About company URL

- Support URL

- Sign up URL

- Forgot username or password URL

Each of these fields changes the URL that all users in the vCloud installation receive. vCloud Director 5.x has no option to customize this per organization.

Public Addresses

When utilizing a load balancer with your vCloud Director installation, the hostname of your vCloud cells is typically not the hostname that the end users will use to access your vCloud installation. In this case, you need to define the URL end users will use to access your cloud. The format should be the entire URL needed (for example, https://<fqdn>/cloud). It is important that you include the full URL; otherwise, the links sent to users via the alerts will likely be broken.

Extensibility

vCloud Director enables you to use an orchestration engine to interact with your cloud deployment. Although configuration of a cloud management system is out of the scope of this book, this is the location where you will configure vCloud to send messages to an AMQP Broker, as well as defining blocking tasks.

NOTE Blocking tasks is a systemwide setting. If a blocking task is defined in vCloud Director, the task must be authorized or allowed by your AMQP server before the task will complete. This can cause an outage if the AMQP server is offline or hung. If blocking tasks are configured, you must ensure that you configure the timeout and the timeout action appropriately to your organization.

The default actions can be configured as

- **Abort**—This will cause the task to simply stop without giving the user an error.

- **Resume**—This will allow the task to complete as if approved.

- **Fail**—This will alert the user that the task failed due to a blocking task not being cleared.

Federation

The federation defined at the system level affects the system users. At the organization level, there is another Federation tab where you can configure SAML and SSO technologies; this is covered in Chapter 7. The federation options at the system level are to register vCloud Director to vSphere SSO for authenticating System users to vCloud. This works in parallel to the LDAP server settings.

Summary

- We began the chapter talking about vCloud Director's installation requirements, including the supported operating systems.

- We then covered the installation of vCloud Director and the configuration of the options required for vCloud Director.

- Then we covered the configuration and installation of vShield Manager and the pairing of vShield Manager to vCenter.

- Finally, we covered the system configuration options of vCloud Director, LDAP settings, alert settings, and log settings.

Exam Preparation Tasks

Review All Key Topics

Review the most important topics in the chapter, noted with the Key Topic icon in the outer margin of the page. Table 2-2 lists a reference of these key topics and the page numbers on which each is found.

Table 2-2 Key Topics

Key Topic Element	Description	Page
Paragraph	vCloud Cells Concept	14
Figure 2-1	Load Balancer Example	16
Figure 2-3	Mounting an NFS Export	17
Directory Location	Database Configuration	19
Activity 2-3	Creating Certificate Keystore	19
Activity 2-5	Installing vCloud Director	22
Activity 2-6	Deploying vShield Manager	27
Activity 2-7	Configuring vShield Manager	31
Activity 2-8	Registering vShield Manager to vCenter	34
Paragraph	vCloud LDAP Options	38

Definitions of Key Terms

Define the following key terms from this chapter, and check your answers in the glossary.

vCloud Director Cell, Web UI, Proxy Console Service, vCenter Proxy, keytool, vCloud System ID, load balancer, global properties, NFS transfer share

Review Questions

The answers to these review questions are in Appendix A.

1. vCloud Director supports which operating system?

   a. CentOS

   b. Windows 2012

   c. Ubuntu

   d. RHEL

2. vCloud Director supports which of the following database platforms? (Choose all that apply.)

   a. Microsoft SQL

   b. Oracle

   c. Postgres

   d. MySQL

3. vShield Manager is an application that you can install using what?

   a. Red Hat RPMs

   b. An OVF file

   c. Windows Installer

   d. Oracle Linux install package

4. vCloud Director supports which LDAP servers? (Choose all that apply.)

   a. Open Directory

   b. Windows 2003

   c. Windows 2008

   d. Red Hat LDAP

5. Where can blocking tasks be configured? (Choose all that apply.)

   a. Per user

   b. Per Cloud

   c. Per organization

   d. Per provider vDC

6. vShield Manager can be connected to how many vCenters?

   a. 1

   b. 2

   c. 4

   d. 5

7. vCloud Director requires which of the following features from a load balancer?

    a. Cookie persistence

    b. HTTPS offloading

    c. SSL session persistence

    d. Reverse Proxy connections

8. What is required for multiple vCloud Director cells to work properly?

    a. Same subnet

    b. NFS file share

    c. Oracle server database

    d. Red Hat clustering services

This chapter covers the following subjects:

- **Privileges and Roles**—This section explains roles and privileges, discusses the predefined roles in vCloud Director, and demonstrates how to create custom roles.

- **Users and Groups**—In this section, you learn about users and groups, where they can be defined in vCloud Director, and how to define local users and import users and groups from an LDAP provider.

- **LDAP Integration**—This section covers integrating vCloud Director with an LDAP provider, the LDAP authentication methods, and using Kerberos.

This chapter covers a portion of the VCP-IaaS Exam Objectives 2.1 and 2.2 and VCP-Cloud Exam Objectives 9.1 and 9.2.

CHAPTER 3

Administer vCloud Users, Roles, and Privileges

Users, roles, and privileges are essential security concepts to understand when administering a vCloud Director environment. In this chapter, we first explore the differences between roles and privileges, the predefined roles within vCloud Director, and the use of custom roles. Then we move on to exploring the various locations in vCloud Director where users can be defined or imported. Finally, we look at configuring vCloud Director to connect to Active Directory (AD) and other Lightweight Directory Access Protocol (LDAP) sources to import users and groups from a centralized directory service.

"Do I Know This Already?" Quiz

The "Do I Know This Already?" quiz enables you to assess whether you should read this entire chapter or simply jump to the "Exam Preparation Tasks" section for review. If you are in doubt, read the entire chapter. Table 3-1 outlines the major headings in this chapter and the corresponding "Do I Know This Already?" quiz questions. You can find the answers in Appendix A, "Answers to the 'Do I Know This Already?' Quizzes and Review Questions."

Table 3-1 "Do I Know This Already?" Foundation Topics Section-to-Question Mapping

Foundations Topics Section	Questions Covered in This Section
Privileges and Roles	1–3
Users and Groups	4–5
LDAP Integration	6–8

1. Which of the following is NOT a predefined role in vCloud Director?

    a. vApp User

    b. System Administrator

    c. Organization Administrator

    d. Organization User

2. Which three actions can vApp Users perform on a vApp?

   a. Suspend a vApp

   b. Edit vApp Properties

   c. Create a vApp

   d. Delete a vApp

   e. Add a vApp

3. Which of the following roles is able to configure organizational LDAP settings?

   a. System Administrator

   b. Organization Administrator

   c. root

   d. vApp Author

4. The default System Administrator username is what?

   a. Admin@system-domain

   b. User-defined

   c. root

   d. Administrator

5. Which two actions can be performed on Groups?

   a. Imported to the vCloud Director system administrators

   b. Created in the vCloud Director system administrators

   c. Imported to a vCloud Director organization

   d. Created in a vCloud Director organization

6. After importing an LDAP user as a system administrator, where is the user's password stored?

   a. The user table in the vCloud Director database

   b. The password table in the vCloud Director database

   c. The local user database created when LDAP integration is configured

   d. The LDAP directory

7. Which of the following is NOT a supported LDAP source?

    a. Windows 2008 Active Directory

    b. Windows 2003 Active Directory

    c. Windows 2000 Active Directory

    d. Linux OpenLDAP

8. Which of the following are supported authentication methods when integrating with LDAP?

    a. OpenLDAP Kerberos

    b. Windows 2003 Kerberos

    c. Windows 2008 Kerberos

    d. None of the above

Foundation Topics

Privileges and Roles

vCloud Director controls access and privileges through role-based access control (RBAC). RBAC is a common access control model where rights to an object are granted based on job function. Privileges (also known as *rights*) are granted to a particular job role, and users (or groups of users) are then assigned to a role. For example, rather than granting specific privileges to user Ned and his Accounting Department, we grant privileges to the Accounting role and then assign the Accounting role to Ned and the other accountants in his department. Do not confuse roles with groups, however. Whereas a user can be a member of several groups, that user can be assigned to only one role within an organization.

What Are Privileges?

Privileges specify which actions a user can and cannot perform. Examples include accessing a virtual machine (VM) console, publishing or sharing a catalog, editing the properties of an organization virtual datacenter (VDC) network, and deleting a disk from a VM. Individual privileges are combined into roles, granting role holders the collection of privileges specified. There are more than 50 individual privileges that can be granted in vCloud Director.

What Are Roles?

Roles are collections of privileges that map to job functions. In a vCloud environment, administrators of a provider VDC require different privileges than administrators of an organization VDC. Similarly, end users within an organization require fewer privileges than an administrator. Combining the privileges necessary for common job functions into roles simplifies the process of defining which operations users are able to perform.

In vCloud Director, there are six built-in roles, each with a predefined set of privileges. The system administrator can modify the predefined roles and also has the ability to create custom roles. We explore these roles in the next section.

Predefined Roles in vCloud Director

vCloud Director includes the following predefined roles:

- System Administrator
- Organization Administrator
- Catalog Author
- vApp Author

- vApp User
- Console Access Only

To access the roles in vCloud Director, click the **Administration** tab at the System level and select **Roles** from the left menu, as shown in Figure 3-1.

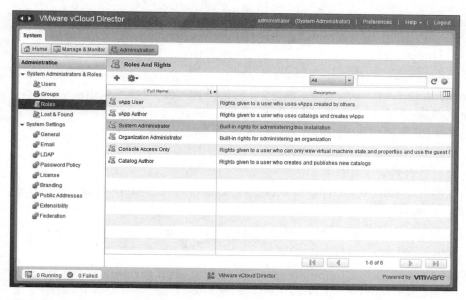

Figure 3-1 Selecting Roles in vCloud Director

The System Administrator role has ultimate authority over the entire vCloud Director installation, with the ability to add, delete, or modify almost any object within the infrastructure.

NOTE   The System Administrator role is the only system-level role available, and it cannot be deleted or modified. However, it can be copied.

The initial System Administrator account username and password are created during the installation of vCloud Director. After installation, that account can be used to add more users to the System Administrator role if necessary. System Administrators have Organization Administrator rights to all organizations within the vCloud infrastructure.

Each organization defined in vCloud Director is administered by users assigned the Organization Administrator role. Users assigned this role can manage a single organization, or multiple organizations, as needed. Organization Administrators are allowed to manage the settings, catalogs, and users within their organizations, as well as set machine policies such as quotas, limits, and leases (if allowed by the system administrator). In vCloud Director 1.5, Organization Administrators were not allowed to create any organization networks—they were only permitted to view and edit their organization networks. With vCloud Director 5.1, Organization Administrators can now create routed and isolated organization networks, but a system administrator must still create external networks and direct-connected organization networks. Organization Administrators can also edit some settings, such as DHCP settings, VPN settings and tunnels, and firewall rules, in their edge gateways in vCloud Director 5.1.

The Catalog Author role has all the rights of the vApp Author role (which we review shortly), as well as the ability to create and publish catalogs within an organization. However, the system administrator controls whether an organization can publish its catalog to other organizations.

Activity 3-1: Allowing an Organization to Publish Catalogs

To allow an organization to publish catalogs, a system administrator must complete the following steps:

1. Select the **Manage & Monitor** tab at the System level, and select **Organizations** from within the left pane.

2. Right-click the organization to be modified (or highlight it and select the gear icon); then select **Properties** from the drop-down list, as shown in Figure 3-2.

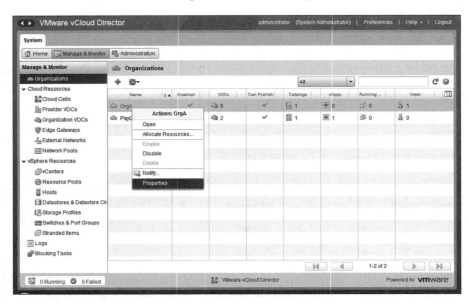

Figure 3-2 Modifying an Organization

3. Select the **Catalog Publishing** tab.

4. Select the **Allow Publishing Catalogs to All Organizations** option, as shown in Figure 3-3.

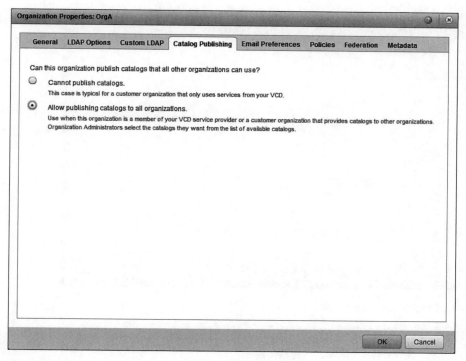

Figure 3-3   Allowing an Organization to Publish Catalogs

5. Click **OK**.

Activity 3-2: Publishing a Catalog for Public Use

After a system administrator has allowed an organization to publish catalogs, an organization administrator or catalog author completes the following steps to publish the selected catalog:

1. From the organization level, select the **Catalogs** tab.

2. Select **My Organization's Catalogs** from the left pane.

3. Select the **Catalogs** tab within the My Organization's Catalogs heading.

4. Right-click the catalog to be published (or highlight it and select the gear icon); from the drop-down list, select **Properties**, as shown in Figure 3-4.

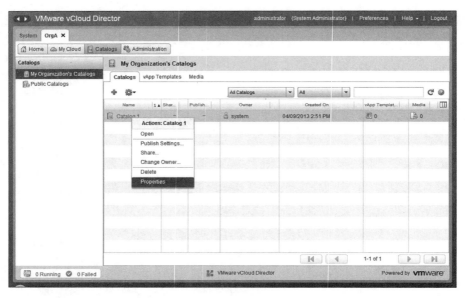

Figure 3-4   Modifying an Organization Catalog

5. Select the **Publishing** tab.

6. Select the **Publish to All Organizations** option, as shown in Figure 3-5.

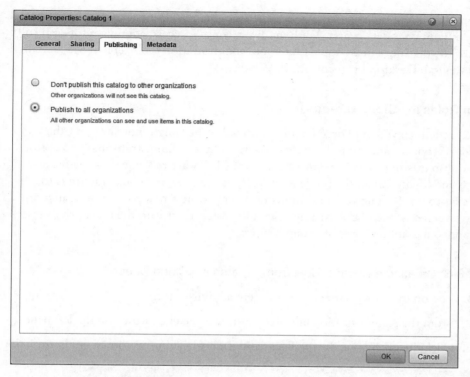

Figure 3-5   Publishing a Catalog

    7. Click **OK**.

Members of the vApp User role are not allowed to create vApps, but they can delete them, edit their properties, and copy or move them. vApp users can perform power functions (start, stop, rest, suspend) and modify properties that are not resource-related (for example, CPU, memory, and hard disk allocations).

The vApp Author role includes all the rights of the vApp User role, along with the ability to create and modify vApps and the resource settings on machines within a vApp. vApp Authors can create vApps from a catalog (either organizational or public) or build them from scratch by adding individual machines from templates. vApp Authors can also modify the CPU, memory, and hard disk allocations of VMs within a vApp and change the ownership of an existing vApp.

The Console Access Only role is the most restricted role. It allows the role holder to remotely access the console of VMs in a vApp but does not allow management of any properties or power controls. This role is targeted at administrators who require direct console access to a VM. This should not include all administrators of a VM but should, instead, be a limited subset. Restrict direct console access to a vApp in vCloud Director to the same staff that you would restrict access to physical machines in your data center. Without direct console access, administrators can still access the machines in a vApp with remote administration tools such as SSH (Linux) and Remote Desktop Protocol (RDP, Windows).

Custom Roles in vCloud Director

The predefined vCloud Director roles outlined earlier might not always fit the needs of your organization. In these cases, the system administrator has two options: modify an existing role or create a custom role. VMware recommends against directly modifying any of the predefined roles, so the recommended practice is to create a custom role. The system administrator can create a new role from scratch or, better yet, copy one of the existing roles and customize it with the exact privileges he wants to grant to a user or group of users.

Activity 3-3: Creating a Custom Role from Scratch in vCloud Director

1. Log on to vCloud Director as a system administrator.

2. From the Administration tab at the system level, click **Roles** on the left pane.

3. Click the green + below the Roles and Rights heading, as shown in Figure 3-6.

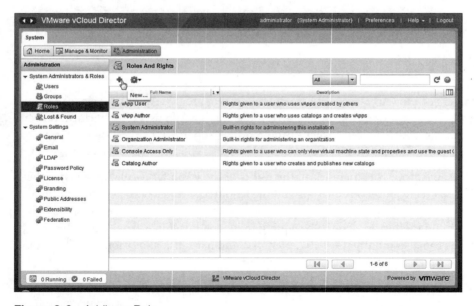

Figure 3-6   Adding a Role

4. Provide a Name and Description (optional) for the new role.

5. Check the box next to each privilege you want to grant.

6. Click **OK** to save your settings (see Figure 3-7).

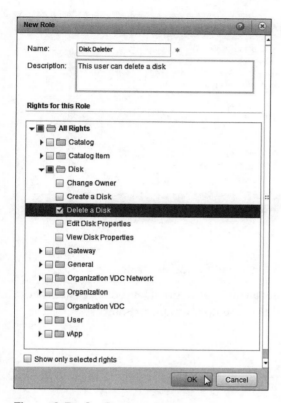

Figure 3-7   Configuring a New Role

Activity 3-4: Creating a Custom Role by Copying an Existing Role in vCloud Director

1. Log on to vCloud Director as a system administrator.

2. From the Administration tab at the system level, click **Roles** in the left pane.

3. Highlight the role you want to copy and right-click it (or press the gear icon); then select **Copy to** as shown in Figure 3-8.

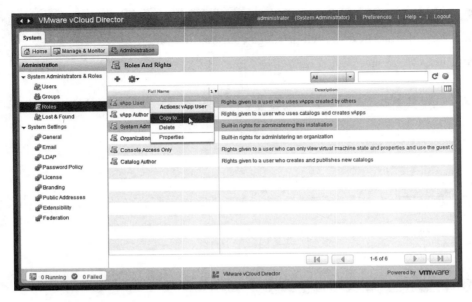

Figure 3-8   Copying a Role

4. Provide a Name and Description (optional) for the new role.

5. Check the box next to each privilege you want to grant, and remove the check next to any privileges that copied that you do not want to grant.

6. Click **OK** to save your settings.

Activity 3-5: Modifying an Existing Role in vCloud Director

1. Log on to vCloud Director as a system administrator.

2. From the Administration tab at the system level, click **Roles** in the left pane.

3. Highlight the role you want to modify and right-click it (or press the gear icon); then select **Properties**.

4. Add or remove the check box next to privileges you want to add or remove from the role.

5. Click **OK** to save your settings.

NOTE   Modifying the predefined roles is not recommended.

NOTE   The System Administrator role cannot be modified.

Activity 3-6: Deleting an Existing Role in vCloud Director

1. Log on to vCloud Director as a system administrator.

2. From the Administration tab at the system level, click **Roles** in the left pane.

3. Highlight the role you want to delete and right-click it (or press the gear icon); then select **Delete**.

4. Click **Yes** to confirm the delete operation or **No** to cancel.

NOTE   Deleting any of the predefined roles is not recommended.

NOTE   The System Administrator role cannot be deleted.

Troubleshooting Roles and Privileges

Creating and assigning custom roles are often exercises in trial and error. The system administrator should grant the minimal amount of privilege necessary for a user to perform her job—no more and no less. Creating custom roles and determining the appropriate privilege therefore requires administrators to test custom roles, either with their own test account or with the end user. These tests involve logging in with the test account or working with the end user to assess and validate the functionality of the role. Does the user have enough rights? Does the user have too many rights? Again, determine the minimal and appropriate rights for the user through an iterative, trial-and-error process.

Users and Groups in vCloud Director

The initial system administrator account is created during install; all other system or organizational users must be created or imported after installation is complete. Users and groups in vCloud Director can be defined at the local system or organization level or imported from an external LDAP identity source. Each organization (and the vCloud Director system itself) has separate settings for its users. The following options exist for defining or importing users or groups in vCloud Director 5.1.

System Administrators can be sourced from the following locations:

- Local users defined in vCloud Director and stored in the database

- Individual users or groups imported from an external LDAP source (AD or OpenLDAP)

- Users or groups imported from vCenter Single Sign-On (SSO) (a new option in vCloud Director 5.1)

Organization users can be sourced from the following locations:

- Local users defined in vCloud Director and stored in the database

- Individual users or groups imported from an external LDAP source (AD or OpenLDAP)

- Users or groups imported from VMware Horizon Application Manager or other third-party Security Assertion Markup Language (SAML) identity provider

All users in vCloud Director must have one and only one role within an organization, but a single user can be imported to multiple organizations. When a user is created or imported at the system level, the user is automatically granted the role of system administrator. When a user is created or imported to an organization, you must select a role for the user.

Local Users

Local users are created at either the vCloud Director system level or individually at each organizational level. These users are stored in the vCloud Director database, along with a salted and hashed form of their password.

Activity 3-7: Adding a Local System Administrator to vCloud Director

1. Log in to vCloud Director as a system administrator.

2. From the Administration tab at the system level, click **Users** in the left pane.

3. Click the green **+** below the **Users** heading in the right pane, as shown in Figure 3-9.

4. Fill in the details for User Name, Password, and Confirm Password. Note that the System Administrator role is automatically selected and cannot be changed.

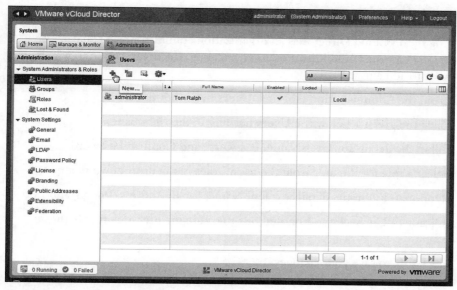

Figure 3-9 Adding a Local System Administrator

5. (Optional) Fill in the details for Full Name, Email Address, Phone, and IM.

6. (Optional) Uncheck the **Enabled** box to create the user and disable the account. Figure 3-10 shows the dialog box in which these actions take place.

Figure 3-10 Creating a New User

7. Click **OK** to save your changes.

Activity 3-8: Adding a Local User to an Organization

1. Log in to vCloud Director as an organization administrator. (You can also log in as a system administrator and navigate to the organization to which you want to add a user.)

2. From the Administration tab, click **Users** in the left pane.

3. Click the green **+** below the **Users** heading in the right pane.

4. Fill in the details for User Name, Password, and Confirm Password.

5. Select a role for the user from the list of roles in the drop-down menu.

6. (Optional) Fill in the details for Full Name, Email Address, Phone, and IM.

7. (Optional) Uncheck the **Enabled** box to create the user and disable the account.

8. Click **OK** to save your changes.

LDAP Users and Groups

LDAP users and groups can be imported at a system or organizational level only after LDAP integration has been configured. Details on configuring LDAP integration are provided in the next section.

Activity 3-9: Importing an LDAP User as a System Administrator

After configuring LDAP server settings for the vCloud Director system (as detailed in the next section, "LDAP Integration"), a system administrator must import users or groups to make them available for authentication. Follow these procedures to import users:

1. Log in to vCloud Director as a system administrator.

2. From the Administration tab at the system level, click **Users** in the left pane.

3. Click the **Import Users** button, as shown in Figure 3-11.

4. Select **LDAP** from the **Source** drop-down box.

5. Type a full or partial user name in the search box, and click **Search**.

6. Highlight the desired user and click **Add**, as shown in Figure 3-12.

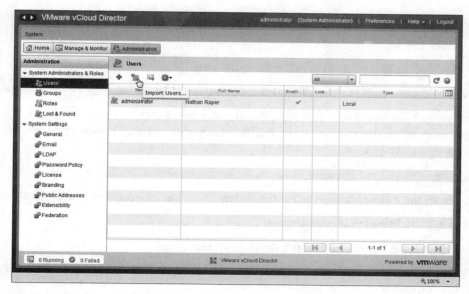

Figure 3-11 Import LDAP User

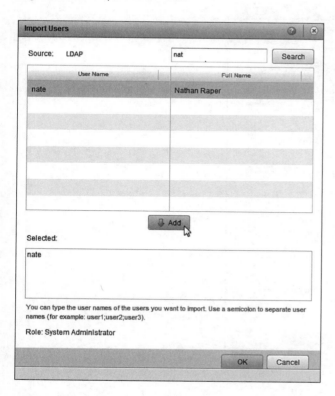

Figure 3-12 Select an LDAP User to Import

7. Repeat steps 5 and 6 to add each additional user.

8. Click **OK**.

Activity 3-10: Importing an LDAP Group as a System Administrator

After configuring LDAP server settings for the vCloud Director system, you must import users or groups to make them available for authentication. Follow these procedures to import groups:

1. Log in to vCloud Director as a system administrator.

2. From the Administration tab at the system level, click **Groups** in the left pane.

3. Click the **Import Groups** button.

4. Select **LDAP** from the **Source** drop-down box.

5. Type a full or partial group name in the search box and click **Search Groups**; an example is shown in Figure 3-13.

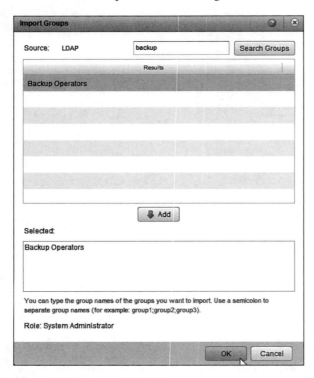

Figure 3-13   Import LDAP User

6. Highlight the desired group and click **Add**.

7. Repeat steps 5 and 6 to add each group.

8. Click **OK**.

Activity 3-11: Importing an LDAP User to an Organization

After configuring LDAP server settings for an organization, a system or organization admin must import users or groups to make them available for authentication. Follow these procedures to import users:

1. Log in to vCloud Director as an organization administrator. (System administrators can't add an LDAP user to an organization.)

2. From the Administration tab, click **Users** in the left pane.

3. Click the **Import Users** button, as indicated in Figure 3-14.

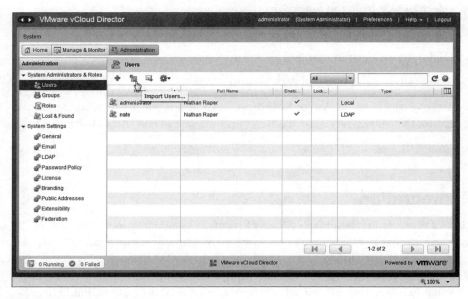

Figure 3-14 Import LDAP User

4. Select **LDAP** from the Source drop-down box.

5. Type a full or partial username in the search box, and click **Search**.

6. Highlight the desired user and click **Add**.

7. Repeat steps 5 and 6 to add each additional user.

8. Assign a role from the Assign Role drop-down box. If you are importing multiple users who should be assigned different roles, you can edit them after importing.

9. Click **OK**.

Activity 3-12: Importing an LDAP Group to an Organization

After configuring LDAP server settings for an organization, you must import users or groups to make them available for authentication. Follow these procedures to import groups:

1. Log in to vCloud Director as an organization administrator. (System administrators can't add LDAP groups to an organization.)

2. From the Administration tab, click **Groups** in the left pane.

3. Click the **Import Users** button.

4. Select **LDAP** from the Source drop-down box.

5. Type a full or partial username in the search box, and click **Search**.

6. Highlight the desired user and click **Add**.

7. Repeat steps 5 and 6 to add each additional user.

8. Assign a role from the Assign Role drop-down box. If you are importing multiple groups that should be assigned different roles, you can edit them after importing.

9. Click **OK**.

LDAP Integration

Instead of creating local users in vCloud Director, a system administrator can integrate an external LDAP source at the system level, at any organizational level, or both. Integrating vCloud Director with an external LDAP source allows the system administrator to import users and groups and some of their properties. This is a manual two-step process: the administrator must first integrate vCloud Director with an external LDAP source and then must import users and groups. When importing users, other information, such as email address, group memberships, and telephone information, can also be synchronized with the LDAP source. Note that the user password is not imported or stored for LDAP users.

vCloud Director 5.1 supports Linux OpenLDAP and Windows Active Directory as LDAP sources, with four possible methods of authentication based on the version. Table 3-2 lists the supported LDAP sources and their corresponding authentication methods.

Table 3-2 Supported LDAP Sources and Authentication Methods

Operating System	LDAP Server	Authentication Methods
Windows 2003	Active Directory	Simple, Simple SSL, Kerberos, Kerberos SSL
Windows 2008	Active Directory	Simple
Windows Server 2008 R2	Active Directory	Simple, Simple SSL, Kerberos, Kerberos SSL
Linux	OpenLDAP	Simple, Simple SSL

LDAP integration can be configured at a system level, and organizations can inherit that configuration. However, when a single LDAP source is used for more than one organization in vCloud Director, separate organizational units should be specified for each organization. Alternatively, distinct LDAP sources can be specified for individual organizations. In either case, only a system administrator can configure LDAP integration. Organization administrators cannot create or modify LDAP integration settings, but they can specify the synchronization frequency.

NOTE vCloud Director cannot modify the information in a configured LDAP source. The connection is a one-way "pull" from LDAP. User and group information must be modified at the LDAP source, and then the organization must be resynchronized with LDAP.

LDAP Authentication Methods

When configuring LDAP settings, you must select an authentication method: Simple or Kerberos. Both methods can be optionally configured with Secure Sockets Layer (SSL), giving you the four options listed in Table 3-2.

Simple Authentication

Simple authentication forwards the user's Distinguished Name (DN) and password to the LDAP authentication server for validation. If authentication is successful, vCloud Director logs the user in. Simple authentication should never be used without configuring SSL settings. If SSL configuration settings are not specified, the user DN and password are sent in clear text and anyone capturing network traffic can gather this information. Furthermore, if SSL is not configured, then there is no way for the server to be authenticated. Best practice dictates that you should always use SSL with Simple authentication. Alternatively, use Kerberos authentication when using AD as an LDAP identity source.

Activity 3-13: Configuring LDAP Integration for vCloud Director Using Simple Authentication

The procedure for connecting to an LDAP server using Simple authentication is the same whether you are connecting to an AD infrastructure or an OpenLDAP infrastructure:

1. Log in to vCloud Director as a system administrator.

2. From the Administration tab at the system level, click **LDAP** in the left pane.

3. In the Server box, enter the name or IP address of an LDAP server.

4. In an Active Directory domain, you can specify the domain name and vCloud Director will query DNS for a domain controller. This provides a measure of redundancy.

5. Enter the Port—the default ports are 389 for LDAP and 636 for secure LDAP (LDAPS).

6. Type the Base Distinguished Name. The base distinguished name is the root the connection vCloud Director makes to the LDAP directory. All user or group accounts that you want to add must reside at this level or within a sub-OU. For example, if the domain name is thevsg.local, enter **DC=THEVSG,DC=LOCAL**.

   Steps 2–6 are shown in Figure 3-15.

NOTE   VMware recommends connecting to the root of the LDAP tree.

Figure 3-15   Configure LDAP Server Settings

7. If you will be using SSL (recommended), check the **Use SSL** box and set the options:

   ■ **SSL Certificate**—Browse to the location of the certificate for the domain.

   ■ **SSL Key Store (JCEKS)**—Browse to the location of the keystore.

8. Enter the Key Store Password.

9. Select **Simple** from the Authentication Method drop-down box.

10. Enter the User Name and Password for the LDAP connection. The username must be in the form of domain\user or UPN format. Leave these blank if anonymous read connections are allowed (this is rare).

11. Click **Apply** to save the new settings, as shown in Figure 3-16.

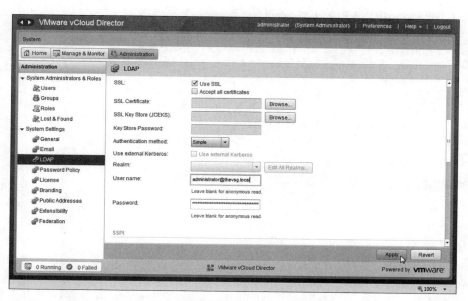

Figure 3-16   Import LDAP Server Settings, cont.

Kerberos Authentication

Kerberos is a ticket-based authentication system in which both the server and user must prove their identities. Kerberos authentication uses symmetric key cryptography by default, so usernames and passwords are never exposed in clear text the way they are when Simple authentication is used without SSL. Kerberos with SSL uses certificate-based authentication and provides another level of security when authenticating to a Windows Kerberos environment. Kerberos must be configured before it can be used with LDAP authentication.

> **NOTE**   Kerberos authentication is not supported by vCloud Director when connecting to OpenLDAP.

Activity 3-14: Configuring LDAP Integration for vCloud Director Using Kerberos

1. Log in to vCloud Director as a system administrator.

2. From the Administration tab at the system level, click **LDAP** in the left pane.

3. Under Authentication Method, select **Kerberos** from the drop-down box.

4. Click the **Edit All Realms** button, as shown in Figure 3-17.

Figure 3-17   Add/Edit Kerberos Realm

5. In the Edit Realms screen, on the Realm tab, click the **Add** button shown in Figure 3-18.

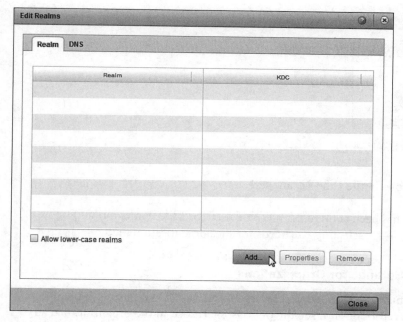

Figure 3-18   Import LDAP User

6. Fill in details for the Kerberos realm:

   ▪ **Realm**—Type the name of the Windows domain. You must use all up-percase letters unless you have selected Allow Lower-Case Realms on the previous screen.

   ▪ **KDC**—The Key Distribution Center (KDC) is any Windows domain controller that vCloud Director is able to contact.

7. Click **OK** to add the realm (see Figure 3-19).

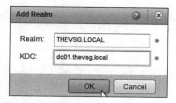

Figure 3-19   Import LDAP User

8. In the Edit Realms screen, click the **DNS** tab.

9. On the DNS tab, click **Add**.

10. Enter a DNS server in the DNS box and select a realm from the drop-down box.

11. Click **OK**, as shown in Figure 3-20.

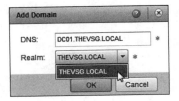

Figure 3-20   Import LDAP User

12. Select **Close** in the Edit Realms screen.

After Kerberos has been configured, it can be used for LDAP integration. Follow the steps in Activity 3-13, selecting **Kerberos** for the authentication method in step 8.

Configure LDAP Settings for Organizations

A system administrator must configure organizational LDAP settings—the organization administrator does not see the options for LDAP in the organizational administration settings.

There are three options for integrating LDAP within an organization, as shown in Figure 3-21.

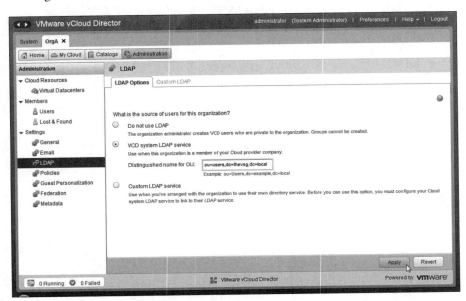

Figure 3-21   Import LDAP User

When an organization chooses not to integrate with an LDAP service, all users must be configured locally in the vCloud Director organization and groups cannot be used.

The organization might choose to use the same LDAP infrastructure that is configured at the vCloud Director system level. This is common for businesses that provide different vCloud Director organizations to their business units. In this case, you can specify a base OU for user and group accounts. When the same LDAP infrastructure is used for multiple organizations, it is recommended that each organization have a separate organizational unit in the LDAP tree.

Finally, the organization might choose to use its own custom LDAP service. In this case, the system administrator follows the same steps as those in Activity 3-13 (Simple Authentication) or Activity 3-14 (Kerberos Authentication).

Activity 3-15: Configuring LDAP Integration for an Organization

1. Log in to vCloud Director as a system administrator.

2. From the Manage and Monitor tab at the system level, click **Organizations** in the left pane.

3. Double-click the organization for which you want to configure LDAP settings.

4. Click the **Administration** tab.

5. Click **LDAP** in the left pane.

   There are three options (see Figure 3-21):

   - **Do Not Use LDAP**—This option is the default and turns off LDAP for the organization.

   - **VCD System LDAP Service**—This option uses the LDAP settings configured at the system level:

     — **Configure the Distinguished Name for OU**—When using the same LDAP settings as the system, it is recommended that each organization be rooted in a unique OU within the LDAP tree. This unique root is configured here.

   - **Custom LDAP Service**—This option provides the opportunity to connect to a separate LDAP infrastructure than what is configured at the system level:

     — Select the **Custom LDAP service** option.

     — Click the **Custom LDAP** tab.

     — Follow the instructions in Activity 3-13 or Activity 3-14, making sure to navigate to the correct organization prior to step 2.

6. Click **Apply** to save your settings.

Additional LDAP Options and Actions

Several other actions can be performed by a system administrator when administering LDAP for vCloud Director. The most important of these are testing LDAP settings, setting the LDAP synchronization interval, and manually synchronizing vCloud Director organizations or the system itself with the configured LDAP provider.

Activity 3-16: Testing System LDAP Settings

After System LDAP settings are configured, use the following procedure to test the settings:

1. Log in to vCloud Director as a system administrator.

2. From the Administration tab at the system level, click **LDAP** in the left pane.

3. Click the **Test LDAP Settings** button shown in Figure 3-22. There should be a green check mark with the word Connected at the top of the dialog box (see Figure 3-23).

Figure 3-22   Test LDAP Settings

4. Enter a User Name to Search For in the box and click **Test**, as shown in Figure 3-23.

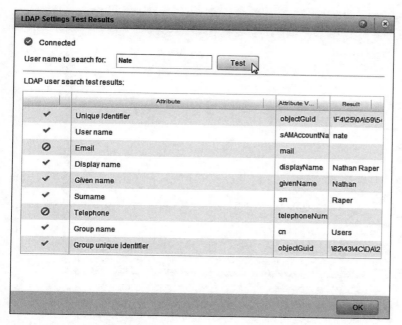

Figure 3-23   Search LDAP for a User

5. Review the results and click **OK**.

Activity 3-17: Setting the LDAP Synchronization Interval

By default, vCloud Director synchronizes with LDAP once every 24 hours. This can be changed to as little as one hour with the following procedure:

1. Log in to vCloud Director as a system administrator.

2. From the Administration tab at the system level, click **General** in the left pane.

3. Under the LDAP Synchronization heading, select the interval in hours, as shown in Figure 3-24. The shortest interval is one hour.

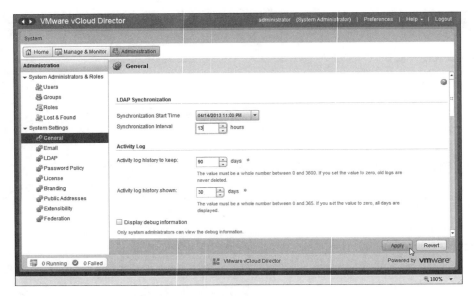

Figure 3-24 LDAP Synchronization Interval

4. Click **Apply**.

Activity 3-18: Manually Synchronizing with the LDAP Server

Occasionally the system administrator might need to manually synchronize the
vCloud Director system or an organization with LDAP to recognize recent changes:

1. Log in to vCloud Director as a system administrator.

2. From the Administration tab for the system or organization, click **LDAP** in
   the left pane.

3. Click the **Synchronize LDAP** button shown in Figure 3-25.

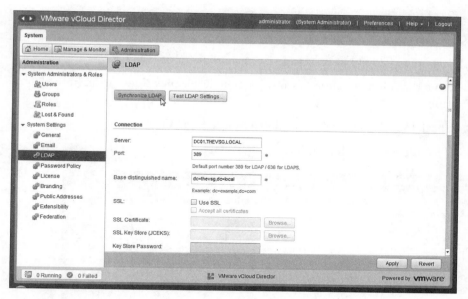

Figure 3-25 Manually Synchronize with the LDAP Server

Federation with vCenter Single Sign-On and Horizon Application Manager

In addition to connecting to an LDAP infrastructure, vCloud Director can be configured to integrate with vCenter SSO for authentication. When configured to connect to the vCenter SSO Repository, users and groups that have been configured in vCenter SSO can be imported for use in vCloud Director in much the same way LDAP users and groups are imported. vCenter SSO users can be imported only as system administrators. However, at an organizational level, vCloud Director can be integrated with an external SAML provider such as VMware Horizon Application Manager. This provides an alternative to LDAP for connecting to an external identity and authentication provider.

These options are not currently part of the exam blueprints for VCP-IaaS or VCP-Cloud and is not tested in the current version of the exam. Make sure to download the latest version of the blueprint, as the exam is occasionally updated. A VMware exam tests only the topics that are on the blueprint.

Activity 3-19: Configuring vCloud Director to Connect to a vCenter Single Sign-On Repository

1. Log in to vCloud Director as a system administrator.

2. From the Administration tab at the system level, click **Federation** in the left pane.

3. Check the box next to **Use vSphere Single Sign-On**.

4. Click the **Register** box shown in Figure 3-26.

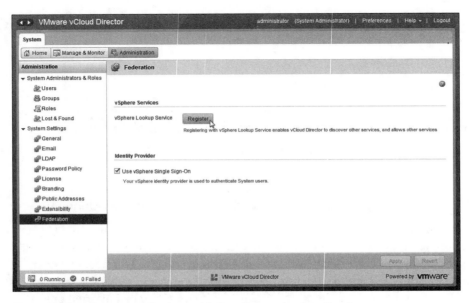

Figure 3-26 Prepare to Register with the vSphere Lookup Service

In the Register With Lookup Service dialog box (shown in Figure 3-27), you need to

- Enter the Lookup Service URL.

- Enter the SSO Admin User Name—by default, this is admin@system-domain, but you might have configured a different admin user in vCenter SSO.

- Enter the SSO Admin User Password.

- Enter the vCloud Director URL.

- Click **OK**.

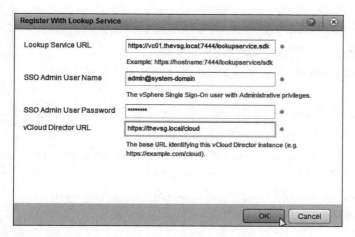

Figure 3-27   Register with the vSphere Lookup Service

5. Click **Apply** to save your settings.

Troubleshooting LDAP Integration Issues

LDAP integration issues can be caused by any number of misconfigured settings. In troubleshooting, it is always best to start as simple as possible and increase complexity from there. Though it is not recommended for long-term use, be sure that Simple authentication over port 389 without SSL works before attempting to configure SSL or Kerberos authentication. Make sure that name resolution is possible and DNS is configured correctly. Use an IP address in place of the server name for the LDAP settings. Use the root of the domain tree for the base distinguished name, and be sure that it is in lowercase as the example suggests.

When configuring Kerberos, it is vital that name resolution and time settings be correct. Always use the fully qualified domain name (FQDN) of a server. Use network time protocol (NTP) servers on all systems, including the vCloud Director server, to ensure that the time on all systems is identical. Windows Active Directory and Kerberos do not function properly if system time is not accurate. Kerberos tickets are time-stamped, and if the time between two systems is off by more than five minutes (by default), this can cause tickets to be rejected and authentication to fail.

Summary

In this chapter, we explored the following main topics:

- vCloud Director uses the common security concept of Role-Based Access Control (RBAC).

- Privileges are also called *rights* and roles are collections of privileges/rights that map to job functions

- There are built-in roles in vCloud Director. If these roles do not adequately map to a particular job function, custom roles can be defined.

- Users and groups can be defined locally in vCloud Director or imported from an external LDAP or SAML provider.

Exam Preparation Tasks

Review All the Key Topics

Review the most important topics in the chapter, noted with the Key Topic icons in the outer margin of the page. Table 3-3 lists a reference to these key topics and the page numbers on which each is found.

Table 3-3   Key Topics

Key Topic Element	Description	Page
Section	Privileges and Roles	48
Section	Predefined Roles in vCloud Director	48
Paragraph	System administrator privileges	49
Paragraph	Initial system administrator username and password	49
Paragraph	Organization administrator role	49
Activity 3-1	Allowing an Organization to Publish Catalogs	50
Activity 3-2	Publishing a Catalog for Public Use	51
Paragraphs	vApp author, vApp user, and Console Access Only roles	53
Section	Custom Roles in vCloud Director	54
Activity 3-5	Modify an Existing Role in vCloud Director	56
Note	The system administrator role cannot be modified.	57
List	Available sources for system administrators	58

Key Topic Element	Description	Page
List	Available sources for organization users	58
Activity 3-7	Adding a Local System Administrator to vCloud Director	58
Activity 3-8	Adding a Local User to an Organization	60
Activity 3-9	Importing an LDAP User as a System Administrator	60
Table 3-2	Supported LDAP Sources and Authentication Methods	65
Activity 3-13	Configuring LDAP Integration for vCloud Director Using Simple Authentication	66
Activity 3-14	Configuring LDAP Integration for vCloud Director Using Kerberos	68
Activity 3-15	Configuring LDAP Integration for an Organization	71
Activity 3-17	Setting the LDAP Synchronization Interval	73
Section	Troubleshooting LDAP Integration Issues	77

Definitions of Key Terms

Define the following key terms from this chapter, and check your answers in the glossary:

privileges, rights, role, LDAP

Troubleshooting Scenario

You have configured LDAP integration at the vCloud Director system level with secure LDAP (LDAPS), but when you test your settings, the connection fails. How would you troubleshoot this problem? What steps can you take?

Review Questions

Answers to review questions are in Appendix A.

1. Which two roles are predefined in vCloud Director 5.1? (Choose two.)

   a. Organization Author

   b. Organization Administrator

   c. vApp Administrator

   d. Console Access Only

2. In vCloud Director 5.1, which action can be taken on the system administrator role?

   a. Edited

   b. Deleted

   c. Copied

   d. Renamed

3. What is the default login and password for vCloud Director 5.1?

   a. root/vmware

   b. admin/vmware

   c. User-defined

   d. administrator/VMware1!

4. In vCloud Director 5.1, the organization administrator can perform which two actions? (Choose two.)

   a. Set quotas and limits on vApps

   b. Deploy new vShield Edge devices for his organizations

   c. Configure LDAP binding for his organization

   d. Create organization networks

5. When should you create a custom role?

   a. During installation

   b. Each time a new user is added to an organization

   c. When one of the predefined roles is full

   d. When one of the predefined roles is not adequate for the user's needs

6. What is the minimum role that can create or modify roles with similar or lesser privileges?

   a. System Administrator

   b. Organization Administrator

   c. vApp Author

   d. Catalog Author

7. Which two sources are supported for LDAP users? (Choose two.)

    a. Windows 2000 Active Directory

    b. Windows 2003 Active Directory

    c. Windows 2008R2 Active Directory

    d. Linux OpenLDAP when using Kerberos

8. When configuring an LDAP infrastructure, what does VMware recommend for the base distinguished name configuration?

    a. The Users OU

    b. The root of the LDAP tree

    c. The Groups OU

    d. A domain controller

9. Which two authentication methods do not send usernames and passwords in clear text? (Choose two.)

    a. Kerberos

    b. Simple

    c. Advanced

    d. Simple with SSL

10. What is the default LDAP synchronization interval in vCloud Director 5.1?

    a. 1 minute

    b. 1 hour

    c. 12 hours

    d. 24 hours

This chapter covers the following subjects:

- **Installing vCenter Chargeback Manager**—This section explains the requirements needed to install vCenter Chargeback Manager 2.5, provides the procedure for installation, and discusses creating vCenter Chargeback Manager 2.5 clusters.

- **Configuring Chargeback Users, Roles, and Privileges**—This section discusses users, roles, and privileges in vCenter Chargeback Manager 2.5.

- **Configuring and Managing Chargeback Cost Elements, Pricing Models, and Costing**—This section discusses the core vCenter Chargeback Manager concepts of costing and pricing.

- **vCenter Chargeback Manager Reporting**—This section discusses the available reports and the procedure for generating and scheduling a report.

This chapter covers a portion of the VCP-IaaS Exam Objective 1.1 along with all of Objectives 3.1–3.3 and a portion of the VCP-Cloud Exam Objective 8.1 along with all of Objectives 10.1–10.3.

CHAPTER 4

Configure and Administer Chargeback

Chargeback is unlike anything else you have experienced as an administrator. But in the Cloud Computing era, charging business units and departments for the cost of their virtual resources is becoming more important. Why?

Virtualization has created a new challenge in measuring resource utilization on shared infrastructure. Gone are the days when an application was tied to a physical server or group of servers that could very easily be accounted for and billed (or charged up-front) to the application owner. With virtualization and cloud computing, there is no longer a one-to-one relationship between an application and infrastructure resources. Infrastructure is shared.

With this shared infrastructure, rather than charging for infrastructure as a whole, we must break down infrastructure into components. vCenter Chargeback Manager 2.5 connects to vCenter Server, vCloud Director (vCD), and vCloud Networking and Security (vCNS, formerly vShield) to collect usage statistics on individual components of virtual machines (VMs). vCenter Chargeback Manager 2.5 stores this usage information in a database that can be used to create reports and billing information.

"Do I Know This Already?" Quiz

The "Do I Know This Already?" quiz enables you to assess whether you should read this entire chapter or simply jump to the "Exam Preparation Tasks" section for review. If you are in doubt, read the entire chapter. Table 4-1 outlines the major headings in this chapter and the corresponding "Do I Know This Already?" quiz questions. You can find the answers in Appendix A, "Answers to the 'Do I Know This Already?' Quizzes and Review Questions."

Table 4-1   "Do I Know This Already?" Foundation Topics Section-to-Question Mapping

Foundations Topics Section	Questions Covered in This Section
Installing vCenter Chargeback Manager	1–4
Configuring Chargeback Users, Roles, and Privileges	5–8
Configuring and Managing Chargeback Cost Elements	9–12
vCenter Chargeback Manager Reporting	13, 14

1. VMware vCenter Chargeback Manager 2.5 can be installed on which two operating systems? (Choose two.)

   a. Windows Server 2003 R2

   b. Windows Server 2003 with SP2

   c. Red Hat Enterprise Linux 6.0

   d. Windows Server 2008 R2

2. The minimum amount of supported RAM to install vCenter Chargeback Manager 2.5 is:

   a. 1GB

   b. 2GB

   c. 4GB

   d. 8GB

3. What is the minimum version of vCenter Server that is supported with vCenter Chargeback Manager 2.5?

   a. Virtual Center 2.5

   b. vCenter Server 4.0

   c. vCenter Server 4.1

   d. vCenter Server 5.1

4. What is the default username for first login to vCenter Chargeback Manager 2.5?

   a. Admin

   b. Administrator

   c. Super user

   d. User defined

5. Which two are privileges that can be assigned to a resource type? (Choose two.)

    a. Create

    b. Modify

    c. No Access

    d. Delete

6. Which two are default roles in vCenter Chargeback Manager 2.5? (Choose two.)

    a. Fixed Cost Update

    b. Report Scheduler

    c. Report Generator

    d. Dependent Resource Update

7. Which two roles have the Create privilege on the vCenter Server resource? (Choose two.)

    a. Hierarchy Manager

    b. vCenter Guest User

    c. Superuser

    d. Administrator

8. vCenter Chargeback Manager 2.5 users can be created from which two sources? (Choose two.)

    a. Local

    b. OpenLDAP repository

    c. Imported from vCloud Director

    d. Imported from Active Directory

9. Computing resources can be measured by which three attribute values? (Choose three.)

    a. Usage

    b. Overage

    c. Reservation

    d. Allocation

    e. Committed

10. What is the definition of base rate?

   a. The global rate that is charged for each individual unit of chargeable computing resource that is used, reserved, or allocated

   b. The fixed rate that is charged for each individual unit of chargeable computing resource that is used, reserved, or allocated

   c. The global rate that is charged for a collection of computing resources that are used, reserved, or allocated

   d. The fixed rate that is charged for a collection of computing resources that are used, reserved, or allocated

11. Which statement best describes a rate factor?

   a. The global rate charged for units of computing resources

   b. A cost that does not vary

   c. A collection of chargeable computing resources

   d. The multiplier used to modify the rate everyone pays

12. Which one of the following refers to a billing policy?

   a. The global rate charged for units of computing resources

   b. A cost that does not vary

   c. A collection of chargeable computing resources

   d. The multiplier used to modify the rate everyone pays

13. Which three are built-in reports in vCenter Chargeback Manager 2.5? (Choose three.)

   a. Allocation Report

   b. Usage Report

   c. Cost Report

   d. Showback Report

   e. Resource Summary

14. Which two reports can be scheduled in vCenter Chargeback Manager 2.5? (Choose two.)

   a. Allocation Report

   b. Usage Report

   c. Cost Report

   d. Showback Report

Foundation Topics

Installing vCenter Chargeback Manager

Before you can begin to have visibility into shared infrastructure costs and charge customers for their use, you must first install and configure Chargeback. Let's walk through the requirements and the installation of vCenter Chargeback Manager 2.5.

Hardware Requirements

The following is a list of hardware required prior to installation:

- 2.0 GHz or faster processor
- Minimum 4GB RAM
- 2GB minimum available disk space; 3GB recommended
- 10/100 Mb Ethernet Adapter; 1GB recommended

Additional resources are recommended if you are running the load balancer and multiple data collectors on the same system as vCenter Chargeback Manager 2.5. Note that each data collector requires a minimum of 1GB RAM, so if multiple data collectors will be installed, then additional memory will be necessary.

Supported Operating Systems

vCenter Chargeback Manager 2.5 supports the following operating systems:

- Windows Server 2003 R2 / 2003 with Service Pack 2
- Windows Server 2008 R2 / 2008 with Service Pack 2

Operating systems that are 64-bit are preferred for the additional addressable memory they provide.

Software Requirements

The following is a list of software and configuration requirements that should be in place prior to installation:

- Synchronized system time on all components
- Visual C++ 2005 Redistributable package
- Windows Firewall exceptions for HTTP, Load Balancer, and HTTPS

Supported Database Management Systems

vCenter Chargeback Manager 2.5 requires a database for storing information and supports the following versions of Microsoft SQL Server and Oracle:

- Microsoft SQL Server 2008 R2 (Standard, Enterprise)
- Microsoft SQL Server 2008 with SP2 (Express, Standard, Enterprise, Datacenter)
- Microsoft SQL Server 2005 with SP4 (Standard, Enterprise, Datacenter)
- Oracle 11g, Release 1 or 2 (Standard, Enterprise)
- Oracle 10g, Release 1 or 2 (Standard, Enterprise)

NOTE You should install the database and the vCenter Chargeback Manager 2.5 server components on separate servers.

Use the vCenter Chargeback Manager 2.5 Database Size Calculator tool to estimate the size of the Chargeback Manager database. The tool is available at www.vmware.com/support/pubs/vcbm_pubs.html.

You might need to select a previous release of vCenter Chargeback Manager 2.5 to view this file.

Supported Web Browsers

vCenter Chargeback Manager 2.5 supports the following web browsers:

- Internet Explorer 7/8
- Firefox
- Adobe Flash Player (10.1 or greater is required)

Supported vCenter Server Versions

vCenter server versions that are supported include

- vCenter Server 5.1
- vCenter Server 5.0 Update 1b
- vCenter Server 4.1 (all releases)
- vCenter Server 4.0 (all releases)

CAUTION If you are using vCenter Server 5.0, ensure that you are running Update 1b or later before integrating with vCenter Chargeback Manager 2.5. Releases prior to Update 1b have known issues.

Supported vCloud Director Versions

vCD versions supported by vCenter Chargeback Manager 2.5 include

- vCloud Director 1.5 and later

Activity 4-1: Installing vCenter Chargeback Manager 2.5

1. Log on to the system where vCenter Chargeback Manager 2.5 will be installed.

2. Run the installer file vCenter-CB.exe, as shown in Figure 4-1.

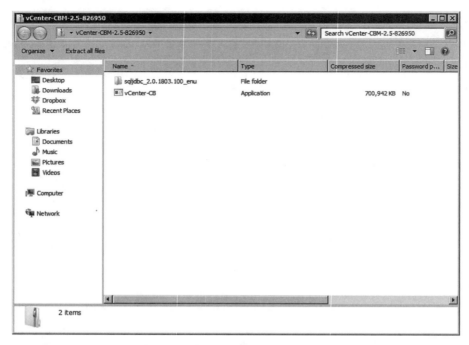

Figure 4-1   Running the vCenter-CB.exe Chargeback Installer

3. Read and accept the License Agreement; then click **Next** as shown in Figure 4-2.

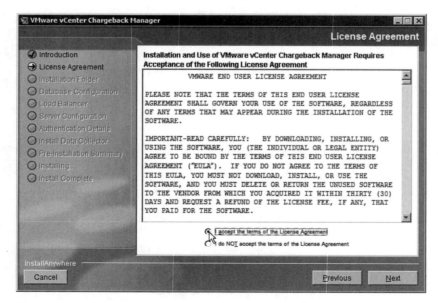

Figure 4-2   vCenter Chargeback Manager 2.5 License Agreement

4. Accept or change the installation folder and click **Next**, as shown in Figure 4-3.

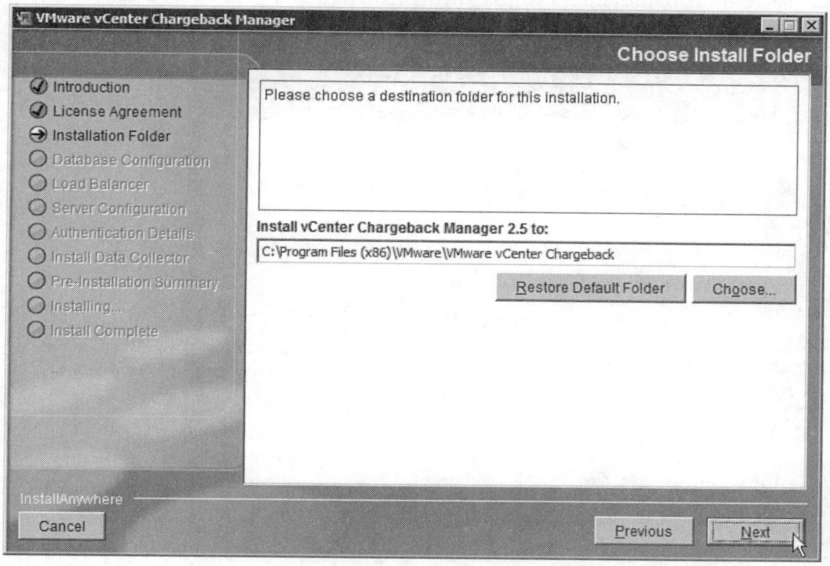

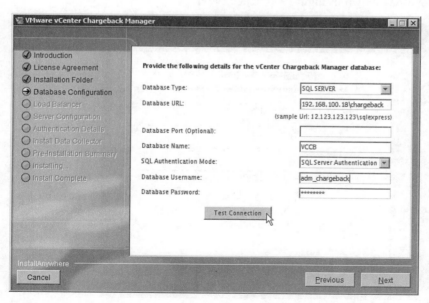

Figure 4-3   Choose Install Folder for vCenter Chargeback Manager 2.5

5. Provide the details for the vCenter Chargeback Manager database, click the **Test Connection** button, and click **Next** when finished. This is shown in Figure 4-4.

Figure 4-4   vCenter Chargeback Manager 2.5 SQL Server Database Configuration

6. The first instance of Chargeback Manager installs a load balancer; enter the details for the load balancer server as shown in Figure 4-5 if you're performing the initial install. Click **Next**.

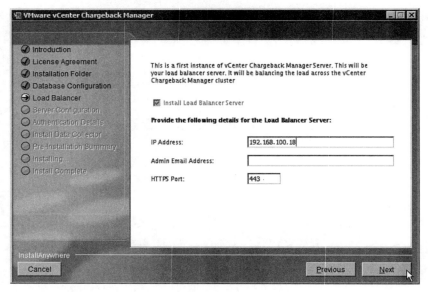

Figure 4-5   Load Balancer Configuration Details

7. Check the box for **Install vCenter Chargeback Manager Server** and fill in the details as shown in Figure 4-6. Click **Next**.

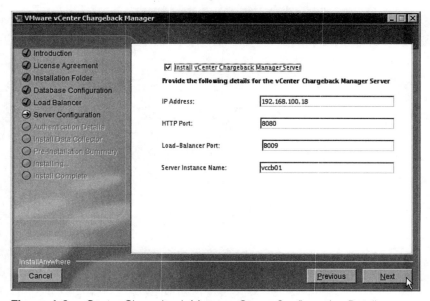

Figure 4-6   vCenter Chargeback Manager Server Configuration Details

8. Create the first administrator/super user account by filling in the username and password as shown in Figure 4-7. Click **Next**.

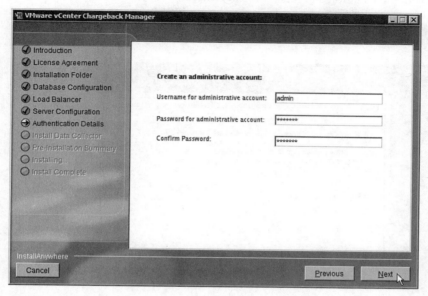

Figure 4-7 Create the Initial Chargeback Manager Account

9. Choose the data collectors to install. These are vCenter, vCD, and vShield Manager, as shown in Figure 4-8.

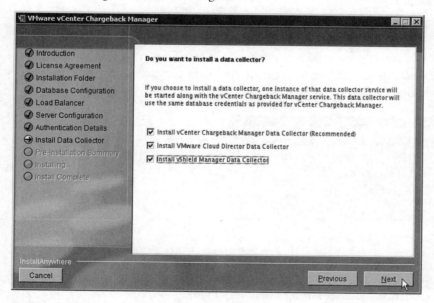

Figure 4-8 Choose the Data Collectors to Install

10. Provide details for any data collectors.

11. Review the installation summary and click **Install**.

12. When the installer completes, the URL for the vCenter Chargeback Manager 2.5 is displayed, as shown in Figure 4-9. Be sure to note the URL.

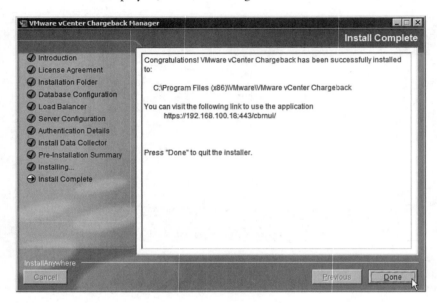

Figure 4-9 Installation Summary

13. You are prompted to generate the default certificate or generate your own certificate; if you choose to generate the default certificate, no other information is necessary. If you choose to generate your own certificate, you are prompted for additional information (see Figure 4-10).

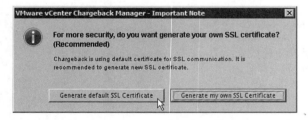

Figure 4-10 Generate the vCenter Chargeback Manager Certificate

14. Connect to the URL; enter the required license information and the super user credentials you set during install (see Figure 4-11).

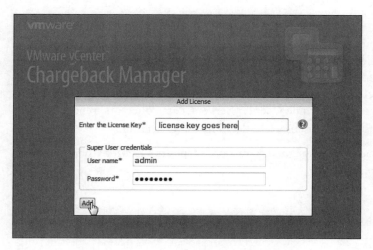

Figure 4-11   Enter the vCenter Chargeback Manager 2.5 License Key

vCenter Chargeback Manager Clusters

A cluster of vCenter Chargeback Manager 2.5 servers can be created for redundancy and load distribution. Each member of the cluster accesses the same database. The first installation of vCenter Chargeback Manager 2.5 must include the installation of the load balancer, and all requests are directed through the load balancer regardless of the number of vCenter Chargeback Manager 2.5 servers in a cluster. Creating a cluster by adding vCenter Chargeback Manager 2.5 servers to the infrastructure is a straight-forward and simple process.

During step 5 in Activity 4-1, if the installer is able to connect to an existing database, you are prompted to use the existing database. After the additional vCenter Charge-back Manager 2.5 instance is installed, you must manually add it to the cluster with the **ModifyLBWorkers** command and then restart the load balancer service.

Configuring Chargeback Users, Roles, and Privileges

Users, roles, and privileges in vCenter Chargeback Manager are configured sepa-rately from vCD. The only user that initially will be present for Chargeback is the Super User/Administrator account you configured during installation. You must create additional users or import users from an Active Directory Lightweight Direc-tory Access Protocol (LDAP) server. For those users to be able to perform tasks in Chargeback, you need to assign roles to them. There are several default roles, each having privileges that define how a user can interact with the available resource types. However, these roles might not suit your needs, in which case you can create additional roles containing the privileges you need for a particular user and use case. This section explores each of these topics.

Privileges

In Chapter 3, "Administer vCloud Users, Roles, and Privileges," you learned that privileges are also called *rights* and that they specify which actions a user can and cannot perform. In vCenter Chargeback Manager 2.5, privileges are set on resource types, which are the elements or objects within vCenter Chargeback Manager 2.5. Some sample resource types include vCenter Servers, data collectors, reports, and schedules. Resource types are discussed in detail in a later section.

The five privileges that can be assigned to resource types in vCenter Chargeback Manager 2.5 are as follows:

- Create

- Read

- Update

- Delete

- Entity cost modify

Resource Types

Privileges are assigned to the various resource types in vCenter Chargeback Manager 2.5 and collected into roles. The resource types in vCenter Chargeback Manager 2.5 are listed in Table 4-2.

Table 4-2   Resource Types in vCenter Chargeback Manager 2.5

Resource Type	Description
vCenter Server	This is the vCenter Server or Servers that are added to the vCenter Chargeback Manager 2.5 infrastructure. Users must have the read privilege on each vCenter Server to see its entities or add them to a hierarchy.
vCenter Server Entity	The entities (virtual machines) in the vCenter Server hierarchy. Permissions cannot be directly assigned to this resource type.
Data Collector	Data collectors that have been registered with vCenter Chargeback Manager 2.5. Administrators have the read privilege on data collectors, whereas super users have the full privilege. Permissions cannot be directly assigned to this resource type.
LDAP Server	LDAP servers that have been configured for authentication in vCenter Chargeback Manager 2.5. Permissions cannot be directly assigned to this resource type.

Resource Type	Description
SMTP Server	Simple mail transfer protocol (SMTP) servers that have been configured for mail relay in vCenter Chargeback Manager 2.5. Super users have the full privilege on this resource type. Permissions cannot be directly assigned to this resource type.
Chargeback Hierarchy	Logical hierarchies that have been configured in vCenter Chargeback Manager 2.5. Users must have the read privilege on the hierarchy to be able to see the hierarchy.
Chargeback Hierarchical Entity	Any entity created or added to a vCenter Chargeback Manager 2.5 logical hierarchy. Users must have the read privilege on the entity and on the hierarchy containing the entity to access it.
Attribute	Any attribute created or imported to vCenter Chargeback Manager 2.5. Permissions cannot be directly assigned to this resource type.
Tier	Storage tiers created in vCenter Chargeback Manager 2.5. Users must have the read privilege on the vCenter Server hosting the storage to see storage tiers.
Pricing Model	Pricing models created in vCenter Chargeback Manager 2.5. The read privilege is required on a pricing model to use it for reporting and cost configuration.
Cost Template	Cost templates created in vCenter Chargeback Manager 2.5. The read privilege is required on cost templates to use them for cost configuration.
Fixed Cost	Fixed costs configured in vCenter Chargeback Manager 2.5. The read privilege is required on cost templates to use them for cost configuration.
Report	Reports created in vCenter Chargeback Manager 2.5. The read privilege is required on a report to view or run the report.
Schedule	Report schedules created in vCenter Chargeback Manager 2.5. The read privilege is required on schedules to view the schedule.
Role	User roles created in vCenter Chargeback Manager 2.5. Permissions cannot be directly assigned to this resource type, and only administrators and super users can create roles.
Billing Policy	Billing policies created in vCenter Chargeback Manager 2.5. The read privilege is required on a billing policy to use it for reporting and cost configuration.
Automatic Report Scheduler	Automatic report schedulers created in vCenter Chargeback Manager 2.5. The read privilege is required to access this resource type and its schedules.

NOTE You cannot directly assign permissions on the following resource types (and they do not appear when defining a custom role):

- Data Collector
- LDAP Server
- SMTP Server
- vCenter Server Entity
- Attribute
- Role

Roles

In Chapter 3, you learned that roles are collections of privileges that map to job functions. In vCenter Chargeback Manager 2.5, you assign roles to users to grant privileges on different resource types. There are some predefined roles in vCenter Chargeback Manager, but—as with the predefined roles in vCD—these might not suit your needs. When a predefined role would grant too much or too little access to Chargeback resource types, you should create a custom role.

The default, predefined roles in vCenter Chargeback Manager 2.5 are

- Super User
- Administrator
- Hierarchy Manager
- Report Generator
- vCenter Guest User
- No Access
- Dependent Resource Update
- Dependent Resource Read

Activity 4-2: Creating a Custom Role in vCenter Chargeback Manager 2.5

1. Log on to vCenter Chargeback Manager.

2. Click the **Users & Roles** tab, as shown in Figure 4-12.

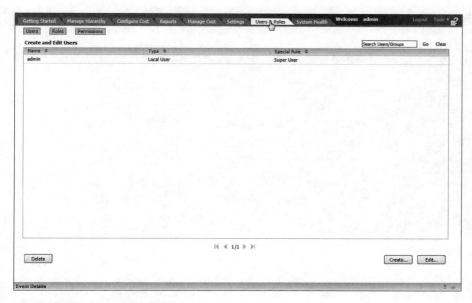

Figure 4-12   Users & Roles Tab

3. Click the **Roles** button, as shown in Figure 4-13.

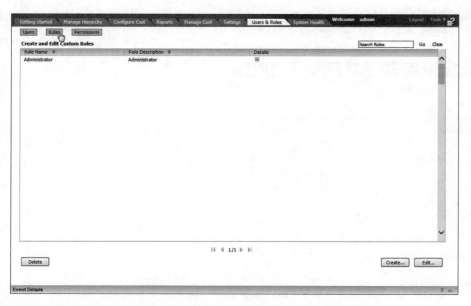

Figure 4-13   Create and Edit Custom Roles Screen

4. Click the **Create** button, as shown in Figure 4-14.

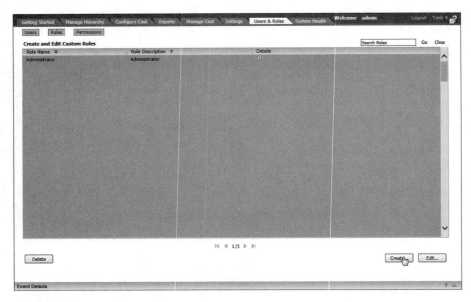

Figure 4-14 Create a Custom Role

5. Enter a name and an optional description for the new role.

6. Check the box for each necessary permission, and then click **Create** (see Figure 4-15).

Figure 4-15 Create Role Screen

Activity 4-3: Modifying a Role in vCenter Chargeback Manager 2.5

1. Log on to vCenter Chargeback Manager.

2. Click the **Users & Roles** tab.

3. Select the role to modify and click **Edit**, as shown in Figure 4-16.

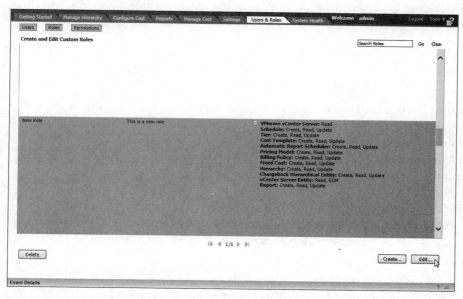

Figure 4-16   Edit a Role

4. Make the desired changes and click **Save**.

NOTE   Default roles cannot be modified.

Activity 4-4: Deleting a Role in vCenter Chargeback Manager 2.5

1. Log on to vCenter Chargeback Manager.

2. Click the **Users & Roles** tab.

3. Select the role to delete and click **Delete**.

4. Confirm the delete by clicking **OK**, as shown in Figure 4-17.

Figure 4-17   Delete a Role

Users

As with vCD, the initial administrator account username and password are created during installation. In the case of vCenter Chargeback Manager, that user is referred to as the super user and is given the default Super User role. (Default roles in vCenter Chargeback Manager are discussed in a later section.) This is the only user that exists after installation. Users can be configured locally or imported from an Active Directory LDAP server. LDAP groups can also be imported from an Active Directory LDAP server. To import LDAP users or groups, you must first enable LDAP integration of vCenter Chargeback Manager with an LDAP server. Only users with the Super User or Administrator role can create a local user or import an LDAP user or group.

Activity 4-5: Creating a Local User in vCenter Chargeback Manager 2.5

1. Log on to vCenter Chargeback Manager.

2. Click the **Users & Roles** tab.

3. Click the **Users** button.

4. Click **Create**.

5. On the Add User Account screen, select **Local** for the User Type and fill in the details for User Name, Password, and Confirm Password. You can choose to assign a role now or later.

6. Click **Add**, as shown in Figure 4-18.

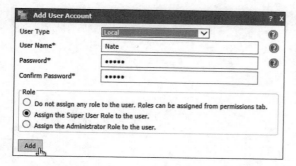

Figure 4-18   Add User Account Screen

Activity 4-6: Configuring an LDAP server

1. Log on to vCenter Chargeback Manager.

2. Click the **Settings** tab.

3. Click the **LDAP Servers** button.

4. Click **Add**.

5. Fill in the details for the following values (see Figure 4-19):

   - **Server Name**—A friendly name to assign the server.

   - **Server Address**—The IP address of the LDAP server.

   - **User Name**—The user account for LDAP authentication in the form of user@domainname (preferred) or domain\user format.

   - **Password**—The password for the user.

   - **BaseDN (optional)**—The BaseDN is the root of the connection vCenter Chargeback Manager makes to the LDAP directory. All user or group accounts that you want to add must reside at this level or within an organizational unit beneath the root connection.

   - **Port**—A port where the LDAP server is listening (port 389 is the default).

   - **LDAP Limit**—The maximum number of users and groups to return and display. The default is 500.

   - **Enable LDAPS checkbox**—Select this to enable LDAP over secure sockets layer (SSL).

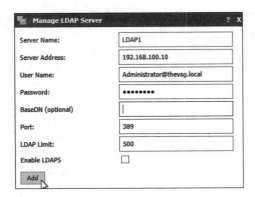

Figure 4-19 Configure LDAP Server Integration

Activity 4-7: Importing an LDAP User or Group in vCenter Chargeback Manager 2.5

1. Log on to vCenter Chargeback Manager.

2. Click the **Users & Roles** tab.

3. Click the **Users** button.

4. Click **Create**.

5. On the Add User Account screen, select **LDAP User** or **LDAP Group** for the User Type.

6. Select an LDAP Server from the drop-down list.

7. Select the LDAP User(s) or LDAP Group(s) you want to import.

8. Assign the Administrator role or choose to assign a role at a later time.

9. Click **Add**.

During local or LDAP user or group creation, you have the option to assign a role after the user is created. Follow the steps in Activity 4-8 to assign a role to a user or group after it is created.

Activity 4-8: Assigning a Role to a User in vCenter Chargeback Manager 2.5

1. Log on to vCenter Chargeback Manager.

2. Click the **Users & Roles** tab.

3. Click the **Permissions** button.

4. In the middle of the screen, search for and select the user to modify, as shown in Figure 4-20.

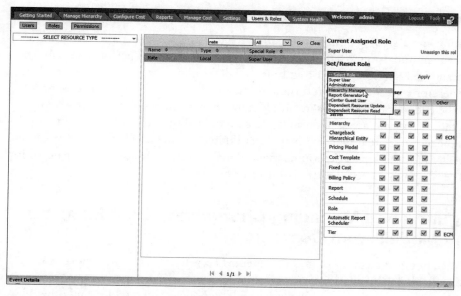

Figure 4-20   Select a User, and Set or Reset a Role

5. In the Set/Reset Role section, click the drop-down box and select a new role for the user. This is also shown in Figure 4-20.

6. Click **Apply**, as shown in Figure 4-21.

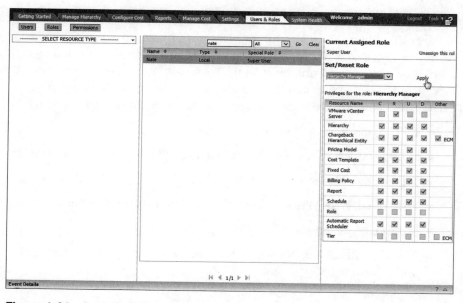

Figure 4-21   Apply Role Changes for a User

Troubleshoot Users, Roles, and Privileges

Creating and assigning custom roles often is an exercise in trial and error. Always grant the minimal amount of privileges necessary for a user to perform her job—no more and no less. Creating custom roles and determining the appropriate privileges will therefore require you to test these roles, either with your own test account or with the end user. These tests involve logging in with the test account or working with the end user to assess and validate the functionality of the role. Does the user have the appropriate privileges? Is the user limited to only performing the functions her role requires? Again, determine the minimal and appropriate set of privileges for the user through an iterative, trial-and-error process.

Configuring and Managing Chargeback Cost Elements, Pricing Models, and Costing

Understanding and configuring the elements necessary for creating reports is the most difficult part of administering vCenter Chargeback Manager. In this section, we discuss cost elements, pricing models, billing policies, hierarchies, and other elements related to vCenter Chargeback Manager and preparing for report generation.

Cost Elements

Cost elements are the basis for costing and billing and must be configured to generate Chargeback reports for billing or show back purposes. The available cost elements that must be configured are

1. **Chargeable Computing Resource**—Any computing resource to which you want to assign a cost. Computing resources can be measured by the following attributes: usage (actual utilization of the resource), reservation (the amount of resource reserved), or allocation (the amount of resource allocated). The chargeable computing resource cost element has the following components:

    - **CPU** usage, measured in GHz.

    - **vCPU**, measured as the number of virtual CPUs in a virtual machine.

    - **Memory** usage, measured in GB.

    - **Disk Read**, **Disk Write**, or **Disk Read and Write**, measured in GB/hour.

    - **Storage** usage, measured in GB.

    - **Network Received, Network Transmitted, or Network Received and Transmitted**, measured in GB/hour.

When the data collectors for vCD and vShield Manager are installed, the following attributes are also available:

- **Count of Networks**, measured as the number of network segments that belong to an organization, an organization vDC, or a vApp.

- **Enabled IPsec VPN Tunnel Count**, measured as the number enabled.

- **NAT**, **DHCP**, **Firewall**, **Load Balancer**, and **Static Routing** services, measured by whether the individual network service is enabled.

- **Gateway HA enabled**, measured by whether high availability (HA) is enabled on the network gateway.

- **Full Gateway Configuration**, measured by whether the full gateway configuration is used.

- **External Network Transmit**, measured as MB uploaded.

- **External Network Receive**, measured as MB downloaded.

- **External Network Transmit Rate**, measured as the upload rate in MB/hour.

- **External Network Receive Rate**, measured as the download rate in MB/hour.

2. **Base Rate**—The global rate that is charged for each individual unit of chargeable computing resource that is used, reserved, or allocated.

3. **Rate Factor**—The multiplying factor to be used with the base rate to charge a premium for or provide a discount for a resource. A rate factor greater than 1 increases the base cost, while a rate factor of less than 1 decreases the cost.

4. **Fixed Cost**—A cost that does not vary. These can be recurring costs that are the same at each billing cycle or they can be one-time costs.

5. **Billing Policy**—A billing policy is a collection of chargeable computing resources that is combined with both the base rate for the resource and any fixed costs. You can use built-in billing policies or create your own.

6. **Pricing Model**—The pricing model defines the currency to be used, the billing policy in effect, and the base rates for the chargeable computing resources to be used.

7. **Cost Template**—Cost templates are made up of entity-specific cost configuration details.

Billing Policies

We mentioned previously that the billing policy is the cost element that determines which computing resources to charge for, along with the base rates and fixed costs for each. An explanation of the roughly 30 billing policies is outside the scope of this book and the exams, but each policy is shown in the following list. The title of each billing policy explains what is being considered for costing; for full details, consult the product documentation:

- Actual Usage
- Allocation Based
- CPU Reservation
- Fixed Cost
- Fixed Cost and Actual Usage
- Fixed Cost and Allocation
- Fixed Cost and CPU Reservation
- Fixed Cost and Maximum of CPU Usage and CPU Reservation
- Fixed Cost and Maximum of Memory Usage and Memory Reservation
- Fixed Cost and Maximum of Usage and Reservation
- Fixed Cost and Memory Reservation
- Fixed Cost and Reservation
- Fixed Cost and vCPU Count and Memory Size
- Maximum of CPU Usage and CPU Reservation
- Maximum of Memory Usage and Memory Reservation
- Maximum of Usage and Reservation
- Memory Reservation
- Reservation Based
- VMware vCloud Director Billing Policy—Actual Usage
- VMware vCloud Director Billing Policy—Allocation Pool
- VMware vCloud Director Billing Policy—Networks
- VMware vCloud Director Billing Policy—Overage Allocation Pool
- VMware vCloud Director Billing Policy—Pay As You Go Fixed Charging

- VMware vCloud Director Billing Policy—Pay As You Go Resource Based Charging

- VMware vCloud Director Billing Policy—Reservation Pool

- vCPU Count and Memory Size

If a default billing policy does not fit your needs, you can create a custom billing policy, as described in Activity 4-9.

Activity 4-9: Creating a Custom Billing Policy

1. Log on to vCenter Chargeback Manager.

2. Click the **Manage Cost** tab.

3. Click the **Billing Policy** button.

4. Click **Create**, as shown in Figure 4-22.

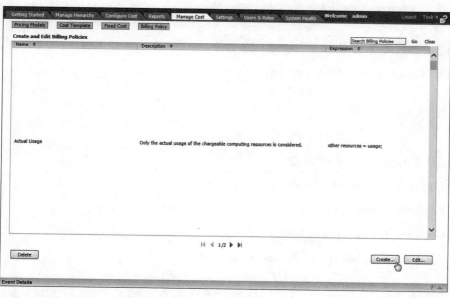

Figure 4-22   Create a Custom Billing Policy

5. Provide a name and a description for the new policy on the General tab.

6. Click the **Expression** tab.

7. Select a resource and an attribute (allocation, usage, or reservation), an operator, conditions that apply, and any custom expression you want to include, as shown in Figure 4-23.

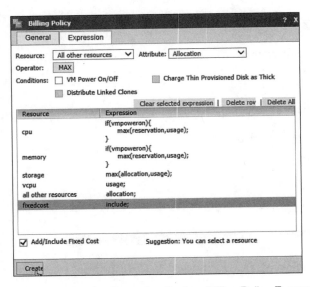

Figure 4-23   Configure the Custom Billing Policy Expression

8. Click **Create**.

Activity 4-10: Editing a Billing Policy

1. Log on to vCenter Chargeback Manager.

2. Click the **Manage Cost** tab.

3. Click the **Billing Policy** button.

4. Click the **Edit** button, as shown in Figure 4-24.

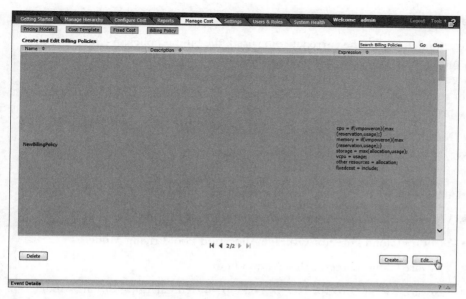

Figure 4-24   Edit a Custom Billing Policy

5. Edit the name, description, or expressions as necessary.

NOTE   Only custom billing policies can be edited; default policies are not editable.

Hierarchies

In vCenter Chargeback Manager 2.5, a hierarchy is a collection of vCenter Server entities and vCenter Chargeback Manager 2.5 entities to which you want to apply a pricing model. vCenter Server entities include virtual machines, ESXi hosts, data centers, clusters, resource pools, and folders. vCenter Chargeback Manager 2.5 entities can be custom-created or synchronized with a vCenter Server hierarchy. vCenter Chargeback Manager 2.5 entities are frequently configured as collections of vCenter Server entities used by departments or billing units. Note that vCenter Chargeback Manager 2.5 entities can contain entities from multiple vCenter Servers and multiple vCenter Chargeback Manager 2.5 entities.

Manage Cost/Pricing Models

Pricing models define the currency to be used, the billing policy in effect, and the base rates for the chargeable computing resources being used. Prior to vCenter Chargeback Manager 2.5, pricing models were referred to as cost models, so you might continue to see references to that term. After a hierarchy has been created and a pricing model selected or defined, basic reports can be generated.

The Default Chargeback Pricing Model is defined when installing the vCenter Server data collector. Several other pricing models are installed with the vCD data collector:

- VMware Cloud Director Actual Usage Pricing Model
- VMware Cloud Director Allocation Pool Pricing Model
- VMware Cloud Director Overage Allocation Pool Pricing Model
- VMware Cloud Director Reservation Pool
- VMware Cloud Director Pay As You Go—Fixed Charging Pricing Model
- VMware Cloud Director Pay As You Go—Resource Based Charging Pricing Model
- VMware Cloud Director Networks Pricing Model

Default pricing models do not include base rates or fixed costs, so these must be defined or included before using one of the default pricing models. If the default pricing models do not fit your needs, you can create custom pricing models.

Activity 4-11: Creating a Custom Pricing Model

1. Log on to vCenter Chargeback Manager.

2. Click the **Manage Cost** tab.

3. Click the **Pricing Models** button.

4. Fill in the necessary details on each tab:

   - **General tab**—Provide the name, description, and currency for the pricing model, as shown in Figure 4-25.

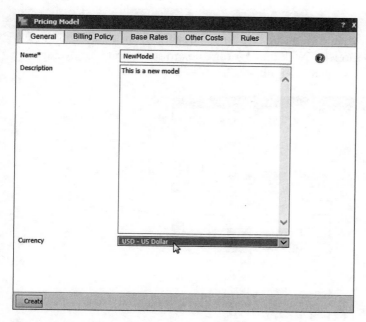

Figure 4-25   General Tab, Custom Pricing Model

- **Billing Policy tab**—Set the effective billing period and select a billing policy as shown in Figure 4-26.

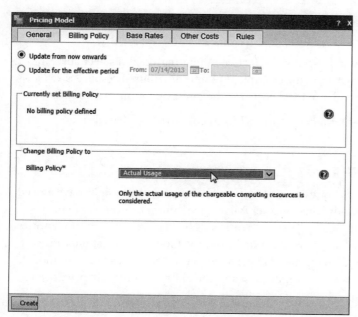

Figure 4-26   Billing Policy Tab, Custom Pricing Model

- **Base Rates tab**—Set the effective billing period and the base rate and duration for each computing resource that will be considered as part of this pricing model. Check the **Overage** box to set the rate for overage usage. This is shown in Figure 4-27.

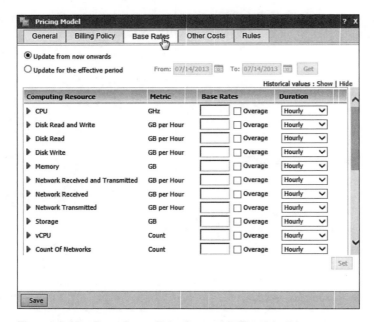

Figure 4-27   Base Rates Tab, Custom Pricing Model

- **Other Costs tab**—Set the effective billing period and select costs for additional vServices (for example, HA and distributed resources scheduler [DRS]) and any fixed costs for the guest operating system.

- **Rules tab**—Define any optional fixed cost attribute-based rules.

Configure Entity-level Costs

Pricing models define base rates on a global scale. However, you might have a need to charge for the use of individual entities (virtual machines) or groups of entities differently, or you might need to associate different fixed costs with specific entities. Entity-level costs can be viewed or modified from the Configure Cost tab of the entity. Note that you must have the read privilege on the entity, the pricing model, and the hierarchy to view the configuration and the entity cost modify privilege to change the configuration.

Physical Infrastructure Costing

vCenter Chargeback Manager 2.5 enables you to charge for physical resources in addition to the virtual resources in vCenter Server, vCD, and vShield Manager. Physical infrastructure costing is accomplished by setting rate factors at the Hosts and Clusters or Datastore levels. Rate factors are considered on hosts and clusters in the absence of any entity-level costs associated with the hierarchy being used for the billing report. To configure a rate factor at the Hosts and Clusters level, follow the steps in Activity 4-12.

Activity 4-12: Setting Rate Factors for Hosts and Clusters

1. Log on to vCenter Chargeback Manager.

2. Click the **Configure Cost** tab.

3. Click the **Edit Infrastructure Cost** button.

4. Select **Hosts & Clusters** from the drop-down list, as shown in Figure 4-28.

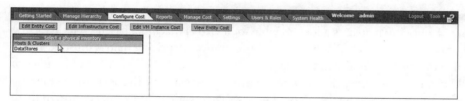

Figure 4-28   Select the Hosts & Clusters Physical Inventory Item

5. Select the cluster or host on which to assign a rate factor.

6. Select a pricing model from the drop-down list.

7. Set the effective billing period.

8. Specify the rate factors for the selected resource, and click **Update Rate Factors**.

Physical datastore costing enables you to associate costs with individual datastores or with groups of datastores. Groups of datastores are configured as tiers and the associated rate factor corresponds to the tier level of the datastore. Tier 1 datastores, for example, might have a higher rate factor configured than tier 2 or tier 3 datastores. Rate factors also might be defined for storage profiles set in vCenter Server.

Activity 4-13: Setting Rate Factors for Datastores, Datastore Tiers, and Storage Profiles

1. Log on to vCenter Chargeback Manager.

2. Click the **Configure Cost** tab.

3. Click the **Edit Infrastructure Cost** button.

4. Select **DataStores** from the drop-down list.

5. Select the datastore, datastore tier, or storage profile to which to assign a rate factor.

6. Select a pricing model from the drop-down list.

7. Set the effective billing period.

8. Specify the rate factor and click **Set**.

Pricing Matrix for Virtual Machines

Pricing matrices define multiple costs based on bundles of vCPU count and memory. Think of a pricing matrix as a lookup table for a virtual machine, based on its associated pricing model and vCPU/memory configuration. A pricing matrix must be associated with a pricing model and contains multiple entries based on different bundles of vCPU count and memory. Each pricing matrix is associated with a level in the hierarchy, so multiple pricing matrices could be associated with an individual entity. In these cases, you can specify the priority of each pricing matrix on the entity.

vCenter Chargeback Manager Reporting

After pricing models have been defined and hierarchies configured, you can generate reports. These reports include cost reports, usage reports, cost comparison reports, and showback reports:

- **Cost report**—Cost reports show utilization information and the associated cost for each entity in the hierarchy for which the report is being generated. This report is based on the cost associated with the hierarchy and the pricing model that is selected when the report is run.

- **Usage report**—Usage reports show only utilization information; they do not include a cost summary or any cost information.

- **Cost Comparison report**—This report enables you to calculate costs for each hierarchy entity against two pricing models and compare the costs.

- **Showback report**—Showback reports enable you to analyze how costs are distributed among the entities in the hierarchy.

Activity 4-15: Generating a Report

1. Log on to vCenter Chargeback Manager.

2. Click the **Reports** tab and the **Create Reports** button.

3. Select the hierarchy on which you want to report from the **Select Hierarchy** drop-down box on the left of the screen. This is shown in Figure 4-29.

Figure 4-29   Select a Hierarchy for Chargeback Reporting

4. Right-click the hierarchy entity for which you want to generate a report, and select the type of report to run from the drop-down menu. This is shown in Figure 4-30.

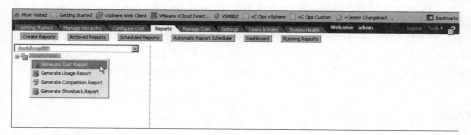

Figure 4-30   Select a Chargeback Report to Run

5. Fill in the details in the wizard. These details vary slightly depending on the type of report you choose.

6. Click **Submit** to submit the report to run.

7. The report displays after it has completed.

Schedule Reports

When creating a report, you have the option to schedule the report to run periodically based on parameters you set. You also have the option to schedule a report that has previously been run. All reports except showback reports can be generated on a schedule you define. To schedule a report during initial report generation, follow the report generation procedure shown previously and set the parameters on the Schedule page. To schedule a report that was previously generated, click the **Schedule Report** icon above the report.

The following are the scheduling parameters you can set:

- **Report creation time**—The time of day (on the vCenter Chargeback Manager 2.5 server) when the report is generated.

- **Recurrence pattern**—How often should the report be generated? The options are daily, weekly, monthly, quarterly, half yearly, yearly, or on a custom schedule.

- **Range of recurrence**—The start date and end date of the report scheduling parameters. Note that you can create a schedule with no end date.

To view a list of scheduled reports, select the **Reports** tab and click **Scheduled Reports**. From this list, you can also edit/reschedule reports or delete report schedules if they are no longer needed.

Manage and Archive Reports

After a report is generated, you can perform a number of actions on it. You can modify a report by removing rows or columns (or rearranging rows and columns), archive, email, schedule, export, or stop a running report. Archiving a report moves it to the Archived Reports page. Archived reports can be exported, emailed, or deleted.

Summary

In this chapter, we explored the following main topics:

- We discussed the requirements, supported operating systems and databases, and the installation procedure for vCenter Chargeback Manager 2.5.

- We discussed configuring users, roles, and privileges. The built-in roles, the resource types, the five privileges that can be assigned to a resource type, and the ways to define a user were covered.

- We also examined the vCenter Chargeback Manager 2.5 cost elements, pricing models, and costing. We explained the definition of cost elements and the available cost elements in vCenter Chargeback Manager 2.5, billing policies, hierarchies, pricing models, and physical infrastructure costing.

- Finally, we looked at vCenter Chargeback Manager 2.5 reporting. The available reports and reporting parameters, scheduling options, and actions that can be taken on a report were discussed.

Exam Preparation Tasks

Review All the Key Topics

Review the most important topics in the chapter, noted with the Key Topic icon in the outer margin of the page. Table 4-3 lists a reference to these key topics and the page numbers on which each is found.

Table 4-3   Key Topics

Key Topic Element	Description	Page
Section	Installing vCenter Chargeback Manager	87
Activity 4-1	Installing vCenter Chargeback Manager 2.5	89
Paragraph	Five privileges available	96
Table 4-2	Resource Types in vCenter Chargeback Manager 2.5	96
Note	Resources that cannot be manually assigned permissions	98
Bulleted list	Default vCenter Chargeback roles	98
Activity 4-2	Creating a Custom Role in vCenter Chargeback Manager 2.5	98
Activity 4-3	Modifying a Role in vCenter Chargeback Manager 2.5	101
Activity 4-4	Deleting a Role in vCenter Chargeback Manager 2.5	101
Activity 4-8	Assigning a Role to a User in vCenter Chargeback Manager 2.5	104
Numbered list	Identify vCenter Chargeback cost elements	106
Bulleted list	Default billing policies	108
Activity 4-9	Creating a Custom Billing Policy	109
Activity 4-10	Editing a Billing Policy	110
Section	Manage Cost/Pricing Models	112
Activity 4-11	Creating a Custom Pricing Model	112
Bulleted list	Report types	116
Activity 4-15	Generating a Report	117
Section	Schedule Reports	117

Definitions of Key Terms

Define the following key terms from this chapter, and check your answers in the glossary:

data collector, cost element, base rate, rate factor, fixed cost, billing policy, pricing model, cost template

Review Questions

Answers to review questions are in Appendix A.

1. Which two methods are valid for deploying vCenter Chargeback Manager 2.5? (Choose two.)

   a. As a virtual appliance managed by vCenter Server 4.x or above

   b. On a virtual machine running Windows Server 2003 R2

   c. On a virtual machine running Windows Server 2008 R2

   d. On a virtual machine running Red Hat Enterprise Linux (RHEL) 6.x

2. Which two are software requirements for installing vCenter Chargeback Manager 2.5? (Choose two.)

   a. Internet Explorer 7 or 8

   b. Correct and synchronized system time

   c. Windows Firewall exceptions for HTTP, HTTPS, and load balancer services

   d. Internet Information Services (IIS) configured for Basic Authentication

3. Which two are supported Database Management Systems for vCenter Chargeback Manager 2.5? (Choose two.)

   a. Oracle RAC

   b. Oracle 11g Release 1

   c. Postgres 8.4

   d. Microsoft SQL Server 2005 SP

4. What is the minimum version of vCenter Server that is supported for integration with vCenter Chargeback Manager 2.5?

   a. Virtual Center 2.5

   b. vCenter Server 4.0

   c. vCenter Server 4.1

   d. vCenter Server 5.1

5. Which two versions of vCloud Director are supported for integration with vCenter Chargeback Manager 2.5? (Choose two.)

    a. vCloud Director 1.0

    b. vCloud Director 1.5

    c. vCloud Director 4.0

    d. vCloud Director 5.1

6. A vCenter Chargeback Manager 2.5 cluster can be created by running which command after installing an additional vCenter Chargeback Manager 2.5 node?

    a. UpdateLoadBalancer

    b. ModifyLoadBalancer

    c. ModifyLBWorkers

    d. UpdateLBWorkers

7. How are users, roles, and privileges created in vCenter Chargeback Manager 2.5?

    a. They are imported from vCloud Director.

    b. They are imported from vCenter Server.

    c. They are configured within the application.

    d. They can be configured within the application or imported from vCD.

8. Which three privileges can be assigned to a resource type in vCenter Chargeback Manager 2.5? (Choose three.)

    a. Read

    b. Modify

    c. Update

    d. Delete

    e. Move

9. Which statement accurately describes a resource type?

    a. Collections of chargeable computing resources

    b. Templates for charging for fixed resources

    c. The basis for costing and billing in a hierarchy

    d. The elements or objects on which privileges are granted

10. Which statement best describes the purpose of a rate factor?

    a. It modifies the cost template to increase or decrease the amount charged for a resource.

    b. It places a cap on the amount that can be charged for a resource.

   c. It modifies the base rate to increase or decrease the amount charged for a resource.

   d. It defines the currency to be used, the billing policy in effect, and the base rate for resources.

11. Which statement best describes the purpose of a pricing model?

   a. It modifies the cost template to increase or decrease the amount charged for a resource.

   b. It places a cap on the amount that can be charged for a resource.

   c. It modifies the base rate to increase or decrease the amount charged for a resource.

   d. It defines the currency to be used, the billing policy in effect, and the base rate for resources.

12. In vCenter Chargeback Manager 2.5, which two authentication sources can be used for users logging in to Chargeback Manager? (Choose two.)

   a. vCloud Director

   b. vCenter Server

   c. Local Chargeback database

   d. Microsoft Active Directory

13. Which two are predefined roles in vCenter Chargeback Manager 2.5? (Choose two.)

   a. Administrator

   b. Root

   c. Super User

   d. Admin

14. How is the initial vCenter Chargeback Manager 2.5 username and password generated?

   a. It is synchronized with the vCD root user.

   b. It is synchronized with vCenter Server administrator user.

   c. It is set by the system to Admin/VMware1.

   d. It is user-configured during installation.

15. Which three are attributes used to measure computing resources? (Choose three.)

   a. Allocation

   b. Commitment

   c. Reservation

    d. Usage

    e. Overage

16. What is a hierarchy in vCenter Chargeback Manager 2.5?

    a. The order in which permissions are applied

    b. A collection of entities to which you apply a pricing model

    c. The order in which costs are applied

    d. A collection of pricing models

17. Which statement accurately describes the base rate in vCenter Chargeback Manager 2.5?

    a. A multiplier for modifying the cost of an individual resource

    b. A collection of chargeable computing resources

    c. The global rate that is charged for individual computing resources

    d. A template that defines the default currency

18. Which three are default reports in vCenter Chargeback Manager 2.5? (Choose three.)

    a. Allocation Report

    b. Usage Report

    c. Cost Report

    d. Showback Report

    e. Resource Summary

19. Which setting cannot be used for recurring scheduled reports?

    a. Daily

    b. Monthly

    c. Hourly

    d. Yearly

20. Which setting is not a valid scheduling parameter that can be set in vCenter Chargeback Manager 2.5?

    a. Report creation time

    b. Recurrence pattern

    c. Recipient email address

    d. Range of occurrence

This chapter covers the following subjects:

- **What Is vCloud Connector?**—This section explains what vCloud Connector does and the features it offers.

- **vCloud Connector Components**—This section outlines the components and their requirements to make Cloud Connector work.

- **vCloud Connector Installation**—This section covers the installation of Cloud Connector and the Cloud Connector components.

- **vCloud Connector Data Flow**—In this section, you learn about the data flow through the various vCloud Connector components.

This chapter covers a portion of the VCP5-IaaS Objective 2.1 and VCP5-Cloud Objective 8.2.

vCloud Connector

vCloud Connector enables you to stretch your cloud between multiple service providers, but do you know how it does this? In this chapter, we cover the two editions of vCloud Connector and what you need to know to be able to pass the VCP-Cloud or VCP-IaaS exams. If you think you have a good grasp on vCloud Connector, take the "Do I Know This Already?" quiz to make sure that you do; if not, read on!

"Do I Know This Already?" Quiz

The "Do I Know This Already?" quiz enables you to assess whether you should read this entire chapter or simply jump to the "Exam Preparation Tasks" section for review. If you are in doubt, read the entire chapter. Table 5-1 outlines the major headings in this chapter and the corresponding "Do I Know This Already?" quiz questions. You can find the answers in Appendix A, "Answers to the 'Do I Know This Already?' Quizzes and Review Questions."

Table 5-1 "Do I Know This Already?" Foundation Topics Section-to-Question Mapping

Foundations Topics Section	Questions Covered in This Section
What Is vCloud Connector?	1–4
vCloud Connector Components	5
vCloud Connector Installation	6
vCloud Connector Data Flow	7

1. vCloud Connector connects to which two VMware products? (Choose two.)

   a. vSphere

   b. vFabric Data Director

   c. vCloud Director

   d. Horizon Mirage

2. vCloud Connector is managed though which VMware product?

   a. vFabric Data Director

   b. vCloud Director

   c. vCenter

   d. vShield Manager

3. vCloud Connector enables catalog synchronization between which cloud technologies?

   a. vCloud to Open Stack

   b. vSphere to vCloud

   c. vCloud to vCloud

   d. vCloud to vFabric

4. What type of synchronization does vCloud Connector enable?

   a. Bidirectional

   b. Just in time

   c. One way

   d. On demand

5. vCloud Connector Server nodes communicate to which two components? (Choose two.)

   a. vCenter Client

   b. vCloud Connector Nodes

   c. vSphere Hosts

   d. vShield Manager

6. vCloud Connector is installable via which method?

   a. OVF Deployment

   b. Red Hat RPM installation

   c. SLES Installable files

   d. Windows Installable file (MSI)

7. vCloud Connector copies data through which objects?

   a. vCloud Connector Node -> vCloud Connector Server

   b. vCloud Connector Node -> vCloud Connector Node

   c. vCloud Connector Server -> vCloud Connector Server

   d. vCloud Connector Server -> vCloud Connector Node

Foundation Topics

What Is vCloud Connector?

vCloud Connector is a product from VMware that is available in two editions, vCloud Connector Core and vCloud Connector Advanced. We cover the Core installation and an overview of the Advanced features. For a deeper dive into the vCloud Connector Advanced features, I recommend heading to the vCloud Connector documentation site at https://www.vmware.com/support/pubs/hybridcloud_pubs.html.

vCloud Connector is an enterprise product that provides a single user interface (UI) for overseeing multiple public and private clouds and for transferring cloud content between these clouds. It allows you to connect multiple clouds, both internal and external, in a single UI.

vCloud Connector Core

The vCloud Connector Core Edition provides an end user with a unified view into an environment containing multiple public and private clouds. This includes cloud instances through the vCloud Hybrid Service and cloud instances through vCloud Service Provider partners. This single UI gives you the ability to see both internal and external cloud installations while allowing you to transfer virtual machines (VMs), vApps, and catalogs from one cloud to another.

Beyond workload transfers, the unified view provided by vCloud Connector enables you to perform basic administration tasks, such as starting and stopping VMs, and basic operations tasks like checking performance and resource utilization.

vCloud Connector Advanced

vCloud Connector Advanced includes all the functionality of the Core Edition, with the added ability to extend a vCloud deployment with the Datacenter Extension feature. This feature allows you to extend a private vCloud Director installation to a public vCloud Director installation. vCloud Connector Advanced also enables you to establish content synchronization between multiple vCloud deployments. The synchronization is one way, meaning that content updated in Catalog A on vCloud A is pushed to Catalog A on vCloud B. Any updates to vCloud B's Catalog A would not be replicated back to vCloud A.

NOTE   Even though vCloud 5.5 introduced the capability to export a vApp with the machine's identity preserved, vCloud Connector 2.5 and older do not support this feature. This causes VMs that are exported using vCloud Connector to lose their identities and hardware configurations.

vCloud Connector Components

vCloud Connector consists of three components. The first component is the UI. To access the UI, you must register your vCloud Connector instance to at least one vCenter Server instance.

NOTE   VMware used to provide an external hosted solution for accessing the vCloud Connector UI; however, this was discontinued in early 2013. At this time, the only way to manage a vCloud Connector installation is through the vSphere Client.

The second component is the vCloud Connector Server. The vCloud Connector Server must be registered to a vCenter Server. This server manages all the worker nodes in a vCloud deployment. This means that this server must be able to communicate with all the vCloud Connector Node servers. (We discuss their function next.) This server is also responsible for all the management tasks in a vCloud Connector deployment.

The third and final component of a vCloud Connector installation is the vCloud Connector Node. The nodes are what actually do the work. These machines execute commands to the vCloud instance to which they are registered. When content is being copied or synchronized across clouds, the node servers are the ones that store and cache the content while it is in flight.

vCloud Connector Installation

Now that we know what the vCloud Connector components do, let's begin installing them so we can learn how they operate.

Install Server

First up, we need to install the vCloud Connector Server.

Activity 5-1: Installing vCloud Connector Server

1. The first thing to do before we can deploy the OVF template is to download it from http://my.vmware.com.

2. Log in to the vCenter Server using the vSphere Client (not the web client) as an administrator. Click **File > Deploy OVF Template**; then select the OVF for vCloud Connector Server, as shown in Figure 5-1.

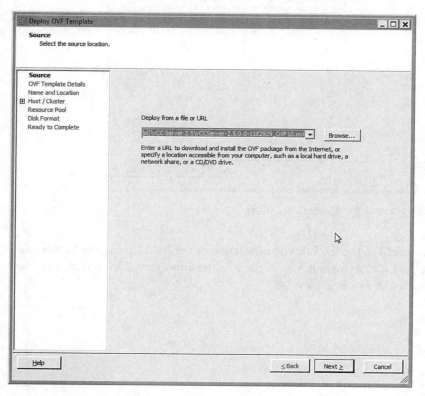

Figure 5-1   vCloud Connector Server OVF Import File Selection

3. After clicking **Next**, you are presented with a screen showing the details of the OVF file, as shown in Figure 5-2. Click **Next** again to open the end-user license agreement (EULA) dialog box.

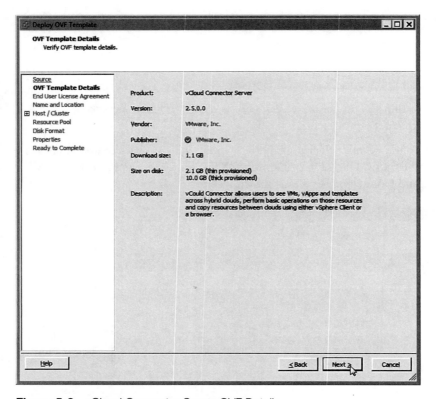

Figure 5-2   vCloud Connector Server OVF Details

4. If you agreed to the EULA, you now name the vCloud Connector Server and select the location for this VM in the vCenter Inventory. This screen and dialog box are shown in Figure 5-3.

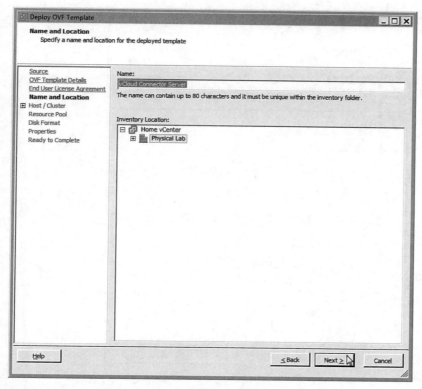

Figure 5-3   vCloud Connector Server OVF Naming

5. Click **Next** to open the Resource Pool selection. Select the location for the VM and to which cluster the VM gets deployed. Figure 5-4 shows the VCP-Book resource pool being selected for the VM to be deployed to.

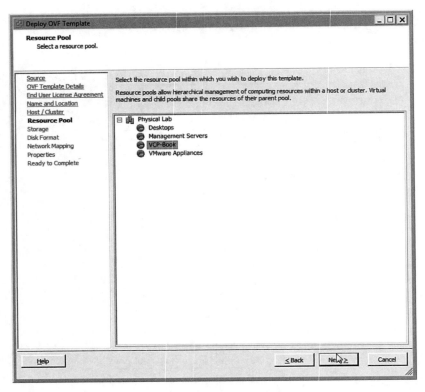

Figure 5-4   vCloud Connector Server Resource Pool Selection

6. Click **Next** to prompt you to select the proper datastore for the VM to be deployed to. After selecting the datastore, you are prompted to select the type of disk to be deployed—Thick Provision Lazy Zeroed, Thick Provision Eager Zeroed, or Thin Provision—as shown in Figure 5-5.

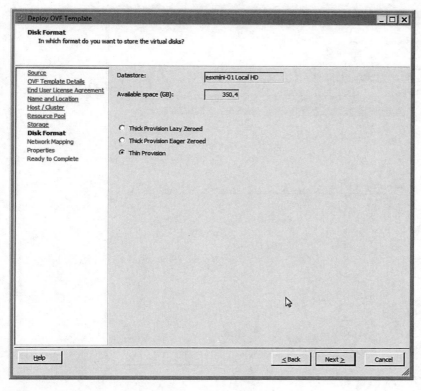

Figure 5-5   vCloud Connector Server Disk Type

7. After choosing the disk type, the next configuration option is the Network Mapping. On this screen, select the destination vSphere Port Group to which the vCloud Connector Server will map, as shown in Figure 5-6.

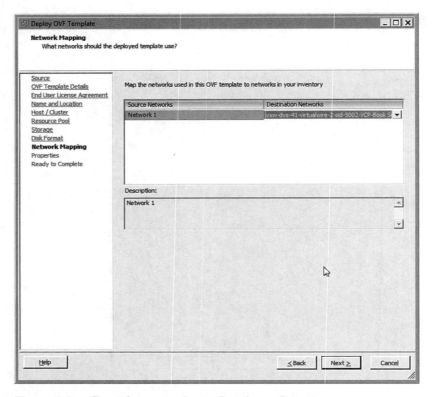

Figure 5-6   vCloud Connector Server Port Group Selection

NOTE   The vCloud Connector Server must be able to connect to the vCloud Connector Nodes and to the vCenter Server that will manage the vCloud Connector environment.

8. The next screen prompts you for your network configuration. Type in the proper settings for your deployment. Click **Next** to get to a final screen, shown in Figure 5-7. If everything looks good, click **Finish** to start the VM deployment.

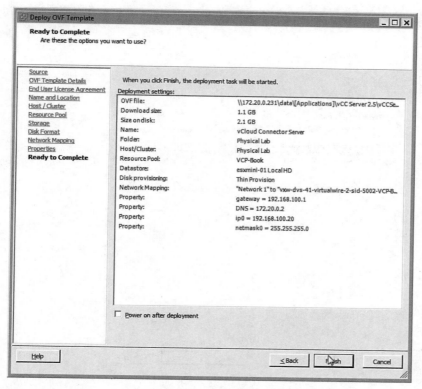

Figure 5-7   vCloud Connector Server OVF Confirmation

Install Nodes

After the server has been deployed, it is time to deploy the vCloud Connector Nodes and register them to the vCloud Connector Server.

Activity 5-2: Installing vCloud Connector Node

1. If you did not download the vCloud Connector Node installation file when you downloaded the vCloud Connector Server file, go back to https://my.vmware.com/web/vmware/downloads to download the vCloud Connector Node OVF.

2. Similar to the vCloud Connector Server steps, you need to log in to vCenter Server using the vSphere Client (not the web client). On each vCenter Server, you will deploy a vCloud Connector Node using the vCloud Connector Node OVF, as shown in Figure 5-8.

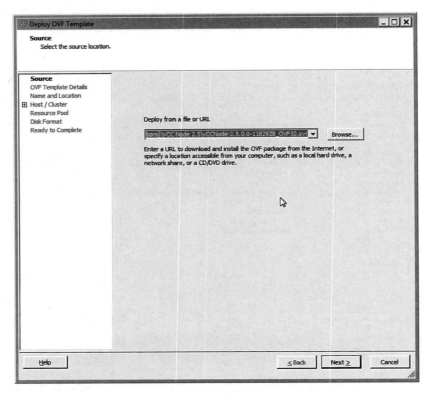

Figure 5-8   vCloud Connector Node OVF Import File Selection

NOTE   Although a vCloud Connector Server can connect via a wide area network (WAN), local area network (LAN), or Internet to your destination vCenter or vCloud Director, a vCloud Connector Node can connect to only a single destination/source.

3. Click **Next** to be brought to the Product Information screen. This shows you the information about the OVF that you are about to deploy. vCloud Connector Node 2.5.0.0 is shown in Figure 5-9.

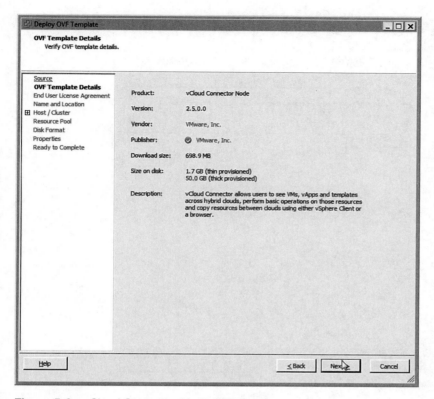

Figure 5-9   vCloud Connector Node OVF Details

4. After you have once again agreed to the EULA, you need to select the location to which the VM should be deployed in the vCenter Server inventory. Figure 5-10 shows the VM being deployed to the Physical Lab datacenter. This screen also enables you to name the VM.

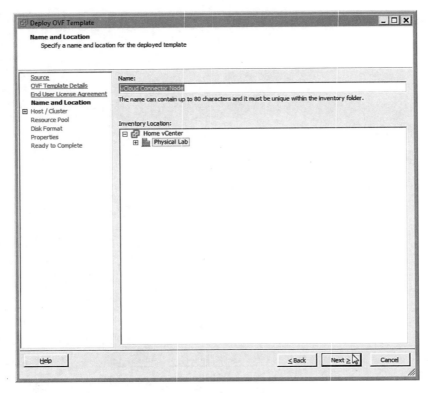

Figure 5-10   vCloud Connector Node OVF Naming

5. Click **Next** to open the Resource Pool selection screen, as shown in Figure 5-11. Select the resource pool where you want to deploy the vCloud Connector Node, and click **Next**.

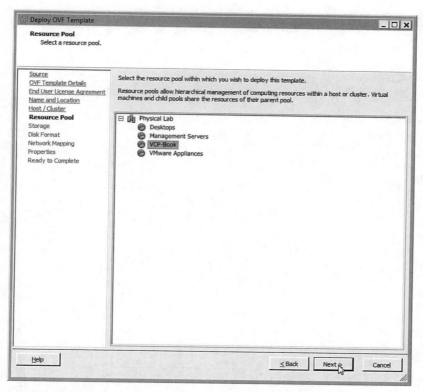

Figure 5-11   vCloud Connector Node Resource Pool Selection

6. The next step is to select a datastore on which to store the vCloud Connector Node. From the Disk Format Selection screen, pick the desired datastore on which the VM will reside. Click **Next** to select the disk type, as shown in Figure 5-12.

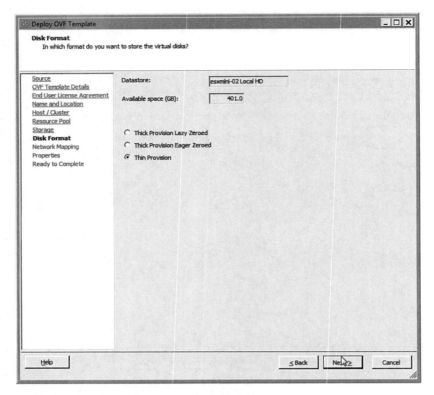

Figure 5-12   vCloud Connector Node Disk Type

7. After clicking **Next**, you are able to select the network port group to which the VM should be deployed, as shown in Figure 5-13.

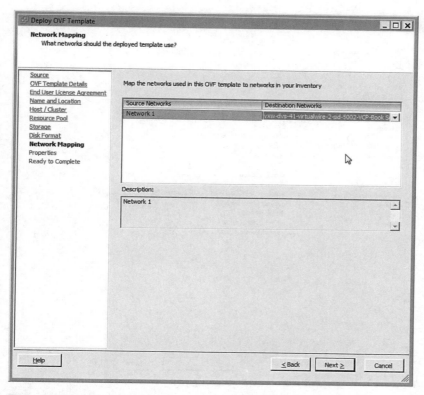

Figure 5-13   vCloud Connector Node Port Group Selection

NOTE   The vCloud Connector Node needs to be able to communicate with the vCloud Connector Server as well as the source of its content (either vCenter or vCloud Director).

8. After typing in the IP information for the vCloud Connector Node, click **Next**. This takes you to the Ready to Complete screen, shown in Figure 5-14. This enables you to confirm your settings prior to deploying the VM. Click **Finish** to complete the deployment of the vCloud Connector Node VM.

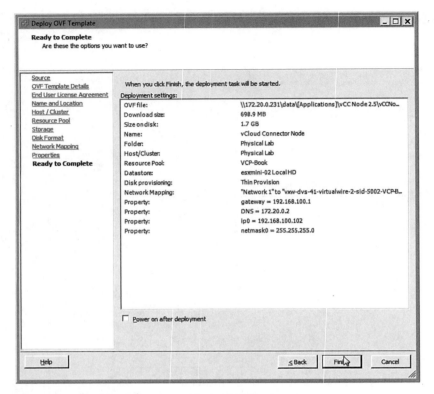

Figure 5-14   vCloud Connector Node OVF Confirmation

vCloud Connector Node VMs can consume a lot of disk space depending on the size of the vApp being moved through them. For clarification as to why so much disk space is needed, refer to the section titled "vCloud Connector Data Flow," later in this chapter. After you have calculated the size of the vApps to be cloned, you will most likely need to add a disk in addition to the 50GB disk that comes with the vCloud Connector Node.

You can also increase the disk size on the vCloud Connector Node VM. For more information on this capability, refer to the vCloud Connector Documentation Center located at http://pubs.vmware.com/hybridcloud-25/index.jsp.

Now that you have a node installed, it is time to register that node to the vSphere or vCloud instance it will connect, as well as the vCloud Connector Server that you installed in Activity 5-1.

Activity 5-3: Registering the vCloud Connector Node

1. Log in to the vCloud Connector Node using the following URL: https://<IPAddress>:5480. The default username is admin, and the default password is vmware.

2. After you have logged in to the vCloud Connector Node server, you are presented with a status page much like the screen shown in Figure 5-15.

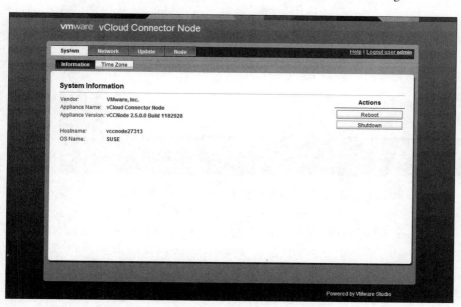

Figure 5-15   vCloud Connector Node Status Screen

3. Select the **Node** tab across the top of the screen. After selecting this tab, you are presented with a screen similar to Figure 5-16. The **Node** tab is where you configure the type of cloud (vSphere or vCloud Director) your vCloud Connector Node will connect to, including whether a proxy server is required to connect to the cloud. There is also an option to ignore the SSL certificate if it is self-signed.

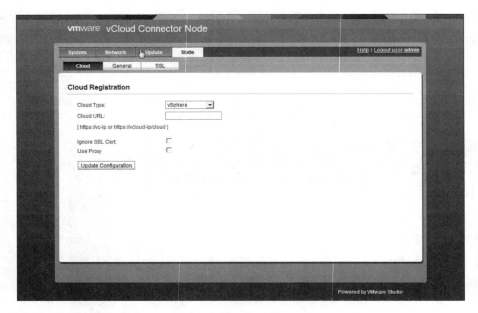

Figure 5-16   vCloud Connector Node Configuration

Now that the vCloud Connector Node is configured for access to a cloud (vSphere or vCloud Director), you need to register the node to the vCloud Connector Server.

4. Log in to the vCloud Connector Server at the following URL: https://<IPAddress>:5480. The default username is admin, and the default password is vmware. Figure 5-17 shows the login screen for your reference.

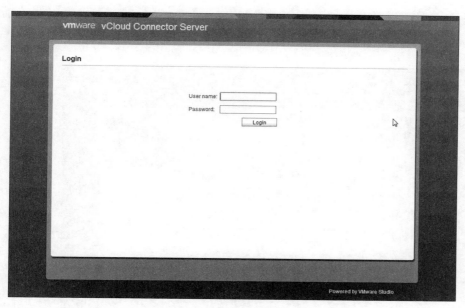

Figure 5-17   vCloud Connector Server Login Prompt

   5. Select the **Nodes** tab across the top, as shown in Figure 5-18. This shows all
   configured vCloud Connector Node Servers, as well as a Local Content Li-
   brary that is located on the vCloud Connector Server.

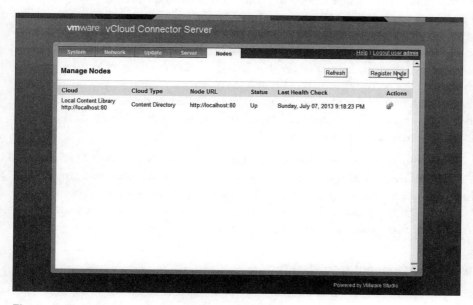

Figure 5-18   vCloud Connector Server Nodes Tab

6. Select the **Register Node** button to launch the Node Info Wizard, as shown in Figure 5-19.

Figure 5-19 vCloud Connector Server Node Register Prompt

Prior to adding the vCloud Connector Node, you need to specify the Node Name and the URL to which the vCloud Connector Node is registered. If the node does not have a DNS entry, an IP address is acceptable. Selecting the Public checkbox indicates that the vCloud Connector Node is outside the local network. The Use Proxy option utilizes the proxy server that is defined on the vCloud Connector Server under the Network tab. The Ignore SSL Certificate option does not validate the trustworthiness of the SSL certificate that is supplied by the destination URL. This does not mean that the connection will be insecure; it simply reflects that the SSL Certificate will not be validated.

The Cloud Info section is next. The Cloud Type indicates to which type of resource you are connecting. The options are vSphere and vCloud. If you are connecting to a vCloud instance, you must specify the organization to which you want to connect. If you are attempting to connect to the system organization, specify System. Provide a username and a password, and then click **Register** to initiate the registration process.

Register vCloud Connector to vCenter

Before you can use the vCloud Connector, you must register it with a vCenter Server instance.

Activity 5-4: Registering vCloud Connector to vCenter

1. Log in to the vCloud Connector Server with a user that has administrator privileges.

2. Select the **Server** tab, and then select the **vSphere Client** option. After the page is loaded, you need to specify how the vSphere Client plug-in will access the vCloud Connector Server URL. You also must supply the vCenter Server IP and a username and password that have administrator access to the vCenter Server. This screen and its options are shown in Figure 5-20.

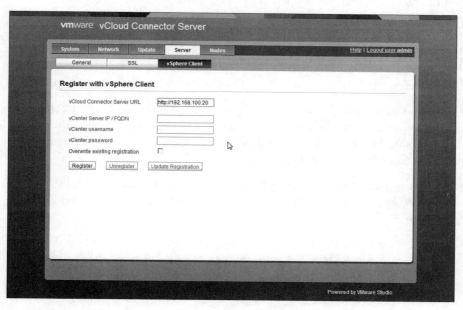

Figure 5-20   vCloud Connector Server vSphere Client Configuration

3. Click the **Register** button, and then open your vSphere Client to access the vCloud Connector UI and advanced features.

For information on how to subscribe to vCloud Catalogs, initiate a content sync, or perform a stretched deploy, refer to http://pubs.vmware.com/hybridcloud-25/index.jsp.

vCloud Connector Data Flow

The data flow through the vCloud Connector environment is network intensive and is generally limited by the speed of the network connecting the nodes and sites.

All VM and vApp data is copied from the source vCenter datastore to the source vCloud Director NFS transfer share and then to the source vCloud Connector node. From there, the data is copied to the destination vCloud Connector node, to the destination vCloud Director NFS transfer share, and finally to the destination vCenter datastore. This means a single catalog item is copied at least five times across the network, depending on the source and destinations.

As a result, it is critical that the network is configured to support the bandwidth required for these operations, and that the operations are planned around peak utilization times. In addition, these operations can be disk intensive, so consideration should be given to storage configuration and placement.

Summary

In this chapter, we briefly covered vCloud Connector and some of its configuration:

- We discussed what vCloud Connector is and what some of its limitations are, most importantly the lack of lossless exports and imports. Although these limitations should not stop you from deploying vCloud Connector, they can limit the use cases for which vCloud Connector can be utilized.

- We also covered the various components of vCloud Connector and how they integrate and operate to achieve content replication and stretch Layer 2 networking.

- Finally, we covered the installation of vCloud Connector Server and vCloud Connector Node VMs to a vCenter Server. We also covered the registration of the components to each other and the registration to vCenter Server.

Exam Preparation Tasks

Review All the Key Topics

Review the most important topics in the chapter, noted with the Key Topic icons in the outer margin of the page. Table 5-2 lists a reference to these key topics and the page numbers on which each is found.

Table 5-2 Key Topics

Key Topic Elements	Description	Page
Section	vCloud Connector Core	127
Section	vCloud Connector Advanced	127
Paragraph	vCloud Connector vCenter Registration	128
Activity 5-1	Installing vCloud Connector Server	129
Activity 5-2	Installing vCloud Connector Node	135
Activity 5-3	Registering the vCloud Connector Node	143
Activity 5-4	Registering vCloud Connector to vCenter	147

Definitions of Key Terms

Define the following key terms from this chapter, and check your answers in the glossary:

vCloud Connector Server, vCloud Connector Node, lossless export

Review Questions

The answers to these review questions are in Appendix A.

1. When creating a vCloud Connector task, which tool do you use?

   a. vCloud Connector API

   b. vCenter Client

   c. vCloud Connector Client

   d. vSphere API

2. vCloud Connector Server completes which tasks in a vCloud Connector Deployment?

   a. Moving the vApps from cloud to cloud

   b. Directing the vCloud Connector node servers

   c. Exporting the vCloud vApp data

   d. Importing the vSphere VM data

3. vCloud Connector's Export does not export which two pieces of information about a VM or vApp? (Choose two.)

    a. NIC configuration

    b. VM identity information (UUID, serial number)

    c. vCPU count

    d. vRAM count

4. What is the URL to configure a vCloud Connector server?

    a. http://<IPaddress>:5380

    b. https://<IPAddress>:5480

    c. http://<IPAddress>:5480

    d. https://<IPAddress>:5380

5. When copying VMs and/or vApp items with vCloud Connector, the data must be copied a minimum of how many times?

    a. 1

    b. 2

    c. 5

    d. 6

6. The vCloud Connector UI can be accessed using which method?

    a. vCloud Director

    b. vSphere Client

    c. vcloud.vmware.com

    d. vCloud Connector Client

This chapter covers the following subjects:

- **External Networks**—This section explains external networks and their operation in vCloud Director.

- **Organization VDC Networks**—This section explains organization virtual datacenter networking.

- **Network Pools**—This section discusses the proper use of Cloud Director Network Pools and their configurations.

- **vApp Networks**—This section covers vApp Networks and their configuration options.

- **Network Services**—This section talks about the network services that the vCloud Director deployed vShield Edges offer and their configurations.

This chapter covers a portion of the VCP-IaaS Exam Objectives 4.1, 4.2, 4.3, and 4.4, and VCP-Cloud Exam Objectives 11.1, 11.2, 11.3, and 11.4.

CHAPTER 6

Configure and Administer vCloud Networking

One of the most complex items in vCloud Director is the networking options and their configuration and administration. This chapter covers the proper configuration of vCloud Networking. It also discusses organization of virtual datacenter networks, as well as vApp networks and their configuration options.

"Do I Know This Already?" Quiz

The "Do I Know This Already?" quiz enables you to assess whether you should read this entire chapter or simply jump to the "Exam Preparation Tasks" section for review. If you are in doubt, read the entire chapter. Table 6-1 outlines the major headings in this chapter and the corresponding "Do I Know This Already?" quiz questions. You can find the answers in Appendix A, "Answers to the 'Do I Know This Already?' Quizzes and Review Questions."

Table 6-1 "Do I Know This Already?" Foundation Topics Section-to-Question Mapping

Foundations Topics Section	Questions Covered in This Section
External and Organization Networking	1–3
Configuring Network Pools	4, 5
vApp Networks	6
Network Services	7–9

1. When a NAT connection is required for external access, which type of network is required?

   a. External – Direct

   b. External – Routed

   c. Internal

   d. None of these options is correct.

2. When using an External – Routed network, which Edge service is not available?

  a. NAT

  b. Firewall

  c. X-Large vShield Edge

  d. DHCP

3. Which network services does an internal network provide?

  a. DHCP

  b. NAT

  c. Firewall

  d. IPsec

4. Which two network pools allow for auto growth and do not require pre-provisioned resources to grow? (Choose two.)

  a. VXLAN

  b. vCD-NI

  c. VLAN

  d. Port-group backed

5. Which two VMware products are not required for VXLAN? (Choose two.)

  a. vSphere ESXi

  b. vCenter Chargeback

  c. vShield Manager

  d. Cloud Connector

6. Which vShield Edge feature is not supported on a Routed vApp Network?

  a. NAT

  b. Firewall

  c. Load balancer

  d. DHCP

7. Which feature does the vShield Load Balancer not include?

    a. SSL Offload

    b. Layer 7 load balancing

    c. TCP port load balancing

    d. Layer 4 load balancer

8. Which features does the vShield Edge DHCP server not support?

    a. Address pools

    b. Custom DHCP options (that is, PXE, Net time)

    c. DHCP Reservations

    d. Lease times

Foundation Topics

One of the hardest concepts to grasp in vCloud Director installations is networking. Even seasoned network professionals find that implementing networking in a vCloud environment can be very confusing. With network configurations required at the External, Organization, and vApp levels, the number of layers can quickly become overwhelming; add in networks that are not routed and you encounter even more confusion.

Throughout this chapter, we cover external networks, organization networks, and vApp networks, including their configuration and consumption.

NOTE   External networks provide connectivity to anything outside the vCloud installation. Organization networks are consumable to the organization that owns the network. vApp networks are usable inside a single vApp.

External Networks

vCloud Director treats any network that can access resources outside of the vCloud instance as an external network. This means an external network could be internal to your company without access to the Internet or it could be a network with a public IP address assigned to it. vCloud Director treats them both the same.

External networks are also the building blocks of organization networks. If your organization needs access to a corporate network or the Internet, it will require an external network to which to pass that traffic. The configuration of an external network is rather simple—after the network is defined in vCenter as a port group across all hosts in the provider virtual datacenter (vDC), it can then be added to vCloud Director.

Activity 6-1: Add External Network to vCloud Director

1. After vSphere networking has been configured in vCenter across all hosts in the provider vDC, log in to vCloud Director as a system administrator.

2. Select the **Manage & Monitor** tab; then select **External Networks**, as shown in Figure 6-1.

3. Select the green plus sign to launch the New External Network wizard, as shown in Figure 6-2.

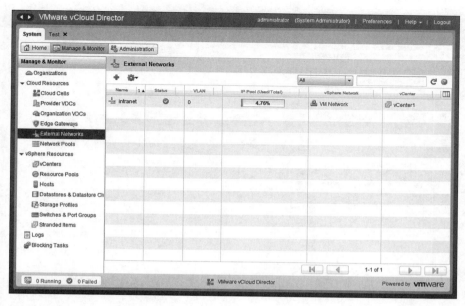

Figure 6-1 External Network Menu

4. After the wizard is launched, select the vCenter and the vSphere Network that vCloud Director will utilize for the external network. The screen and options are shown in Figure 6-3.

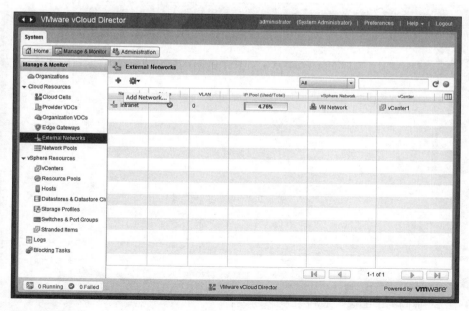

Figure 6-2 Launch New External Network

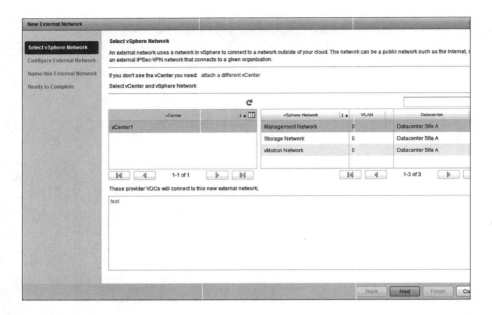

Figure 6-3   External Network vSphere Selection

  5. After clicking **Next**, the Configure External Network screen enables you to specify the new external network's IP settings. This screen is shown in Figure 6-4.

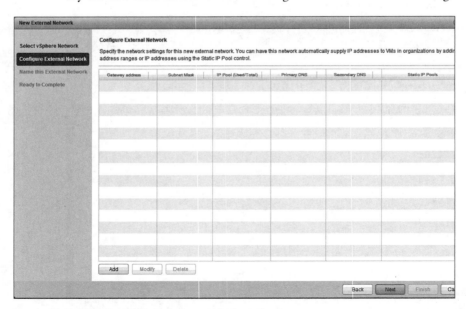

Figure 6-4   Configure External Network Settings

6. Click the **Add** button to launch the Add Subnet wizard. This wizard allows you to configure the gateway, network mask, Domain Name Service (DNS) servers, DNS suffix, and IP ranges, as shown in Figure 6-5.

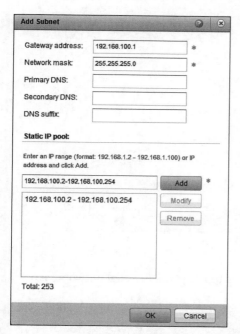

Figure 6-5   External Network Subnet Settings

7. After clicking **OK** on the Add Subnet wizard, you will see a screen similar to Figure 6-6 allowing you to verify the settings before proceeding.

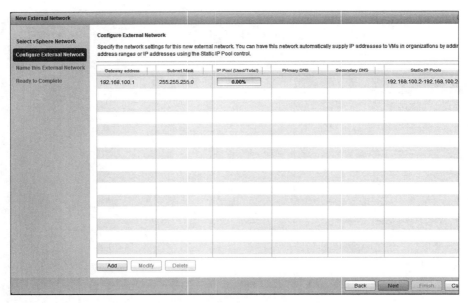

Figure 6-6   Verify External Network Subnet Settings

8. All that is left to complete at this point is to name the external network, as shown in Figure 6-7.

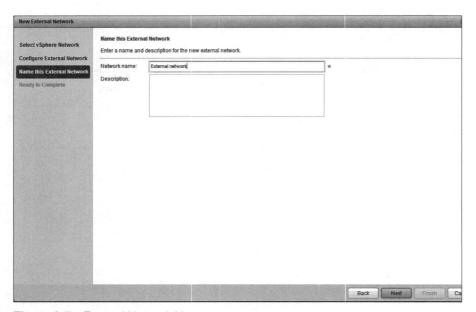

Figure 6-7   External Network Name

9. The final screen, shown in Figure 6-8, allows you to verify the selected network configuration. If everything looks good, click **Finish**; otherwise, click **Back** to correct any problems.

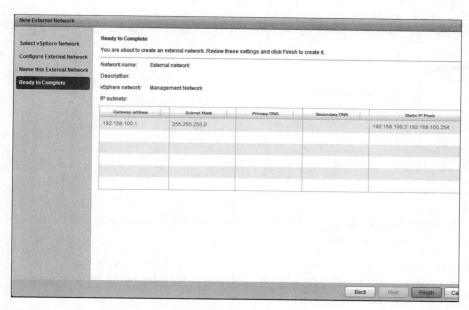

Figure 6-8   Finalize External Network Creation

Configuring and adding an external network is easy, but as with many things in IT, your network configuration is unlikely to remain static. In case you need to modify the existing vCloud Director external networks, follow the steps outlined in Activity 6-2.

Activity 6-2: Modifying External Network Settings

1. After you have logged in to vCloud and proceeded to the External Networks section, right-click the network you want to modify; then select **Properties** as shown in Figure 6-9.

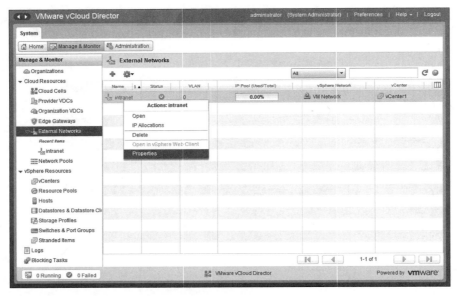

Figure 6-9   Modifying External Network

> **2.** The network properties screen appears with the fields that are editable. You cannot modify the gateway address or the network mask as shown in Figure 6-10, even if the network is not in use.

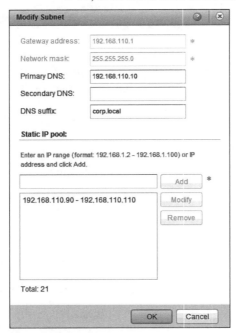

Figure 6-10   Modify Subnet

NOTE   If you need to modify the gateway or subnet of an external network, you must create a new network, migrate the virtual machines (VMs) to that new subnet, and then remove the old subnet.

3. The final tab on the Network Properties screen is the Metadata tab, as shown in Figure 6-11. This tab lets you create metadata items as well as modify those items.

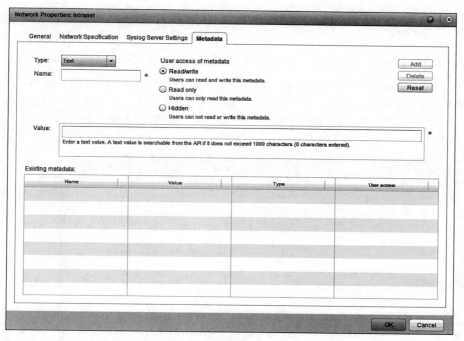

Figure 6-11   External Network Metadata Properties

External Routed Network

Routed external networks are just that: routed connections. vCloud Director deploys a vShield Edge device for each routed network that is created. This device can be configured to provide various network services, including virtual private network (VPN), dynamic host configuration protocol (DHCP) server, DNS Relay, Network Address Translation (NAT), Firewall, Router, and Load Balancer. A routed network consumes a resource out of the network pools in vCloud Director; we cover network pools and their configuration and use later in this chapter. Similar to the external network, also known as an *external direct connected network*, an external routed network refers to a network that provides access to resources outside the cloud.

To configure an external routed network, the following items are required:

- Network pool resource

- External (outside of the cloud) IP

- Internal IP range and subnet

- Default gateway, which will become the internal IP address of the deployed vShield Edge

- DNS

We cover the configuration of the NAT, Firewall, Routing, Load Balancer, DNS Relay, and DHCP server services, in the section called "Managed Network Services."

If your use case or configuration calls for multiple external networks to run on the same logical segment (VLAN) and you will use other methods to control the traffic segmentation, you can enable this under the System Administration tab, General settings as shown in Figure 6-12.

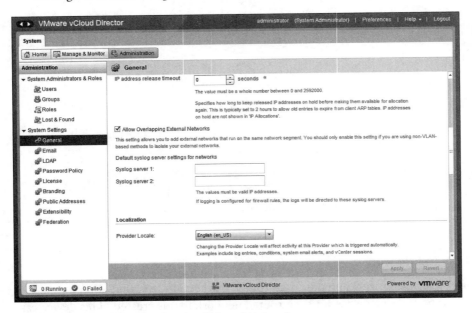

Figure 6-12   Enabling Overlapping External Networks

Organization vDC Networks

vCloud Director has three options for organization networks, including isolated, routed, and direct connect. Each of these can be shared across an organization consuming multiple vDCs or limited to a single vDC. This flexibility allows for a single organization to have separate network security zones without the worry that a secure vApp could be connected to an unsecured network. Unfortunately, this flexibility can also increase the complexity and degree of troubleshooting required to administer networking in vCloud Director.

Types of Organization Networks

Although it would be easy to just say "Give me X type of organization network," that option does not exist in vCloud Director. A few minor configuration tasks need to be done before an organization network is ready to consume. This section examines these configuration tasks for the direct, routed, and isolated versions of the organization vDC network.

NOTE The only network that gets a vShield Edge device is the routed network. Internal and direct organization vDC networks do not receive a vShield Edge device.

Direct Network

Direct networks connect an organization vDC to external network resources by connecting directly to the port group where the external network exists. Any vApp deployed on this network consumes at least one IP address from the IP pool. To reduce the IP consumption, each vApp can be deployed behind a vShield Edge device that will NAT/route to external network resources. These resources could include the Internet, resources external to your company, or anything outside of vCloud Director.

Routed Network

Routed networks are routed connections to an external network. vCloud Director deploys a vShield Edge when a routed network is created. This vShield Edge device can be configured with the VPN, DHCP server, DNS Relay, NAT, Firewall, Router, and/or Load Balancer services. A routed network also consumes a resource out of the network pools in vCloud Director; we cover network pools, their configuration and use in the section titled "Configure and Administer vCloud Network Pools."

NOTE Just as with a direct connected network, the term *external* refers to network resources that exist outside the cloud.

Internal Network

Unlike the two previously mentioned networks, an internal network in vCloud Director is internal to the organization. With the changes that vCloud Director 5.1 introduced to network configuration, an organization network can extend between organization vDCs or can be limited to a single organization vDC.

> **NOTE**   An internal network consumes a resource out of a network pool.

Create, Modify, and Remove Organization Networks

In this section, we discuss the proper way to create, modify, and remove organization networks in vCloud Director.

Activity 6-3: Creating a Routed Network

1. Log in as a system administrator to the organization where you will be creating the routed network. To accomplish this, log in to vCloud Director and from the System interface, select the organization from the Manage & Monitor tab, as shown in Figure 6-13.

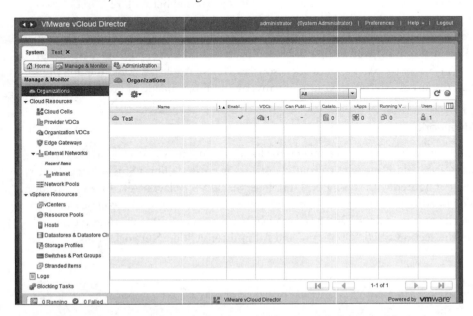

Figure 6-13   Selecting an Organization from the System Administrator View

2. Select the Administration tab inside the organization; then select the organization vDC that will own the routed network.

> **NOTE**   You can share a network between organization vDCs during their creation. You cannot, however, move the network to a different organization vDC after creation.

3. For a routed network, select the **Edge Gateways** tab; then select the green plus sign to add a new Edge gateway, as shown in Figure 6-14.

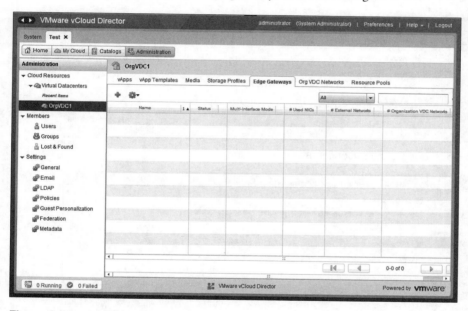

Figure 6-14   Add Edge Gateway

4. You are now able to choose whether to deploy a Compact or Full size Edge gateway device and whether to Enable High Availability. Advanced options also allow you to Configure IP Settings, Sub-Allocate IP Pools, and Configure Rate Limits as needed on the vShield Edge devices. Figure 6-15 shows these options checked; their settings are explained in the following steps.

5. Select the network in the External Network list that this routed network will use, as shown in Figure 6-16.

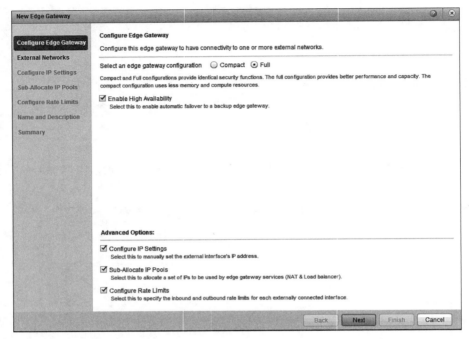

Figure 6-15   Edge Gateway Configuration

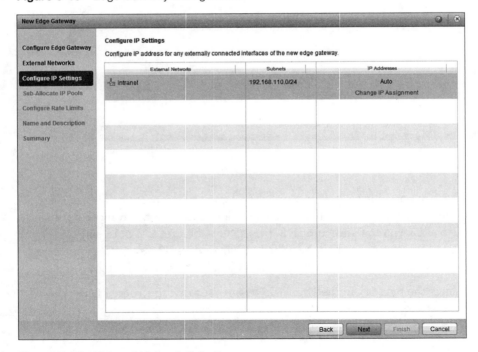

Figure 6-16   External Network Selection

6. Select **Change IP Assignment** for the chosen network to configure the specific IP that the outside interface of the Edge device receives. Figure 6-17 shows the process to configure a specific IP.

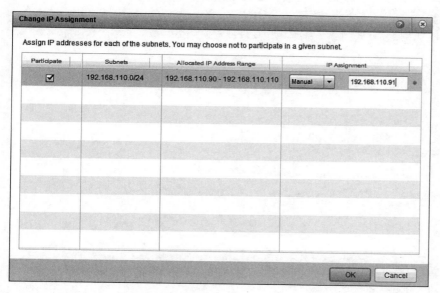

Figure 6-17 External Edge IP Assignments

7. Next up is the configuration of IP pools for the routed network, as shown in Figure 6-18. This will enable you to allocate a pool of IP addresses to the organization to use on the external network (as opposed to a single IP address).

8. Rate limits are the next setting to configure; this lets you limit the amount of data sent over a network. You can set a separate limit for inbound and outbound traffic. In this case, the settings have been applied to the external network, as shown in Figure 6-19.

9. After that, the final step is to name the network and click **Finish**.

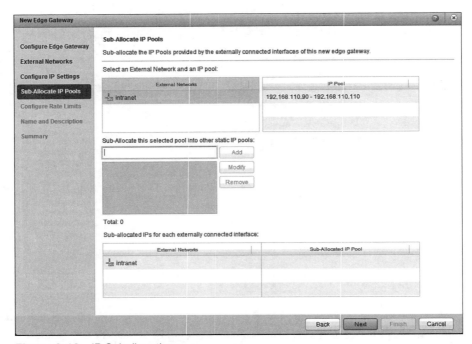

Figure 6-18   IP Suballocations

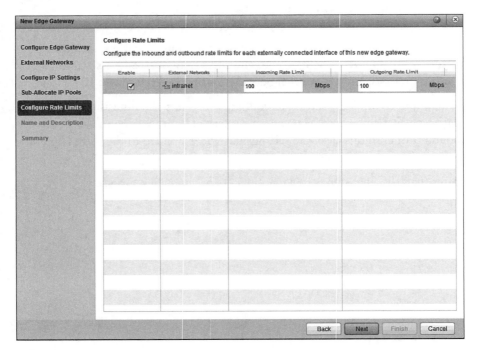

Figure 6-19   Rate Limits

Activity 6-4: Creating a Direct Network

1. To add a direct network to an organization virtual datacenter, select the **Org VDC Networks** tab and click the green plus sign to start the New Organization VDC Network wizard.

2. Select the option **Connect Directly to an External Network** as shown in Figure 6-20.

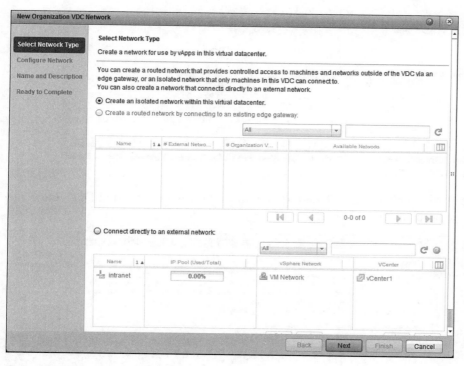

Figure 6-20   Direct External Network Wizard

3. Click **Next**, give it a name, and then click **Finish**. You are finished creating a direct network. The IP settings and other options will be taken from the external network.

Now that we have configured the external networks for our organizations, we need to investigate the configuration of the internal networks.

Activity 6-5: Creating an Internal Organization Network

1. Much like in Activity 6-3, go to the Organization Virtual Datacenter view and select the **Org VDC Networks** tab. Select the green plus sign to launch the New Organization VDC Network wizard, as shown in Figure 6-21.

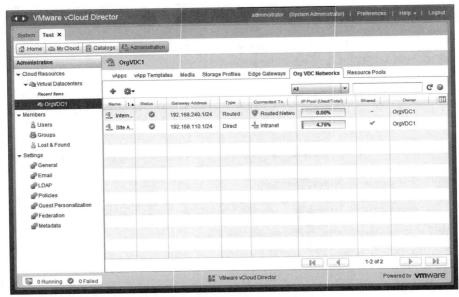

Figure 6-21 New Organization VDC Network

2. Select the **Create an Isolated Network Within This Virtual Datacenter** option, as shown in Figure 6-22.

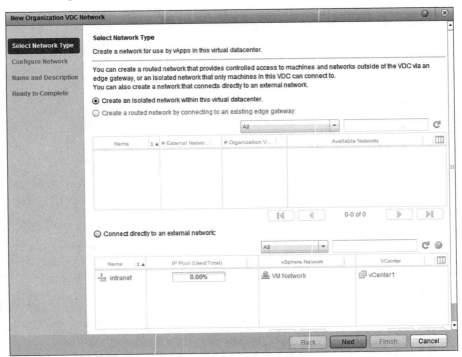

Figure 6-22 Isolated Network Creation

3. Provide the gateway, network mask, DNS servers, and IP pool settings in the appropriate fields, as shown in Figure 6-23.

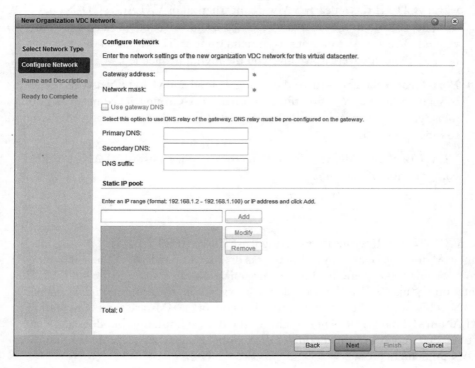

Figure 6-23   Internal Network Configuration

4. Give it a name and click **Finish**; you are done.

Configure and Administer vCloud Network Pools

vCloud network pools are groupings of vSphere networking resources that can be consumed by a tenant of your cloud. These resources can be logical or physical networking resources, but they must be configured by a vCloud system administrator.

Types of Network Pools

- **VXLAN**—Virtual eXtensible Local Area Network (VXLAN) pools provide the ability to extend Layer 2 capabilities in Layer 3 networks by encapsulating Layer 2 logical networks in standard Layer 3 IP packets. Does that scare you? It shouldn't; it is what VLAN is to Layer 2. If you are still scared, keep reading.

- **vCloud Director – Network Isolation (vCD-NI)**—vCD-NI pools work much like VXLAN pools, allowing multiple Layer 3 networks on a single network. vCD-NI was an early VMware incarnation of VXLAN. vCD-NI has been deprecated in the current vCD release and will soon be removed from vCloud Director. We do not recommend using vCD-NI due to this fact, but because the test covers it, we give you the highlights needed.

- **Port-Group Backed**—Instead of using vCloud and vCloud Network Security to segment traffic, you can utilize a normal Port-Group backed network pool. This type of pool requires a higher degree of manual configuration compared to other pool types.

- **VLAN Backed**—Allows vCloud Director to utilize a list of VLANs for the configuration of networks.

VXLAN

The VXLAN is an Internet Engineering Task Force (IETF) standard that defines a framework for overlaying Layer 2 networks on a Layer 3 network. This technology allows for several key benefits. First, an organization can overcome the 4096 VLAN limitation because VXLAN encapsulation allows for up to 16 million networks per VLAN. This calculates to roughly 65 billion networks! VMware's implementation of VXLAN in vCloud 5.1 does not reach this theoretical limitation but does allow for up to 10,000 networks, which doubles the number of networks capable in a standard VLAN implementation.

In addition, VXLAN enables Layer 2 traffic to extend across a Layer 3 network. This allows for Layer 2–specific traffic, such as vMotion, to boldly go where it has not gone before. It also enables VMs in two separate VLANs to communicate with each other.

All of this is done utilizing encapsulation. VXLAN adds information to the packet headers to ensure their proper routing. This additional data requires the underlying network to be configured to support a greater than 1,600 MTU. If this setting is not changed, network packets are dropped and lost.

VXLAN works by creating tunnels. These tunnels are sometimes referred to as *virtual wires*. The endpoint of the tunnel is called a VXLAN tunnel end point (VTEP). VXLAN requires some additional configuration inside vShield Manager to enable a VTEP to be deployed and configured on each host that will connect to a VXLAN network.

Activity 6-6: Enabling VXLAN

1. VXLAN is configured from the vShield Manager web interface. After logging in to vShield Manager, select the datacenter that is to be prepared for VXLAN. (We select the proper cluster in a later step.) Next, select the **Network Virtualization** tab, as shown in Figure 6-24.

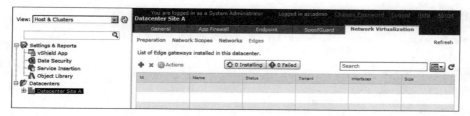

Figure 6-24   Network Virtualization in vShield Manager

2. Select the **Preparation** menu, as shown in Figure 6-25.

Figure 6-25   Preparation of Network Virtualization

3. Then select the **Segment ID** option, as shown in Figure 6-26.

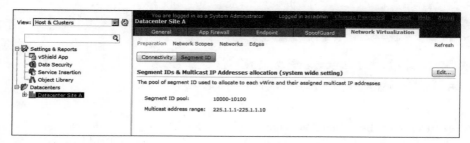

Figure 6-26   Segment ID

4. Select the **Edit** button and provide a value for the Segment ID Pool. This value designates the range of pool IDs that are used for the virtual wires. Next, provide the value for the Multicast Addresses. Each multicast address is associated with a single VXLAN logical Layer 2 network. An example using a pool of 100 segments and 10 multicast addresses is shown in Figure 6-27.

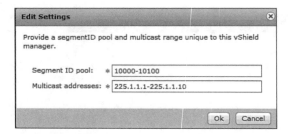

Figure 6-27 VXLAN Segment ID Configuration

> **5.** Click the cluster to be prepared, and then click the **Edit** button. The Prepare Infrastructure for VXLAN Networking window appears, as shown in Figure 6-28.

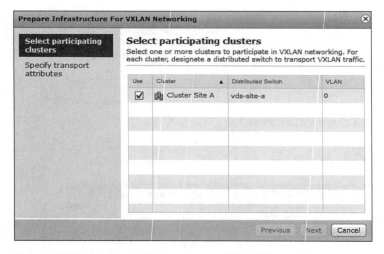

Figure 6-28 Prepare Infrastructure for VXLAN Networking

> **6.** At this point, the vShield Manager deploys VXLAN vmk modules to the vSphere hosts and configures their IP addresses with a DHCP address.

NOTE Static IP addresses should ultimately be configured on the vmks. This can be accomplished by utilizing the vSphere Client to find, select, and configure the vmks on each host.

vCloud Director – Network Isolated Network

The first release of vCloud Director included something called vCloud Director – Network Isolation (vCD-NI), which provides some of the benefits of VXLAN and uses an encapsulation methodology. vCD-NI uses Mac-in-Mac encapsulation, whereas VXLAN uses Mac-in-UDP encapsulation. Even though vCD-NI is still supported in vCloud Director 5.1, it is being deprecated and is not likely to exist in future versions.

NOTE   vCD-NI does not provide all the benefits that VXLAN provides. Because vCD-NI is nonroutable, it does not scale as well as VXLAN does.

vCD-NI requires fewer settings changes than VXLAN on a vSphere host, but it still requires specific settings to be configured on the switching infrastructure. These settings include changing the MTU of the physical switches to 1,600 bytes or higher. This change must be made on all switches where a vCD-NI packet might traverse. Keep in mind that vCD-NI packets transmit only between vSphere hosts.

Port-Group Backed

For an organization looking for absolute control over network resources, port-group backed network pools are a good choice. Port-group backed network pools are directly tied to a port group that must be manually configured in vSphere prior to being consumed in vCloud Director. This means you need to create every network pool item before you need it. Although port-group backed pools can provide tight control and some degree of simplicity in configuration, the process to create them is highly manual. If this pool type is used, you might want to consider scripting or automation to offset the manual work.

NOTE   Port-group backed networking works with both standard and distributed switches.

VLAN-Backed

vCloud Director can dynamically deploy VLAN-based networking for organizations of the cloud. VLAN-backed networking creates a port group on a distributed virtual switch and assigns it to the desired VLAN automatically. One of the requirements of VLAN-backed networking is that vCloud be given a range or series of VLAN IDs that it can use and consume at any time.

Create/Delete a Network Pool

Now that we know all the flavors of network pools in vCloud Director, it is time to create one of each network pool, so keep reading! Keep in mind that VXLAN network pool objects are created automatically when the provider vDC is created in vCloud Director and vShield manager has been configured for network virtualization.

Activity 6-7: Creating a vCD-NI Network Pool

1. After logging in to vCloud Director, select the **Manage & Monitor** tab, select **Network Pools**, and select the green plus to launch the Create Network Pool Wizard, which is shown in Figure 6-29.

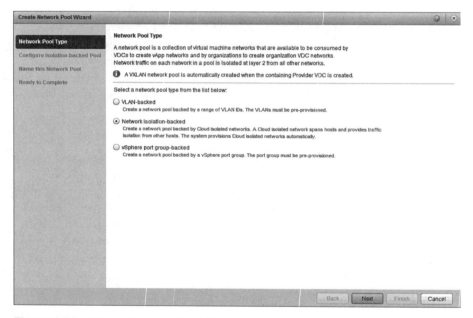

Figure 6-29   Create Network Pool Wizard

2. Select **Network Isolation-Backed** as the network pool type.

3. Configure the number of vCD-NI networks that are required as well as the VLAN ID that the port groups should be created on for the vCD-NI networks. Also select the vCenter Server that the vCD-NI pool should belong to and the vDS on which the port groups should be provisioned. These configuration items are shown in Figure 6-30.

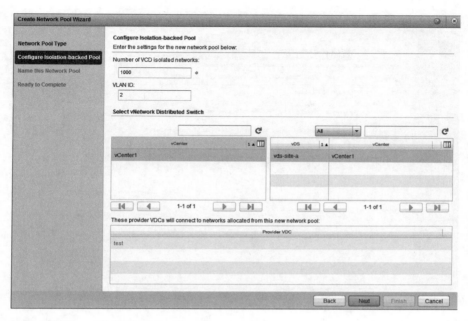

Figure 6-30   vCD-NI Pool Configuration

4. Give the pool a name, verify your settings, and click **Finish**. The pool is now configured in vCloud Director and is ready for use.

Activity 6-8: Creating a Port-Group Backed Network Pool

1. Follow step 1 in Activity 6-6.

2. Select **vSphere Port Group-Backed** as the network pool type, as shown in Figure 6-31.

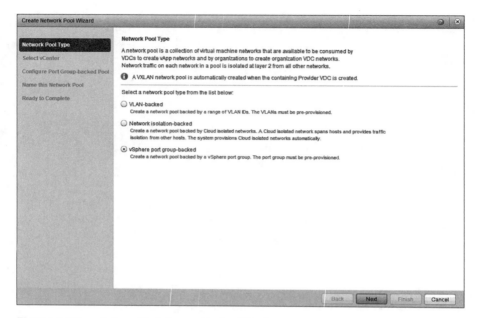

Figure 6-31 vSphere Port-Group Backed Pool

3. Select the vCenter Server where the port groups exist, as shown in Figure 6-32.

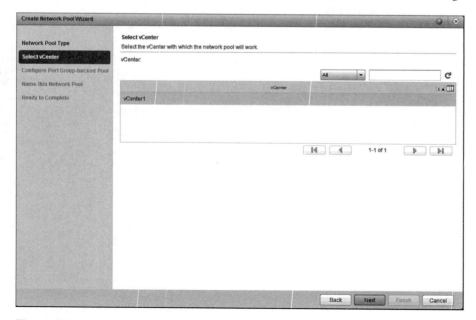

Figure 6-32 vCenter Selection

4. Figure 6-33 shows the adding of port groups that are to be part of this network pool.

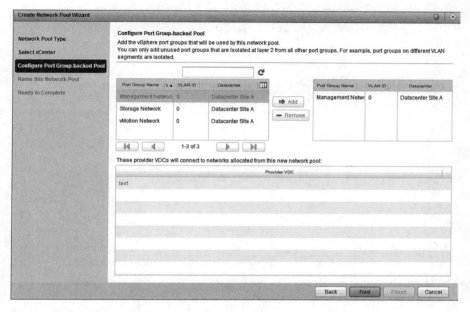

Figure 6-33   Adding Port Groups to the Port-Group Network Pool

5. Give the network pool a name and click **Finish** to complete the wizard.

NOTE   Unlike VXLAN and vCD-NI network pools, a vSphere port-group backed pool must have the port group created before deployment. VXLAN and vCD-NI networks will create pool members on demand as needed.

Activity 6-9: Creating a VLAN-Backed Network Pool

1. Follow step 1 in Activity 6-7.

2. Select **VLAN-Backed** as the network pool type, as shown in Figure 6-34.

3. A VLAN range must be supplied to the network pool. This range does not have to be consecutive; you can add multiple segments as shown in Figure 6-35.

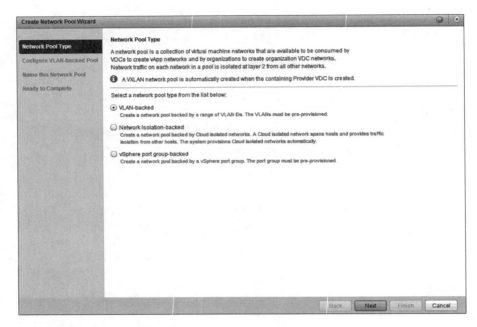

Figure 6-34 VLAN Backed Pool

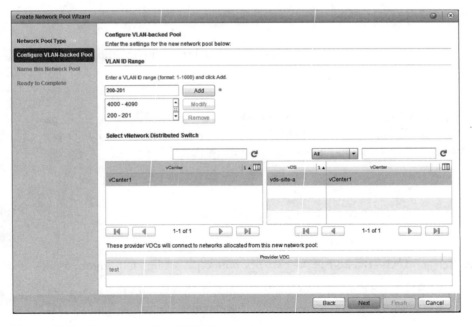

Figure 6-35 Nonconsecutive VLAN Segments

4. After you have added the proper ranges, select the vCenter Server and Distributed Network switch where the network pool will reside.

Troubleshooting Common Network Pool Problems

Network pools are pretty generic, and they either work or they do not. The most common problem with them is the pool being out of resources. To verify the amount of resources left in a network pool, log in to vCloud Director, select **Manage & Monitor**, and then select **Network Pools**. A progress bar shows how much of the pool is used versus what is left. This is shown in Figure 6-36.

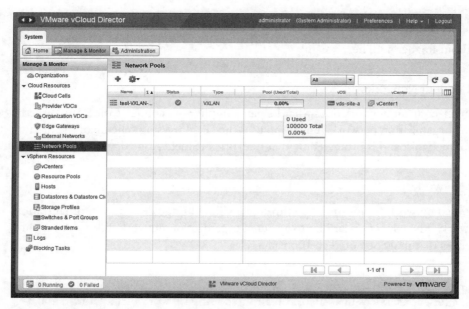

Figure 6-36 Network Pool Usage

Configure and Administer vApp Networks

vCloud Director allows for another layer of networking to isolate applications and tenants. A vApp network is a network that is isolated to a single vApp and cannot span across vApps without an organization network to do so. A vApp network can connect to organization networks through a routed or direct connection. When connecting through a routed network, a resource from the network pool is required. In some cases, there is no need to connect to an external network; in this case, the network is considered to be isolated to the vApp only.

Much like organization networks, a routed connection is made through a vShield Edge device, though there are differences. We cover those differences in this section as well as the configuration of those options.

vApp Network Types

We have covered external networks and organization vDC networks. It is now time to examine vApp networks, the networks that the actual VMs will connect to. That means covering the two vApp network types:

- Direct-Connect networks
- Routed networks

Without further ado, here we go!

Direct-Connect Networks

A direct-connect network does what its name implies—it connects the vApp directly to the organization network. The vApp uses the IP addressing scheme of the organization network and is protected by that network's vShield Edge device.

Routed Networks

A routed network routes the vApp through a vShield Edge device to an organization network. The concept is similar to a routed organization network, but there are differences that must be noted and considered.

> **NOTE**   Network services unavailable on a routed vApp network include the load balancer and VPN services, as well as multi-interface configurations.

Most network services are still available to a routed vApp network, including Firewall, NAT, and DHCP services. These are configured through the Network tab on the vApp Configuration screen. We cover the configuration of a vApp Network vShield Edge device in the next section.

> **NOTE**   Another vApp networking option is fencing. Fenced vApps consist of a routed network with a one-to-one NAT configuration, enabling identical VMs to be deployed on the same network without MAC or IP address collisions.

Managed Network Services

We have discussed the types of vCloud networks and the ways to configure those networks; now we need to discuss the services we can offer on those networks. These options include

- vShield Edge sizing
- DHCP servers
- DNS Relay
- SNAT
- DNAT
- Firewall
- Static routing
- IPsec VPN
- SSL VPN-Plus
- Load balancer
- Third-party support

After that, we cover the configuration of selected services.

vShield Edge Sizing

With the release of vCloud Director 5.1 and vCloud Networking and Security 5.1, vShield Edge devices can now be deployed in three sizes. Two of these can be deployed using vCloud Director. This section discusses the differences between the sizes of vShield Edge devices and their capabilities.

Compact

A compact vShield Edge device is configured with 1 vCPU, 256MB of RAM, and 512MB hard drive space for logs. This size option should be used for minimal workloads where throughput of less than 1Gbps is expected or required. It is not recommended that IPsec VPN or SSL VPN be used on a vShield Edge Compact, due to the overhead of these technologies. The compact size should be utilized more as a vApp router device.

Large

A large vShield Edge device is more suited for >1Gbps traffic and when VPNs, firewalls, and other options are needed. A large vShield Edge device is configured with

2vCPU, 1GB RAM, and a 256MB hard drive. All features are supported with this size option, and these are more commonly deployed for organization networks.

NOTE Even though there is an option for extra-large Edge devices in vCNS, that option is not available in vCloud Director 5.1.

vShield Edge Services

The vShield Edge firewall/router that is deployed for organization networks contains the following configurable items:

Firewall

vShield Edge provides basic firewall services. These services enable you to configure inbound and outbound traffic across multiple network protocols.

Static Routing

A vShield Edge device provides an option for defining static routes, which can be useful when a default gateway might not be enough to enable network traffic to flow properly.

Load Balancer—Layer 4 and Layer 7

vShield Edge in vCloud Director 5.1 introduced the option to configure a load balancer at Layer 4 and Layer 7. In vCloud Director 5.1, the user interface (UI) enables the configuration of the Layer 7 load balancing. If a Layer 4 load balancer is required, it must be configured in vShield Manager. A Layer 7 load balancer directs traffic based on the content of the request, meaning session persistence (that is, cookies, SSL sticky sessions, and so on). vCloud Director requires a Layer 7–type load balancer due to the SSL sticky session configuration.

NOTE A Layer 4 load balancer preserves the original client IP address of the request. This type of load balancer can be used for HTTP pages that do not require any state information or basic TCP load balancing.

High Availability

There are three license levels in vCloud Director, two of which affect the options for vCloud Network and Security. These two versions of vCloud Director Suite are Standard and Advanced. The Standard version does not include the ability to enable high availability (HA) or load balancing. The Enterprise version of vCloud Director Suite includes the same features as the Advanced license for vCloud Network and Security.

DHCP

The vShield Edge can act as a DHCP server for the networks it protects. This option exists on both vApp and organization networks. On an organization network with multiple internal interfaces, you can configure different IP ranges and DHCP settings for each interface. The DHCP server can also dynamically create DNS entries on the vShield Edge's internal DNS server. Static DHCP leases are also available based on the requesting machine's MAC address.

DNS Relay

As a DNS Relay, the vShield Edge is capable of relaying DNS requests out of the protected networks to an authoritative DNS server. The device can also act as a DNS cache for name requests.

NOTE   When acting as a DNS cache, this can complicate troubleshooting procedures because there is now another cache that could contain incorrect information.

SNAT

The vShield Edge device is capable of performing Source Network Address Translation (SNAT). This is configurable on both vApp and organization networks. This configuration enables source IP addresses and ports to be translated to predefined internal IP addresses and ports.

DNAT

As a Destination Network Address Translation (DNAT) device, this enables the vShield Edge to complete translations of IP addresses and ports based on the destination of the network traffic. This option is available on all versions of vCloud Director Suite.

Firewall

A vShield Edge device can act as a Layer 2 and Layer 3 firewall for network traffic destined to a network for which the device routes. This means that traffic between internal interfaces can be filtered as well as traffic from the outside to the inside and the reverse. The firewall is stateful even through failover events when HA is enabled.

Static Routing

The vShield Edge can act as a static router. This is configurable through the vCloud Director web pages as well as the API.

NOTE The vShield Edge is unable to process dynamic routing protocols such as RIP, BGP, and others.

IPsec VPN

vShield Edge devices support site-to-site IPsec VPN tunnels between vShield Edge devices and remote sites. They also support certificate authentication, preshared keys, and IP unicast traffic, but they do not support dynamic routing protocols transmitted over the tunnel.

NOTE Without dynamic routing protocols supported with a site-to-site VPN, all subnets behind each site must be defined and configured prior to traffic being able to route over the VPN connection.

SSL VPN-Plus

vShield Edge provides the capability to be a VPN device for end users, unlike the site-to-site VPN, which requires predefined routes, shared keys, and static IP or DNS resolution. The SSL VPN-Plus enables remote users to connect securely to private networks behind a vShield Edge gateway, allowing access to internal resources. Connections through the SSL VPN-Plus can still be firewalled and filtered just as any other interface or connection.

Layer 7 Load Balancer

vShield Edge provides load balancing for HTTP, HTTPS, and TCP traffic types. Load balancing at Layer 7 of the OSI model enables web applications to autoscale and SSL communications to be balanced.

With the load balancer, you can map public IPs or external IPs to a predefined set of internal IP addresses, called a *server pool*. The load balancer can also complete checks of the internal servers to ensure that they are operational before allowing traffic to flow to them.

Third-Party Support

vCloud Network and Security enables third-party network services to be managed through the vShield Edge and Manager interfaces. This lets a third party replace or add to the services offered in a cloud. For example, it could allow a load balancer company to offer a more fully featured load balancer or a large security firm to offer IPS/IDS services through vCloud Director.

Configuring vShield Edge Services

Activity 6-10: Configuring a DHCP Server

1. In the Organization VDC, select **Edge Gateways**, right-click, and select **Configure Services**.

2. As shown in Figure 6-37, select **Enable DHCP**.

3. Click the **Add** button in the lower-right corner.

4. When adding a DHCP pool, the Applied On network selection is the network interface on which the DHCP server will listen. As shown in Figure 6-38, the range is set for the pool of IPs and the lease times for those IPs are defined.

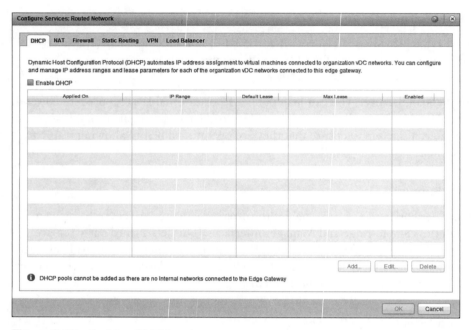

Figure 6-37 Enabling DHCP

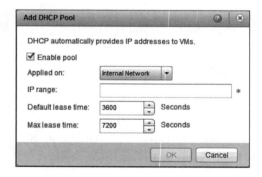

Figure 6-38 DHCP Pool Settings

Activity 6-11: Configuring NAT Rules

NOTE In DNAT, the requested or destination IP is changed. In SNAT, the requesting or source IP is changed.

1. In the Edge gateway properties, select the **NAT** tab and select the type of rule to add—either SNAT or DNAT. Figure 6-39 shows a SNAT rule being added, and Figure 6-40 shows a DNAT rule being added.

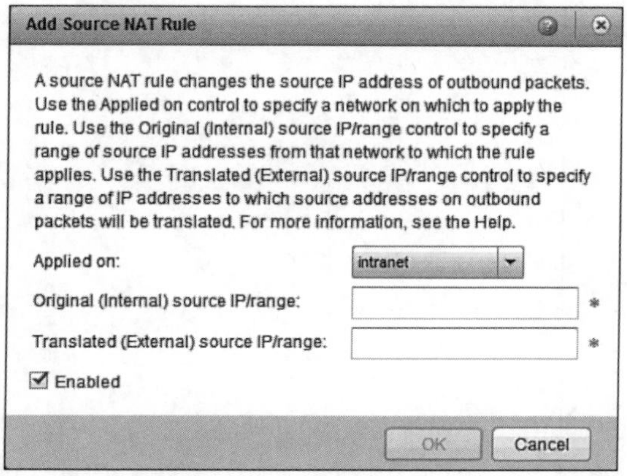

Figure 6-39 SNAT Rule Creation

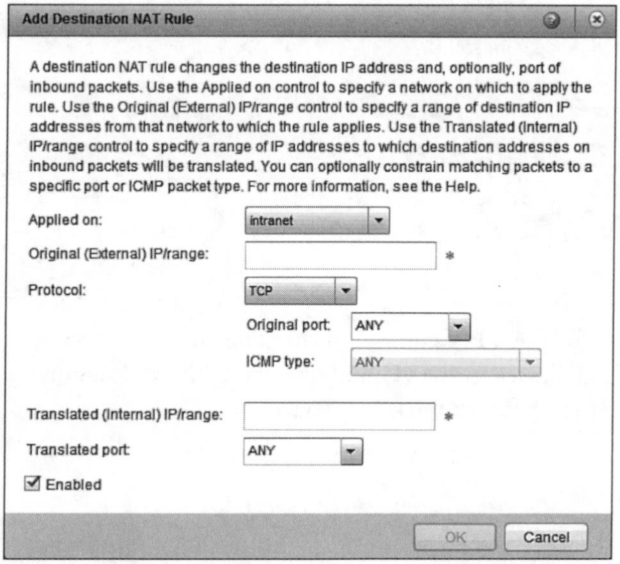

Figure 6-40 DNAT Rule Creation

Activity 6-12: Creating a VPN Session (IPsec and SSL)

1. In the Edge Gateway properties, select the **VPN** tab; then enable VPN connectivity by selecting the **Enable This VPN Configuration** check box shown in Figure 6-41.

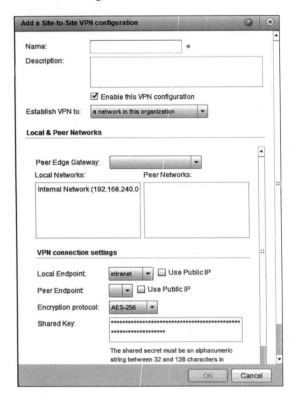

Figure 6-41   Enabling VPN

2. Select the destination type for the VPN configuration. The endpoint device can be another vShield Edge device in the vCloud or outside the vCloud installation, or it can be an IPsec VPN-compatible device.

Summary

We began the chapter talking about vCloud networking and how networking can be the most complex and tricky subject in a vCloud Director installation. To make the complex topic of networking easier to understand, we broke it into these parts:

- We determined that an external network is considered to be any network with access to a network resource outside the cloud installation; it can be on the Internet or an intranet.

- We discussed organization networks and their connection methods to the external networks, including the ability to create an isolated network.

- We discussed the use of network pools, the creation of network pools, and how a network pool is defined.

- We also covered vApp networks and their connection options to organization networks. We determined that a vApp cannot connect directly to an external network and that there must be an organization network between the two, even if the organization network is a direct connected network.

- Finally, we covered the services offered by the vShield Edge devices at the organization network layer and the vApp network layer.

Exam Preparation Tasks

Review All Key Topics

Review the most important topics in the chapter, noted with the Key Topic icon in the outer margin of the page. Table 6-2 lists a reference to these key topics and the page numbers on which each is found.

Table 6-2   Key Topics

Key Topic Element	Description	Page
Activity 6-1	Add External Network to vCloud Director	156
Activity 6-2	Modifying External Network Settings	161
Activity 6-3	Creating a Routed Network	166
Activity 6-4	Creating a Direct Network	171
Activity 6-5	Creating an Internal Organization Network	171
Activity 6-6	Enabling VXLAN	174
Activity 6-7	Creating a vCD-NI Network Pool	178
Activity 6-8	Creating a Port-Group Backed Network Pool	179
Activity 6-9	Creating a VLAN-Backed Network Pool	181
Activity 6-10	Configuring a DHCP Server	189
Activity 6-11	Configuring NAT Rules	190
Activity 6-12	Creating a VPN Session (IPsec and SSL)	192

Definitions of Key Terms

Define the following key terms from this chapter, and check your answers in the glossary:

external network, internal network, direct network, routed network, vShield Edge, IP allocations, VXLAN, vCD-NI, port-group backed, VLAN-backed, vApp network

Review Questions

The answers to these review questions are in Appendix A.

1. When VXLAN is used as a network pool, what must the MTU be set above to ensure network connectivity operates properly?

   a. 1,500

   b. 1,524

   c. 1,600

   d. 9,000

2. Which two features does an external routed network have that a routed vApp network does not have? (Choose two.)

   a. Load balancer

   b. DHCP

   c. DNS Relay

   d. SSL VPN-Plus

3. VXLAN in vCloud 5.1 has a maximum supported network count of how much?

   a. 16,000,000

   b. 1,000,000

   c. 10,000

   d. 1,024

4. After the creation of an external network in vCloud Director, which two settings cannot be changed? (Choose two.)

   a. DNS servers

   b. Default gateway

   c. Subnet mask

   d. IP allocation ranges

5. Rate limiting on an external network works on which traffic direction(s)?

    a. Outbound

    b. Inbound

    c. Inbound and outbound

    d. Inbound, outbound, and pass-through

6. For expected traffic loads of greater than 1Gbps, it is recommended to use which size vShield Edge appliance?

    a. Compact

    b. Large

    c. X-large

    d. Full

7. vShield SSL VPN allows for which type of VPN connection?

    a. Point-to-point

    b. End devices

    c. Mobile devices

    d. Layer 2 connections

This chapter covers the following subjects:

- **What Is a vCloud Director Organization?**—This section explains what a vCloud Director organization is and what an organization's boundaries are.

- **Creating a vCloud Director Organization**—This section demonstrates the configuration options for a vCloud Director organization and how to create a vCloud Director organization.

- **Modifying an Organization**—This section covers the modification of an organization.

- **Configuring an Organization for Federation**—This section covers the configuration of federation.

This chapter covers a portion of the VCP5-Cloud Exam Objective 12.1, VCP5-Cloud Exam Objective 12.2, VCP5-IaaS Exam Objective 5.1, and VCP5-IaaS Exam Objective 5.2.

CHAPTER 7

Configure and Administer vCloud Organizations

In this chapter, we cover the creation of vCloud Director organizations, the modification of vCloud Director organizations, and how to implement federated logins in vCloud Director. We also cover the modification of organization settings, including what can and cannot be changed.

"Do I Know This Already?" Quiz

The "Do I Know This Already?" quiz enables you to assess whether you should read this entire chapter or simply jump to the "Exam Preparation Tasks" section for review. If you are in doubt, read the entire chapter. Table 7-1 outlines the major headings in this chapter and the corresponding "Do I Know This Already?" quiz questions. You can find the answers in Appendix A, "Answers to the 'Do I Know This Already?' Quizzes and Review Questions."

Table 7-1 "Do I Know This Already?" Foundation Topics Section-to-Question Mapping

Foundations Topics Section	Questions Covered in This Section
What Is a vCloud Director Organization?	1
Creating a vCloud Director Organization	2–5
Modifying an Organization	6, 7
Configuring an Organization for Federation	8

1. Users can be logged in to how many organizations simultaneously?
    - a. 2
    - b. 3
    - c. 1
    - d. 4

2. Which field cannot be modified after an organization has been created?
    - a. Name
    - b. Full name
    - c. Description
    - d. Quotas

3. How many different authentication methods can be used for a vCloud Director organization (such as LDAP, local, and so on)?

   a. 1

   b. 2

   c. 3

   d. 4

4. Account lockout settings in vCloud Director apply to which type of authentication?

   a. Local users

   b. LDAP users

   c. SAML users

   d. Federated users

5. At which two points in time during the usage of a vApp do storage leases start? (Choose two.)

   a. Following a power-off action on the vApp

   b. At the vApp creation

   c. While the vApp is running

   d. When the users starts the timer

6. When modifying an organization's default quota, which accounts are affected?

   a. New user accounts.

   b. All existing accounts.

   c. Accounts that have the default quota values.

   d. No accounts will be affected.

7. Which field is required for a user of an organization to receive notifications?

   a. Full Name

   b. Email Address

   c. Quota

   d. Password

8. When configuring a federated authentication source, which two pieces of information are required? (Choose two.)

   a. IDP XML metadata

   b. vCloud organization metadata

   c. Source server address

   d. Service account for authentication

Foundation Topics

What Is a vCloud Director Organization?

In the simplest terms, a vCloud Director organization is a logical grouping of users. However, it is a bit more than that. The organization construct in vCloud Director can be compared to the datacenter construct in vCenter. It is where permissions are defined and is also the location to define lightweight directory access protocol (LDAP) server settings, federations, and the allocation of computer resources to a group of users.

NOTE   vCloud supports one user session per browser. This means that a user can be logged in to only one organization at a time, per browser. If you need to log in to more than one organization, you can use private browsing in modern browsers or use different browsers (such as Internet Explorer and Firefox).

Most vCloud actions are taken inside an organization. This includes the powering on of vApps, creation of catalog items, creation of templates, and so on.

Create an Organization

The first task after configuring the physical resources in a vCloud Director installation is the creation of an organization. It might seem straightforward to create an organization, but there are a few things you need to know and have documented before you begin setting up your first organization. The following list outlines the organization parameters for the creation of an organization:

- **Organization Name**—This field is the end of the URL that every user will use to access your cloud (for example, https://cloud.domain.tld/cloud/org/<orgName>).

NOTE   Careful consideration should be taken before you define this field because it cannot be changed unless you delete and re-create the organization.

- **Organization Full Name**—This friendly name is displayed on the page when users log in to your cloud. This field is changeable by organization administrators and system administrators.

- **LDAP**—How are users going to authenticate to your cloud instance? LDAP, security assertion markup language (SAML), or local users? This is where you configure the LDAP settings. Are users going to use the same LDAP settings as the vCloud Director System? Or are they going to use a custom LDAP server?

- **Local Users**—If you are not using LDAP or SAML, this is where you need to configure local users for your organization. It might be wise to add a local user to get back into your organization if the LDAP or SAML providers are offline; think of it as a fail-safe.

- **Catalog Publishing**—Will this organization be able to publish a catalog to all other organizations and users in your cloud? As discussed in Chapter 8, "Allocate and Manage vCloud Resources," publishing a catalog is an all-or-nothing setting.

- **Email Preferences**—Prior to a vApp being shut down due to a lease expiration, how should vCloud Director notify the user of this impending action? If you would like vCloud to send the owner of the vApp an email, you must specify a simple mail transfer protocol (SMTP) server (hostname, port, authentication).

NOTE If emails are going to be sent to users, the user objects in vCloud must be populated with an email address. If the account is from LDAP, the mail field will be used. If the user account is from a SAML source, this must be defined in the user record from your identity management solution. For proper configuration of SAML, see the section "Configure an Organization for Federation," later in this chapter.

- **Leases**—How long should a workload run in your cloud without action from the end user? vCloud suspends any vApp when the runtime lease is over.

NOTE Storage leases start counting when a vApp is in a powered-off state. An example of this is when the runtime lease expires or when the vApp is newly created. Storage leases always start at the length specified in the vApp's configuration.

When a storage lease expires, vCloud performs either Permanently Delete or Move to Expired Items on the affected vApp. Expired items still count against an organization's virtual machine (VM) count and storage allocation. Permanently Delete means just that—remove the vApp from disk and release all IP bindings that might have been consumed from the network pools.

- **Default Quotas**—This is the first place where you can set a quota on all the VMs and or just the running VMs. This is not the only place, though; this is also defined at the organization virtual datacenter (Org vDC) level and a per-user level. Troubleshooting which quota is expired can be a time-consuming task.

- **Intensive Task Limits**—Limiting the number of current tasks that are considered resource intensive can reduce the chances of a denial of service (DoS) against other tenants. This can be limited on a per-user or per-organization level. Resource-intensive tasks include copying, moving, deploying, and adding vApps to a catalog. All these operations can be intensive on disk input/output operations per second (IOPS).

- **Connections per VM**—This limits the number of VMware Remote Console (VMRC) connections per VM. This does not, however, limit the number of connections via other means such as remote desktop protocol (RDP), virtual network computing (VNC), or other remote access technologies.

- **Password Policies**—When using a local user for the organization, this section enables you to set account lockouts and the length of those lockouts.

Activity 7-1: Creating an Organization

1. After logging in to vCloud Director as a system administrator, select the **Manage & Monitor** tab; then click the green + sign to start the New Organization Wizard, as shown in Figure 7-1.

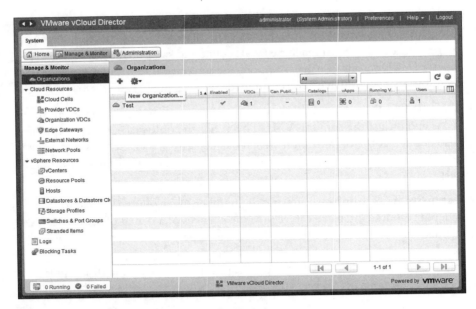

Figure 7-1 Start the New Organization Wizard

2. Specify an organization name, an organization full name, and a description for your organization, as shown in Figure 7-2.

3. The next item that needs to be configured is your LDAP settings, if you are planning to use an LDAP server for user authentication. If not, the next step lets you create local users. You can use the VCD System LDAP Service or a Custom LDAP Service, as shown in Figure 7-3.

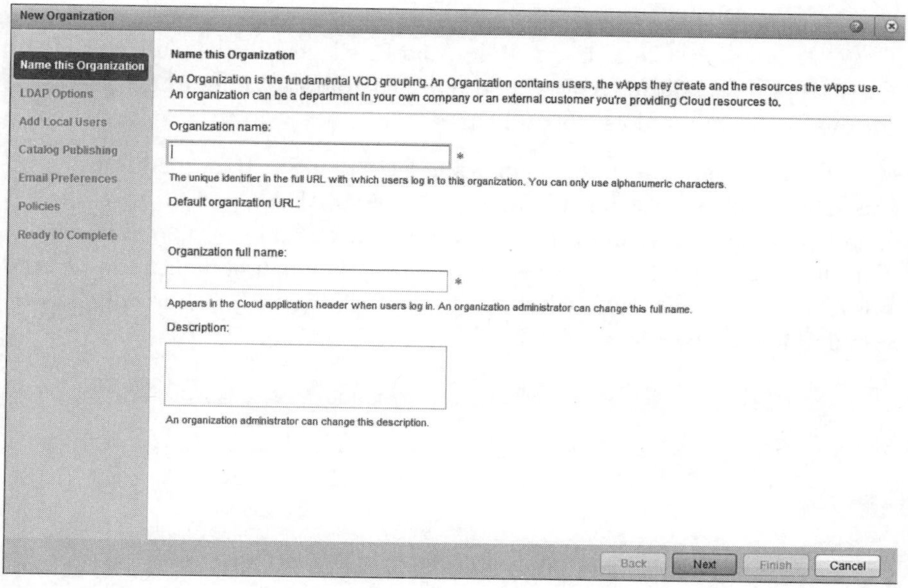

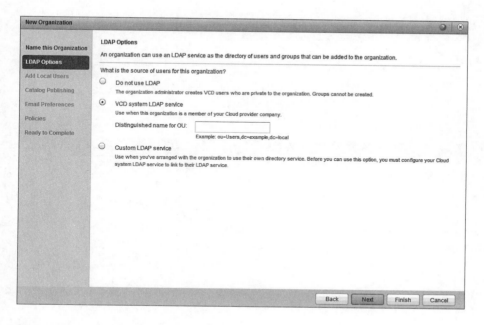

Figure 7-2   Name This Organization

Figure 7-3   LDAP Service Selection

Selecting the VCD system service utilizes the LDAP service defined in Chapter 3, "Administer vCloud Users, Roles, and Privileges." If the Custom LDAP Service option is selected, you will be able to define a separate LDAP service for this organization to use for authentication.

4. Adding local users is next; if you are using LDAP or SAML authentication, this step is optional. Keep in mind, though, that if LDAP or the SAML authentication service is offline, no one will be able to log in to vCloud Director. You should create at least one local user in case the other authentication methods fail. Figure 7-4 shows the local user interface; Figure 7-5 shows the fields required for adding a local user.

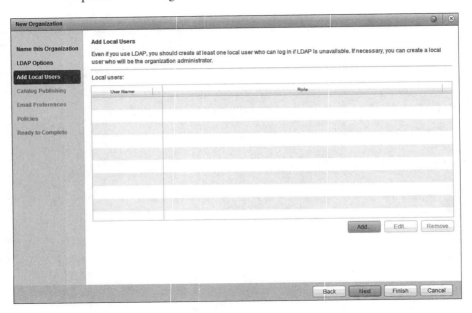

Figure 7-4   Add Local Users

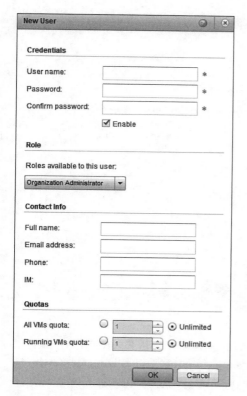

Figure 7-5   New User Dialog Box

NOTE   The email address field is required if the user will receive alerts for lease expirations or emails sent from the organization or system administrator.

5. The configuration step to enable an organization to publish a catalog is next. Keep in mind that unless you restrict the ability for a user to see published catalogs (refer to Chapter 3 for role information), publishing a catalog gives everyone in the cloud access to the vApp templates contained within it. Figure 7-6 shows the publishing option screen, with Cannot Publish Catalogs selected.

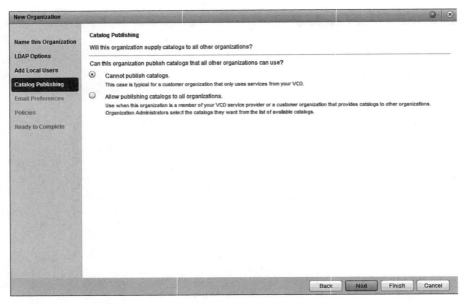

Figure 7-6 Publish a Catalog

6. Next, we configure the email and alert settings, as shown in Figure 7-7. You will define the SMTP server information or simply use the vCloud Director system SMTP settings, as well as configure who is to receive system notification messages.

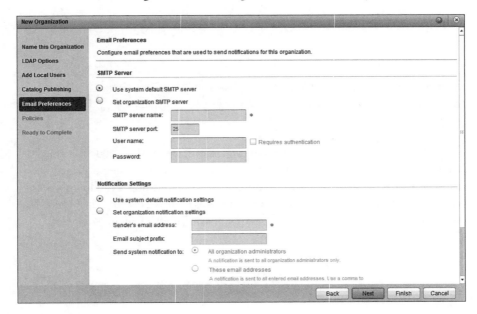

Figure 7-7 Email Configuration Settings

7. Finally, the last page of configuring an organization—and arguably the most important—Policies and Leases. The first section is the lease definition for the organization, as shown in Figure 7-8.

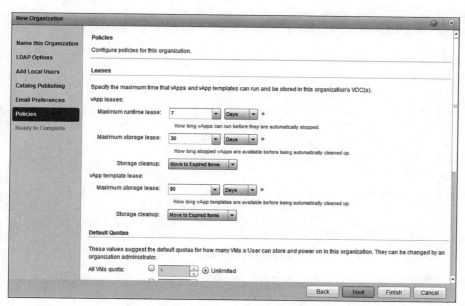

Figure 7-8 Lease Configurations

The second section of policies defines the default quotas for new users, the limits on concurrent tasks, and a password policy if local users are used. Figure 7-9 shows the default quotas, limits, and password policies.

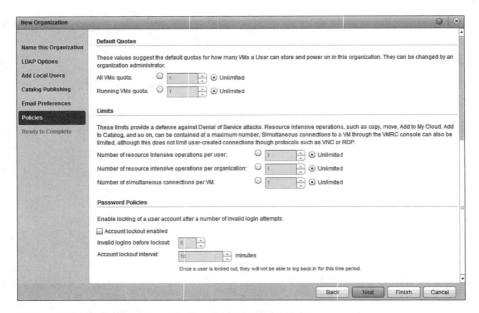

Figure 7-9   Default Quotas, Limits, and Password Policies

NOTE   The default quota applies to new user accounts on their first logins when using LDAP or SAML authentication. Changing this value after users have logged in affects only new users; all existing accounts remain as configured.

    8. Verify the settings on the final screen, and click **Finish** to create the organization.

Modifying an Organization

Now that you have created an organization, it is time to learn how to modify an organization. Although you might never need to modify an organization, something will likely need to be changed at a later date. The modification can be something as simple as changing the storage lease duration or something as complex as changing the LDAP server authentication settings to use Kerberos authentication instead of simple authentication.

NOTE   Keep in mind, though, that you can't change the organization name after creation.

The modification of an organization is much like the creation of the organization, with the difference being that instead of having a nice wizard to modify settings, you access the options through menus.

Activity 7-2: Modifying an Organization

1. Log in to the organization that needs modification, either as a system administrator or an organization administrator logged in to the organization. Select the **Administration** tab, as shown in Figure 7-10.

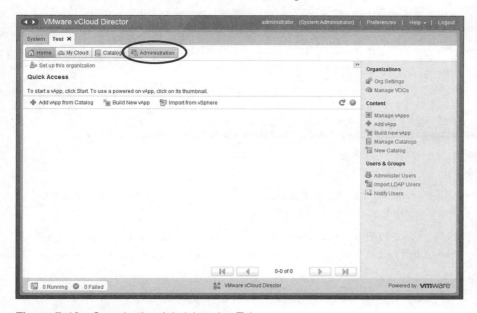

Figure 7-10   Organization Administration Tab

2. From this page, you can access menus based on the change required. To add users, select the **Users** option in the left selection box, as shown in Figure 7-11.

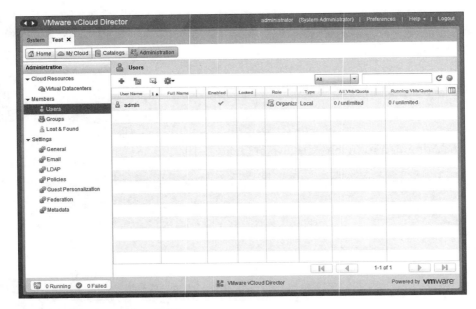

Figure 7-11   Local User Settings

Add a local user by selecting the green + sign and filling in the user information required, as shown in Figure 7-12.

To add an LDAP user, you select the icon to the right of the green + sign, as shown in Figure 7-13; then search for and select the user name as shown in Figure 7-14.

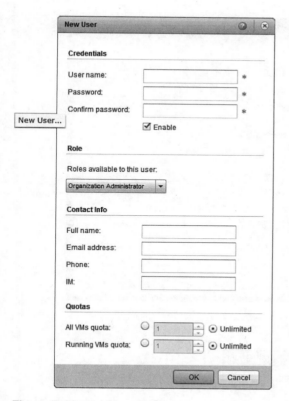

Figure 7-12   Add Local Users

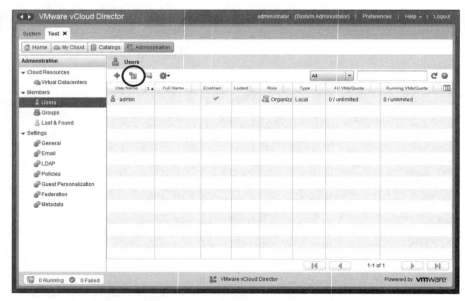

Figure 7-13 Add LDAP Users

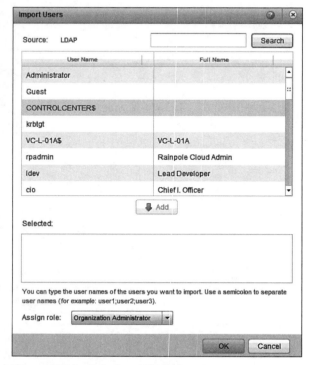

Figure 7-14 Select an LDAP User

For modification of an SAML user, please refer to the section "Configure an Organization for Federation," later in this chapter.

3. To modify a group that has access to vCloud, select the **Groups** option in the left menu, as shown in Figure 7-15.

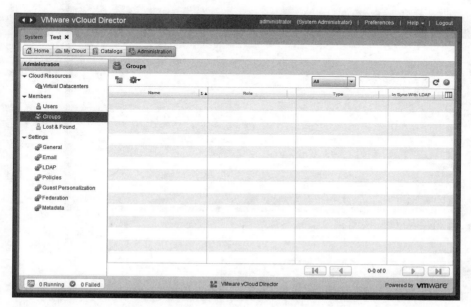

Figure 7-15   Select Groups

NOTE   Only LDAP groups can be searched for. SAML groups require manual entry. vCloud Director has no local group construct, which is why you do not have the ability to add or modify local groups.

To add a group to vCloud Director, click the **Import Groups** icon shown in Figure 7-16; then search for and add the groups, as shown in Figure 7-17.

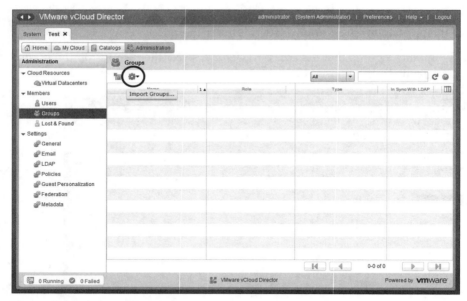

Figure 7-16   Import Groups Icon

Figure 7-17   Import Groups Dialog Box

NOTE   If a user account is granted access to vCloud Director solely on its LDAP group permission, when that group is removed from vCloud Director, the account becomes stranded and the user is no longer able to log in to vCloud Director.

4. The remaining options for modification are similar to the wizard you used to create the organization. For the organization name, use the **General** menu option, shown in Figure 7-18.

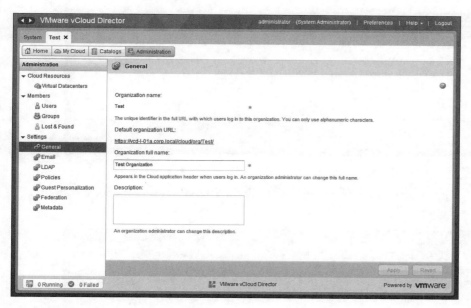

Figure 7-18   General Options

To modify the email settings, SMTP server, and notification addresses, use the **Email** settings menu shown in Figure 7-19.

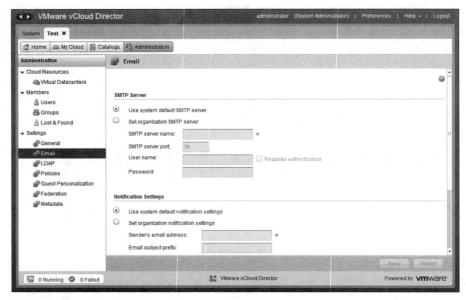

Figure 7-19 Email Settings

LDAP settings can be modified using the **LDAP** settings menu, shown in Figure 7-20.

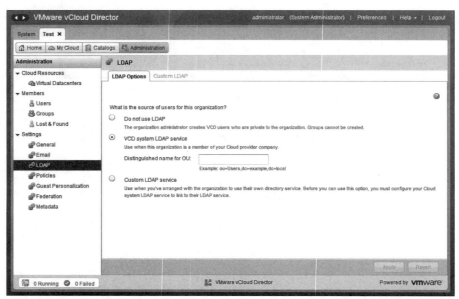

Figure 7-20 LDAP Settings

Organization policies can be modified using the **Policies** menu option, shown in Figure 7-21.

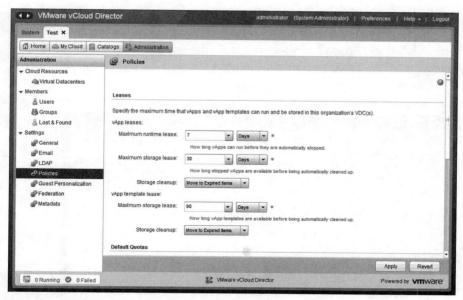

Figure 7-21 Organization Policies

5. **Guest Personalization** enables you to define the default authentication parameters for joining a Windows guest to Active Directory. These settings and options are shown in Figure 7-22.

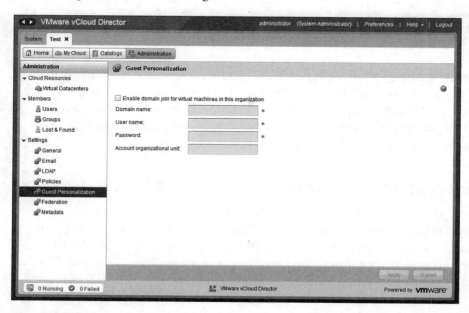

Figure 7-22 Guest Personalization

6. **Organization Metadata** is the last option we cover in this section. The Federation settings are covered in the following section. The Metadata option enables you to store metadata about the organization. Application programming interface (API) and custom portal solutions use organization metadata. Figure 7-23 shows the options for configuring the metadata.

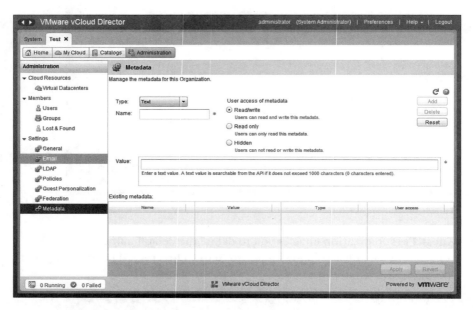

Figure 7-23 Organization Metadata

Even though many of the settings you can modify are defined during the creation of the organization, there are a few that must be done post-creation. These include adding LDAP users and groups to the organization, defining the service account used for joining a machine to an Active Directory domain, configuring federation settings, and setting metadata values.

Configuring an Organization for Federation

vCloud Director 5.1 allows for federation of logins to an organization, meaning vCloud can use an authentication service other than local users or LDAP. Using federation requires certain items from your federation or identity provider (IDP). When using federation for vCloud Director, the service provider is vCloud Director because it is the one that is providing a service to the end user. The IDP is the application or service that authenticates the users (for example, VMware's Horizon or vCenter Single Sign-On [SSO]).

When configuring the response from the IDP, the following sections must be returned in the secure portion of the identity response:

- UserName
- EmailAddress
- FullName
- Groups

The last item is not required for SAML or federation to work, but it simplifies the administration from vCloud Director. With vCloud Director, there is no way to search an IDP for valid usernames like there is with LDAP. As a result, adding users by name can be a long process; groups are easier to add and manage.

Activity 7-3: Configuring Federation in vCloud Director

1. After you're logged in as an organization administrator or system administrator, go to the organization's Administration page. Click **Federation**, and then enable the **Use SAML Identity Provider** option, as shown in Figure 7-24.

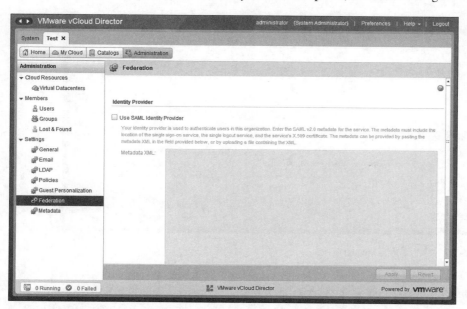

Figure 7-24   Use SAML Identity Provider

2. The Extensible Markup Language (XML) metadata file you got from your SAML/SSO provider should be downloaded to the machine from which these actions are running. When using VMware's Horizon Product, the metadata can be found here:

https://<hostname>/SAAS/API/1.0/GET/metadata/idp.xml

Other products might have a different location for the XML metadata, so refer to their documentation for its location.

NOTE Due to the use of special characters and copy/paste issues, it is not recommended to paste the XML metadata directly into the field. Instead, use the browse/upload function to upload the XML file, as shown in Figure 7-25.

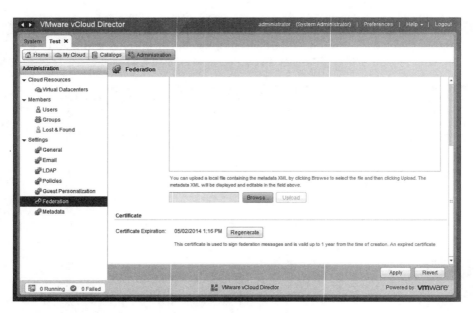

Figure 7-25 XML Metadata Upload

3. You need to close the Organization tab if you are logged in as the system administrator or log out and in again if you're logged in to the organization directly. After you have logged back in to the organization, navigate to the Administration tab, select **Users**, and click the icon next to the green + sign to import users. A new window appears where you can choose SAML as the source, as shown in Figure 7-26. Type in the names of the users who will be granted access to the organization.

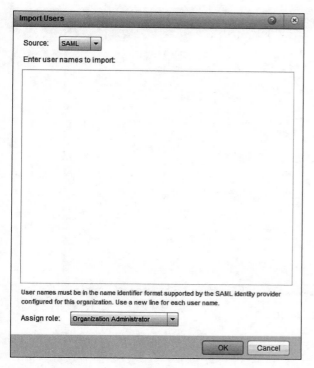

Figure 7-26 Import an SAML User

Now that vCloud Director is set up to utilize a SAML provider for authentication, you must configure the SAML provider to trust and accept requests from vCloud Director.

Export XML Metadata from vCloud Director to Identity Provider

First, you need to export an XML metadata file much like what was downloaded and imported from the SAML provider. The importing of the vCloud Director XML metadata enables the SAML provider to trust and validate requests coming from the vCloud Director organization. This file and related certificates are controlled on the Federation page where we imported the SAML XML file. At the bottom of the page, click the **Regenerate** button to create a new certificate with a validity of one year, as shown in Figure 7-27.

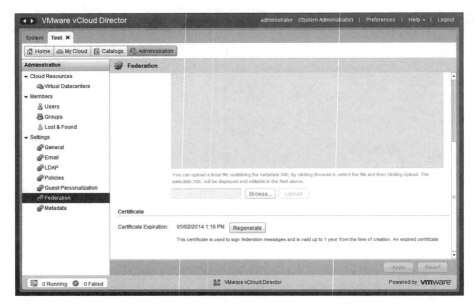

Figure 7-27   Federation Certification Generation

NOTE   Regenerating the certificate invalidates the old certificate, causing an already established relationship to break until the IDP starts to use the newly generated certificate.

After the certificate is generated, you can download it via this web link:

https://<domain>.<tld>/cloud/org/<OrganizationName>/saml/metadata/alias/vcd

Save this file as an XML file and provide the file to your SAML IDP for configuration on their end.

The configuration of the SAML provider is beyond the scope of this book. This section has given you the items required for most SAML or IDP solutions. For additional information, please refer to the SAML or IDP provider's instructions.

Summary

In this chapter, we covered

- The creation of a vCloud organization and the pitfalls that can happen during the initial configuration.

- The management of your organizations, including quotas and limits, what those mean, and how they affect your users. We also covered lease settings and when those leases start and stop.

- Finally, we covered federated logins, the requirements for federation, and the limitations for federation when used in vCloud Director.

Exam Preparation Tasks

Review All the Key Topics

Review the most important topics in the chapter, noted with the Key Topic icon in the outer margin of the page. Table 7-2 lists a reference to these key topics and the page numbers on which each is found.

Table 7-2   Key Topics

Key Topic Element	Description	Page
Bulleted list	Organization parameters	199
Activity 7-1	Creating an Organization	201
Note	Organization name changes after creation	208
Activity 7-2	Modifying an Organization	209
Bulleted list	Identity provider requirements	219
Activity 7-3	Configuring Federation in vCloud Director	219
Section	Export XML Metadata from vCloud Director to Identity Provider	221

Definitions of Key Terms

Define the following key terms from this chapter, and check your answers in the glossary:

organization, federation, SMTP server, quota, runtime lease, storage lease, SAML, IDP, metadata, intensive tasks

Review Questions

The answers to these review questions are in Appendix A.

1. vCloud Director organizations are used to define what?

   a. Groupings of users to access vCloud Director

   b. Access to compute resources

   c. Access to network resources

   d. Access to catalogs

2. When defining an organization, the name of the organization becomes what?

   a. The URL for accessing the organization

   b. A description of the organization

   c. The domain name of the organization

   d. A way to log in to the organization

3. Organization LDAP settings can be configured from how many different LDAP sources?

   a. 1

   b. 2

   c. 4

   d. 8

4. When publishing a catalog, how many organizations can you limit the publishing of the catalog to?

   a. 1

   b. 2

   c. Unlimited—cannot be defined

   d. 4

5. Which two events will cause the storage lease time to begin counting down? (Choose two.)

   a. vApp created

   b. vApp powered off

   c. vApp powered on

   d. vApp owner changes

6. Federated authentication requires which three items to be returned from the IDP? (Choose three.)

   a. User location

   b. Username

   c. Full name of the user

   d. User group

   e. User account status

7. When removing an LDAP group, what happens to the user objects that were granted access through that group?

   a. The access remains unchanged.

   b. The user is no longer able to log in.

   c. The user's account is flagged as disabled.

   d. The user's VMs are powered off and deleted.

This chapter covers the following subjects:

- **What Is a vCloud Resource?**—This section explains vCloud resources, what they are, and how to define them in vCloud Director.

- **Create and Administer Provider vDCs**—This section explains Provider vDCs, their creation, and their administration.

- **Create and Administer Organization vDCs**—This section covers the creation of organization vDCs and their administration.

- **Catalog Management**—In this section, you learn about catalog management, including the population of the vApp Templates and media items.

This chapter covers a portion of the VCP5-Cloud Exam Objective 13.1, VCP5-Cloud Exam Objective 13.2, VCP5-Cloud Exam Objective 14.1, VCP5-Cloud Exam 14.2, VCP-IaaS Exam Objective 6.1, VCP-IaaS Exam Objective 6.2, VCP-IaaS Exam Objective 7.1 and VCP-IaaS Exam Title Objective 7.2.

CHAPTER 8

Allocate and Manage vCloud Resources

Good news, with the introduction of vCloud Director you now have the ability to control the exact amount of resources your end users can consume, while still allowing for multitenancy. This new capability to manage the allocation and consumption of user resources will enable you to accurately assign and monitor resources in the cloud. However, this ability does not come without a price, and the management overhead introduced by vCloud Director must be accounted for. In this chapter, we cover not only how to configure and use these new allocation models, but also their proper usage. Finally, we explore the relationship between allocation models and vCenter Server configuration changes.

"Do I Know This Already?" Quiz

The "Do I Know This Already?" quiz enables you to assess whether you should read this entire chapter or simply jump to the "Exam Preparation Tasks" section for review. If you are in doubt, read the entire chapter. Table 8-1 outlines the major headings in this chapter and the corresponding "Do I Know This Already?" quiz questions. You can find the answers in Appendix A, "Answers to the 'Do I Know This Already?' Quizzes and Review Questions."

Table 8-1 "Do I Know This Already?" Foundation Topics Section-to-Question Mapping

Foundations Topics Section	Questions Covered in This Section
What Is a vCloud Resource?	9
Create and Administer Provider vDCs	1–2
Create and Administer Organization vDCs	3, 4, 6, 7
Catalog Management	5, 8

1. It is possible for more than one resource pool or cluster to be used by a single provider vDC.

    a. True

    b. False

2. When adding storage to vCloud Director, datastores are directly added to the provider vDC.

    a. True

    b. False

3. Where is the limit on CPU resources placed in an Allocation Pool organization vDC?

    a. On individual virtual machines

    b. On the provider vDC

    c. On the organization vDC

    d. On the vCenter Server Cluster

4. When defining a Pay-as-You-Go organization vDC, which three options are defined? (Choose three.)

    a. CPU limit per virtual machine

    b. Memory limit per virtual machine

    c. vCPU count per virtual machine

    d. Maximum number of virtual machines that can be deployed

    e. Maximum RAM allocated to the organization vDC

5. When sharing an item from the catalog, which items are allowed to be shared?

    1. ISO images

    2. vApp templates

    3. Floppy images

    4. vApps

6. A reservation organization vDC allows for the configuration of which two options? (Choose two.)

    a. CPU limit

    b. Memory per VM limit

    c. CPU reservation

    d. Memory limit

7. How many organizations can share an organization vDC?

    a. 1

    b. 2

    c. 3

    d. Unlimited

8. vCloud Director shares a published catalog to how many organizations?

    a. 0

    b. 1

    c. User definable

    d. All organizations

9. vCloud Director provisions resources from which hypervisor?

    a. VMware vSphere

    b. Microsoft Windows Hyper-V

    c. Citrix XEN Server

Foundation Topics

What Is a vCloud Resource?

VMware defines cloud resources in two sections, compute and network resources. vCenter Server clusters and vSphere hosts provide compute resources, while vCloud Networking and Security (in conjunction with vCenter Server) provides the network resources. We covered network resource configuration and allocation in Chapter 6, "Configure and Administer vCloud Networking."

vCloud Director enables compute resources to be provisioned using a provider virtual datacenter (vDC), assigned to organizations through organization vDCs, and finally consumed by users through containers called vApps.

In this chapter, we discuss compute resources and how vCloud Director presents those resources to you, the cloud administrator. Then, we explain how to define the consumption model for those resources, and ultimately how the end user consumes the resources provided.

Create and Administer Provider vDCs

vCloud Director's first abstraction of resources is the provider virtual datacenter, commonly referred to as a provider vDC. A provider vDC takes the compute and memory resources from a vCenter Server resource pool and combines them with one or more available datastores to create a group of resources available within the cloud. These resources are then provisioned to one or more organization virtual datacenters (org vDCs). We cover org vDCs in the next section.

A provider vDC is a combination of one or more resource pools or clusters defined by vCenter Server. If multiple resource pools are provisioned to a single provider vDC, that provider vDC is considered an elastic provider vDC.

What Is an Elastic Provider vDC?

When VMware released vCloud Director 1.5, it incorporated the capability to include more than one resource pool per provider vDC for a Pay-as-You-Go allocation model. With the release of 5.1, VMware expanded this capability to include the Allocation Pool allocation model. When configured with multiple resource pools, these elastic provider vDCs provide the flexibility for cloud resources to be scaled as needed.

NOTE   A cluster in vCenter Server is considered the root resource pool. It is a VMware recommended practice to place provider vDCs at the root level (that is, the cluster) during initial configuration.

Several things must be in place and working for an elastic provider vDC to function properly. First, the resource pools must exist in the same vCenter Server and the same vCenter Server Datacenter. Second, the network pool that is backing the workloads must be capable of being extended to all resource pools used by the provider vDC. This extension is necessary to avoid issues with network communication between virtual machines (VMs). Finally, the storage between the resource pools should be shared. If the storage is not shared, deployment times are greatly extended. This is due to the fact that vCloud Director must export the VM using the Export Open Virtualization Format (OVF) process and then reimport the VM to the other resource pool's storage.

NOTE   Elastic provider vDCs are available only when using the Allocation Pool model or the Pay-as-You-Go model. A provider vDC configured using the Reservation Pool model cannot be used as an elastic provider vDC.

Activity 8-1: Creating a Provider vDC

1. Log in to vCloud Director, and click the **Manage & Monitor** tab.

2. Click the **Provider VDCs** option in the left pane, as shown in Figure 8-1.

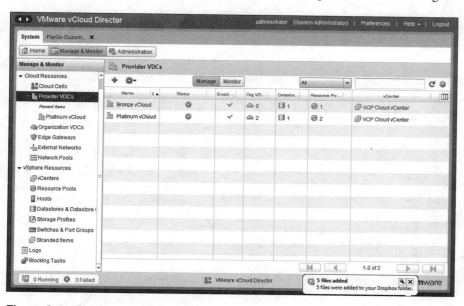

Figure 8-1   Provider vDC Selection

3. Click the green **+** or the blue gear symbol, and select **New Provider VDC**, shown in Figure 8-2.

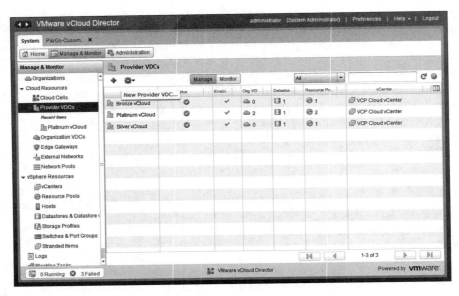

Figure 8-2 Add New Provider vDC

4. Type in a name and description.

> **NOTE** A good use of the Description field is to indicate what the resource pool provides, as shown in Figure 8-3.

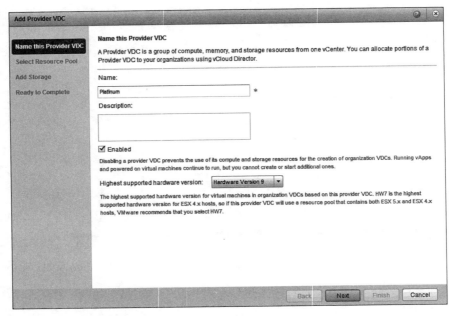

Figure 8-3 Provider vDC Naming

5. Select the highest VM Hardware version that your vSphere installation supports, as shown in Figure 8-4.

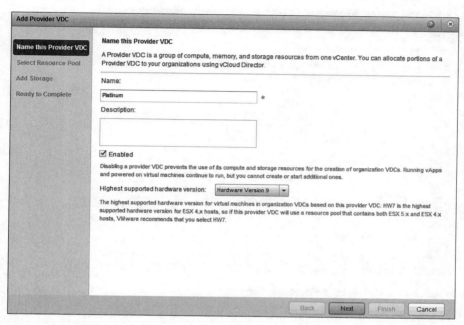

Figure 8-4   VM Hardware Selection

> **NOTE**   Here is a quick reference of VM Hardware versions and the corresponding vSphere version:
>
> - **vSphere 4**—Hardware Version 7
> - **vSphere 5**—Hardware Version 8
> - **vSphere 5.1**—Hardware Version 9

6. Next, as shown in Figure 8-5, select the vCenter Server and the resource pool that this provider vDC will consume.

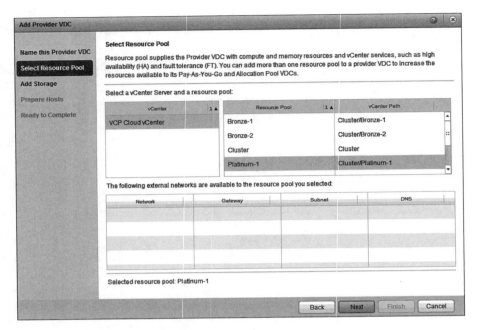

Figure 8-5   vCenter and Resource Pool Selection

NOTE   vCloud Director assumes that there will be no other users of the resource pool allocated to the provider vDC. If other workloads are using this resource pool, they can be starved of resources because vCloud Director will consume and allocate all resources in the pool to the provider vDC.

7. Select the appropriate storage profile for this provider vDC. Figure 8-6 shows the Any profile selected.

8. Click **Finish**.

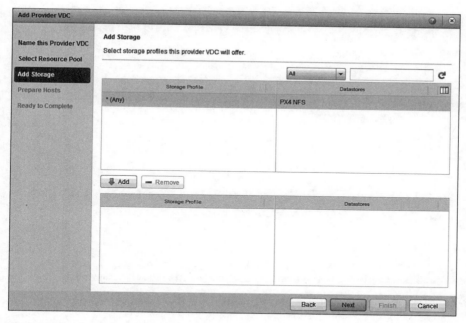

Figure 8-6   Storage Profile Selection

Prepare a Provider vDC

After you have created your first provider vDC, you must prepare the hosts that will provide the physical resources to that provider vDC. Until the hosts are prepared by vCloud Director, they cannot be used to host a vCloud workload.

Activity 8-2: Preparing a Host

1. Click the **Manage & Monitor** tab, and then select the **Provider VDCs** option in the left pane.

2. Find the provider vDC with hosts that need prepared; then right-click it and select **Open**, as shown in Figure 8-7.

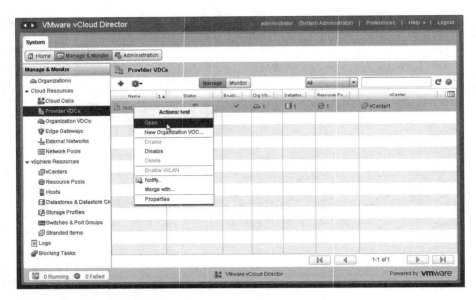

Figure 8-7   Provider vDC Selection

3. As shown in Figure 8-8, select the **Hosts** tab.

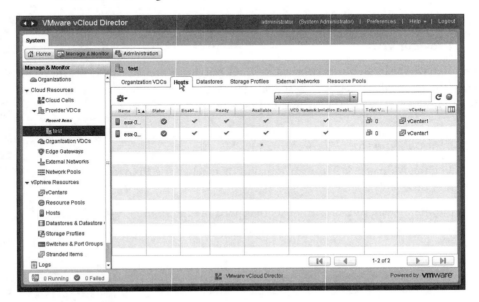

Figure 8-8   Host Selection

4. Select the hosts to prepare; then right-click and select **Prepare Host**, as shown in Figure 8-9.

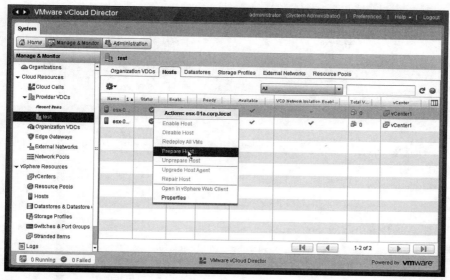

Figure 8-9 Prepare Host Selection

5. Enter a username and password of a user who has administrator privileges on the vSphere host. Figure 8-10 shows an example using root, which is the most common user used.

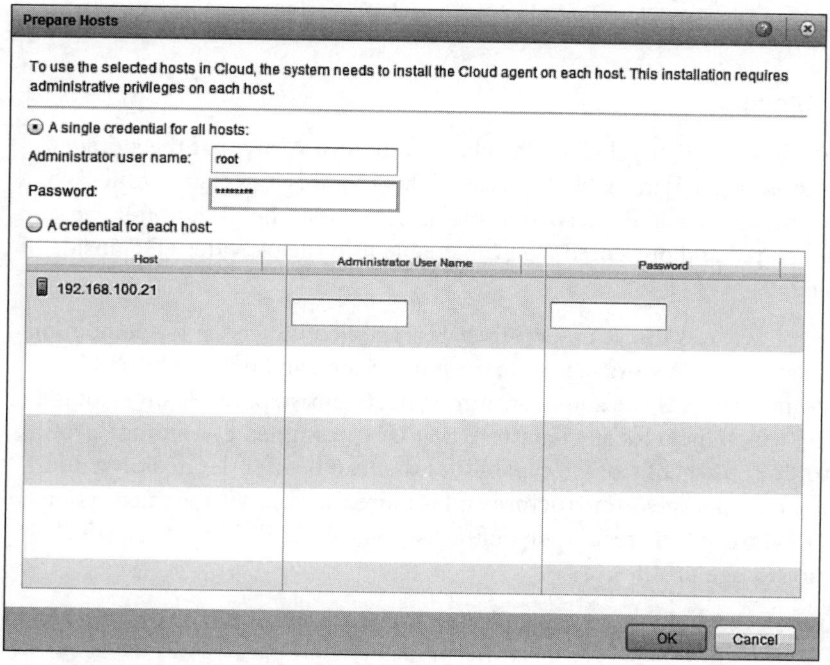

Figure 8-10 Username Input

6. Verify that the hosts have been prepared properly. The host in Figure 8-11 has been successfully provisioned.

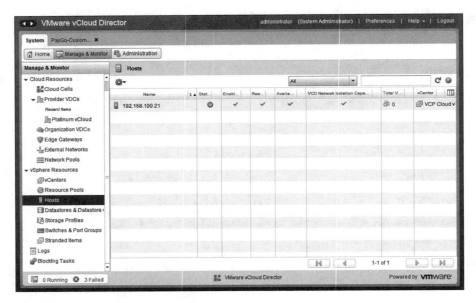

Figure 8-11   Host Successfully Provisioned

Enable Provider Storage

After the hosts have been enabled for the cloud, you must verify that the storage presented to those hosts is available for usage. This requires a storage profile to be created in vCenter Server and attached to the datastores on the hosts. After the storage profile is created and presented, you can enable it in the provider vDC inside of vCloud Director.

vCloud Director 5.1 uses the vCenter Server Storage Profile service for combining and utilizing datastores. A storage profile must be created and defined by a vCenter Server administrator. If the administrator neglects this step, the *(Any) storage profile is used, which includes any datastore that is not assigned to a storage profile. A storage profile consists of storage capabilities that can be user defined or vendor defined. If you have a large infrastructure and require the ability to segment your storage, you might need to create user-defined storage capabilities and selectively assign them to storage profiles.

We cover how to check the storage profile and how to attach it to a provider vDC in Activity 8-3.

Activity 8-3: Assigning a Storage Profile to a Datastore

1. Log in to the vCenter Server to which vCloud Director is attached.

2. Select **Management > VM Storage Profiles > [Datacenter Name]**.

3. Click **Create New VM Storage Profile**.

4. Select a name that is unique to this vCenter Server or Cluster to reduce confusion later, similar to the profile being created in Figure 8-12.

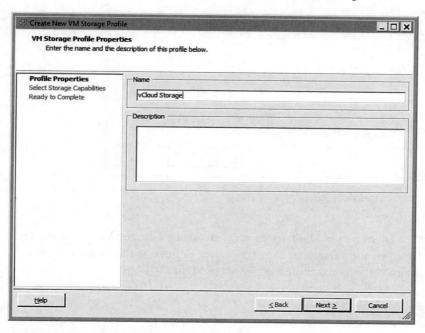

Figure 8-12 Storage Profile Creation in vCenter

5. Select the vendor- or user-defined storage capabilities for this profile. Figure 8-13 shows an NFS profile being selected.

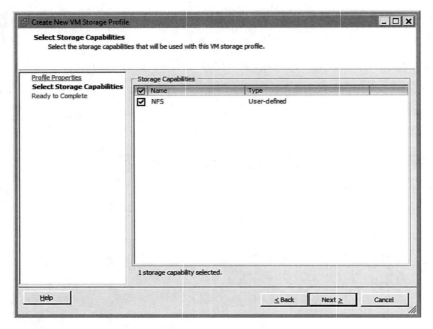

Figure 8-13 Storage Capabilities in vCenter

6. Select the **Inventory > Datastores** and **Datastore Cluster View**. Now select each datastore and verify that the proper user-defined storage capability has been assigned to the datastores, as shown in Figure 8-14.

Figure 8-14 Storage Profile Assignment

vCloud Director should now display the available storage profiles in the system administrator view. If the profiles are not visible, a problem has occurred. Troubleshooting storage profiles is covered in the next section.

Decommission a Provider vDC

In the lifecycle of a vCloud deployment, there might come a time when you need to decommission a provider vDC, or possibly a storage profile. This task is not as simple as just powering on the new provider vDC and powering down the old infrastructure. The process can vary based on the hardware and the use of the hardware that is being replaced. For the purpose of the VCP-Cloud and VCP-IaaS exams, we cover only the disabling and deleting of a provider vDC and the addition of a storage profile to a provider vDC.

Disabling a provider vDC does not power off the existing vApps, stop access to the associated network, or delete files from the storage profile. Disabling the provider vDC stops vCloud Director from adding new workloads to the provider vDC and prevents the powering on of any vApp that might be powered down. You can still migrate vApps or workloads off of the provider vDC.

Activity 8-4: Disabling a Provider vDC

1. Open the vCloud Director user interface (UI), as shown in Figure 8-15.

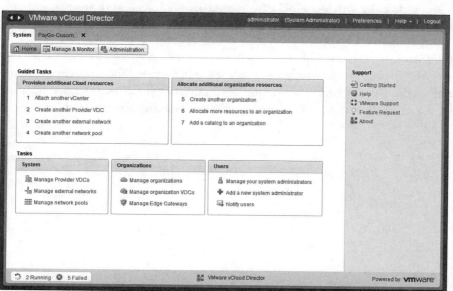

Figure 8-15 vCloud Director UI

2. Select the **Manage & Monitor** tab, and then select the Provider vDCs option in the left pane, as shown in Figure 8-16.

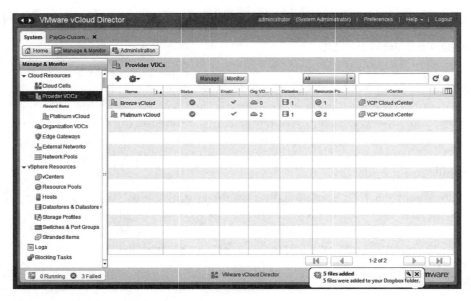

Figure 8-16   Manage & Monitor Tab

3. Right-click the provider vDC that is to be disabled, such as the one shown in Figure 8-17, and then select **Disable**.

After the provider vDC is disabled, you must remove the resources allocated to the provider vDC before it can be removed from vCloud Director. These resources can include networks, vShield Edge devices, storage profiles, org vDCs, catalogs, vApps, and media. We cover the removal of these items in their respective chapters and sections.

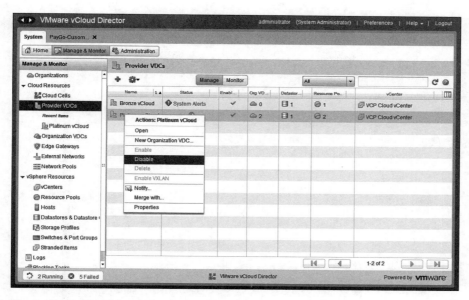

Figure 8-17   Disabling a Provider vDC

Activity 8-5: Deleting a Provider vDC

   1. Open the vCloud Director UI, as shown in Figure 8-18.

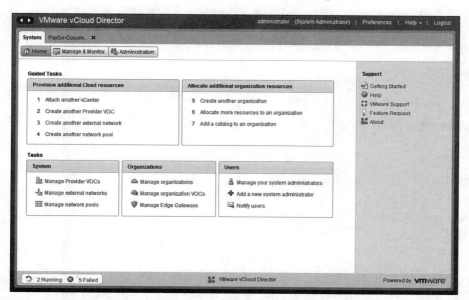

Figure 8-18   vCloud Director Main Page

2. Select the **Manage & Monitor** tab, and then select the provider vDCs option in the left pane, as shown in Figure 8-19.

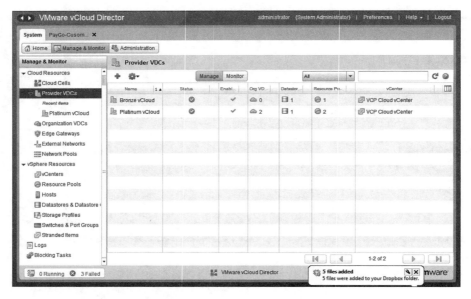

Figure 8-19 Manage & Monitor Tab

3. Right-click the provider vDC that is to be deleted, as shown in Figure 8-20.

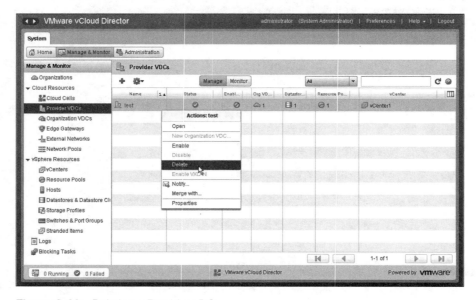

Figure 8-20 Deleting a Provider vDC

4. Select **Delete**.

If the provider vDC still has a resource assigned to it, you will receive an error similar to that shown in Figure 8-21.

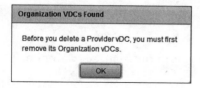

Figure 8-21 Resource Deletion Error

If this happens, find the resource that the error mentions, remove it from the provider vDC, and then attempt the delete operation again. For example, Figure 8-21 shows an error that is a leftover org vDC that must be removed before the provider vDC can be deleted.

After all items are removed, the delete process removes the binding of vCloud Director to the resource pool in vCenter Server. The operation does not remove the vCloud Agents from the hosts—this must be done separately. To do so, navigate to the host tab and select **Disable Host** and **Unprepare Host**, as shown in Figure 8-22.

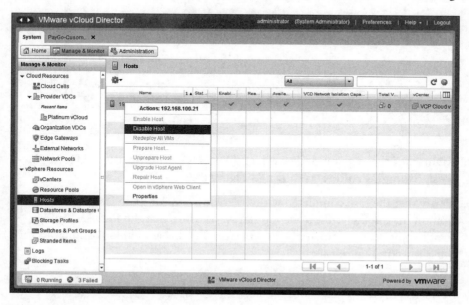

Figure 8-22 Disable and Unprepare a Host

Storage Profile in vCenter

It is common for vCenter Server to take a few minutes to sync newly created and defined storage profiles. To speed up this process, you can force a re-sync operation, which is performed from the system administrator view.

Activity 8-6: Syncing vCenter Storage Profiles

1. Open the **vCenter** Servers view from the left pane of the Manage & Monitor tab, as shown in Figure 8-23.

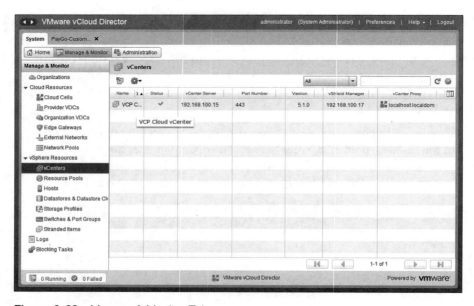

Figure 8-23   Manage & Monitor Tab

2. Right-click the vCenter Server where the storage profile exists, and select **Refresh Storage Profiles**, as shown in Figure 8-24.

3. Verify that the task completed without error by clicking the **Logs** menu option on the left pane. View the log status to ensure that the Refresh Storage Profile operation completed without error. The log should look similar to the one shown in Figure 8-25.

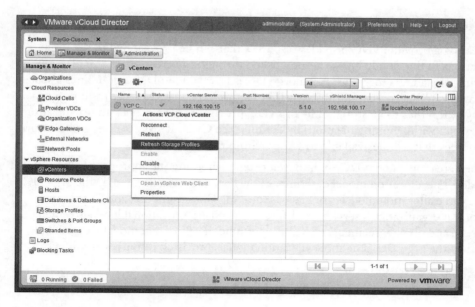

Figure 8-24   Refresh Storage Profiles

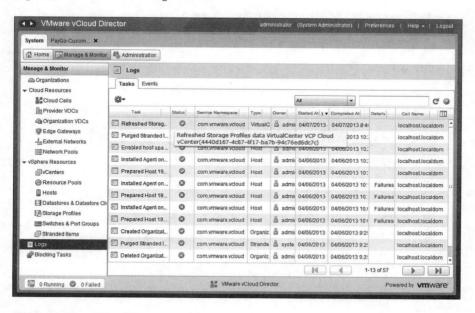

Figure 8-25   vCloud Director Event Log

Create and Administer Organization vDCs

Creating a provider vDC provides resources that can be provisioned to the organizations in the cloud. This is accomplished through the creation of organization virtual datacenters (org vDCs). An org vDC is how vCloud Director defines a space for vApps to be stored and run, as well as a space for CD-ROM (.iso) and floppy image (.flp) files to be stored. The org vDC provisions resources to an organization (or group within an organization) by defining the CPU, RAM, storage, and network resources that will be available to vApps within the org vDC.

When creating an org vDC, an important step is choosing the appropriate allocation model. The allocation model determines how resources are allocated by the org vDC. The three allocation models are Pay-as-You-Go, Allocation Pool, and Reservation Pool. An organization's service-level agreement (SLA), operational level agreement (OLA), and other agreements typically determine the allocation model that will be used by the org vDC. The three allocation models provision resources as follows:

- Pay-as-You-Go
    - Resources are not allocated in advance.
    - Resources are reserved as vApps are powered on.
    - A percentage of resources can be reserved.
    - vCPU speed rating is adjustable.

- Allocation Pool
    - A percentage of resources is allocated in advance.
    - This percentage of resources is reserved.
    - Cloud administrators control the amount of over commit.
    - Resources are sharable between org vDCs.

- Reservation Pool
    - All resources are allocated and reserved in advance.
    - Users are able to adjust individual VM priorities and resources.
    - No sharing of resources with other org vDCs.

Pay-As-You-Go

The Pay-As-You-Go (PAYG) allocation model most closely resembles the Amazon EC2 model, in which the compute resources are defined on a per-VM basis. PAYG allows for performance guarantees on each VM as well as limits for each VM. The benefit of PAYG is that the provider vDC's resources are consumed only when a VM or vApp is powered on.

NOTE PAYG is comparable to how an electric company charges for power. When the lights are on, you are being charged; when they are off, you are charged nothing.

When a VM or a vApp is powered on, vCloud Director places the vApp into the provider vDC that is assigned to the org vDC. After the VM is placed into a resource pool, it is configured with the limits and guarantees that are defined by the org vDC.

PAYG allocation models are unique in that they allow you to place limits on a single VM and not the entire resource pool, while still allowing for a % reservation. A PAYG model is ideal for use cases where noisy neighbors are a concern. PAYG enables you, the cloud administrator, to limit the amount of resources a single VM can consume.

It should be noted that there is some risk with using a PAYG allocation model. Because there are no pre-reserved or committed resources, a VM might be unable to power on if the provider vDC is out of resources.

At some point an org vDC configured with the PAYG allocation model might need to be resized. This can be done, but it does require all vApps to be powered down and backed up before the adjustment can be made. Figure 8-26 shows the PAYG org vDC properties.

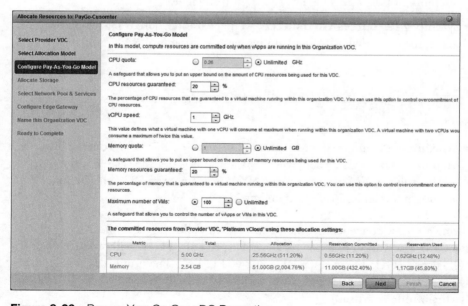

Figure 8-26 Pay-as-You-Go Org vDC Properties

During the creation of a PAYG allocation model, you will define the following:

- **CPU Quota**—This quota is the limit of CPU resources that an organization can consume at any time. This limit can be higher than the actual resources presented, which gives a cloud administrator the ability to overcommit CPU resources provided by the org vDC.

- **CPU Resources Guaranteed**—vCenter Server defines this as the reservation on the VM.

> **NOTE** This can affect the slot sizing for high availability (HA) calculations in vCenter Server.

- **vCPU Speed**—In vCenter Server, this is defined as the limit of a VM's CPU resource. This is a per-CPU value, so the number placed in this field becomes the limit on the CPU of the VM multiplied by the number of vCPUs assigned.

- **Memory Quota**—Much like the CPU quota, this is the limit of memory for an org vDC. This limit will most likely be higher than the physical memory in the backing provider vDCs. Features built in to vSphere such as transparent page sharing, compression, swapping, and ballooning make overallocating memory not only possible but also highly efficient.

- **Memory Resources Guaranteed**—The guarantee here is placed on the VM itself, meaning that a VM will always have X amount of RAM available.

> **NOTE** This might affect the slot sizing for HA calculations in vCenter.

- **Maximum Number of VMs**—It might seem that this field would apply only to powered on VMs or deployed VMs, but this is not the case. For the purpose of this value, a VM is counted as ANY VM in the org vDC. This includes catalog items and powered-off and powered-on VMs.

To bring all these concepts together, consider the following example. An org vDC with a CPU reservation of 20% and a vCPU speed of 2.5GHz will produce a limit of 5GHz with 1GHz being reserved on a 2 vCPU VM. That same VM with 12GB of assigned RAM and a 10% guarantee will have a 1.2GB reservation for RAM (plus the virtualization overhead).

The PAYG allocation method can also present a billing problem to end users in a service provider model. The billing process for PAYG varies and can be unpredictable from month to month. That being said, PAYG does provide the best method of accounting for the actual resources used by an organization because both of the other allocation models require a pre-purchased amount of resources.

Allocation Pool Model

An Allocation Pool is the second most commonly used allocation model in vCloud Director deployments. An Allocation Pool model gives you the ability to overcommit resources while still limiting the amount of resources an organization consumes.

Much like PAYG, an Allocation Pool model can be elastic. This means it can span multiple resource pools inside a single provider vDC. While providing a great deal of flexibility, this can complicate the troubleshooting of resources should a resource-related problem arise.

For example, assume you have a provider vDC with multiple resource pools, with multiple organization vDCs provisioned. A vApp could span resource pools, which could result in decent performance for VMs in one resource pool but heavily over-committed VMs in another resource pool. Because DRS does not balance VMs between resource pools, and vCloud Director's placement engine runs only on power-on, this is a very real concern and possibility.

Unlike a PAYG model, the Allocation Pool model enables you to adjust resources and their commitments without causing a need to redeploy VMs. Figure 8-27 shows the Allocation Org vDC properties page.

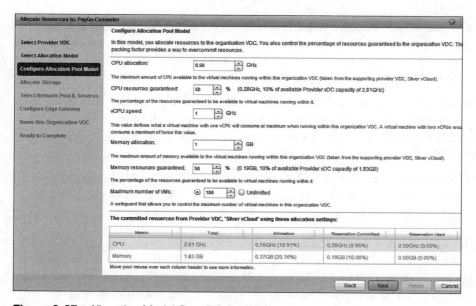

Figure 8-27   Allocation Model Org vDC Properties

During the creation of an org vDC with the Allocation Pool model, you define the following:

- **CPU Allocation**—Like the PAYG allocation model, this is the limit of resources for the entire org vDC. This limit is placed on the resource pool that was created by vCloud Director in vCenter Server. By placing a number higher than the physical resources, you are able to overcommit the CPU resources in the org vDC.

- **CPU Resources Guaranteed**—Unlike the PAYG model, the CPU resource guarantee is not defined on the individual VM. This reservation is placed on the org vDC's resource pool in vCenter Server. What an Allocation Pool model does not protect against is the possibility of a single VM compromising the rest of the machines in the org vDC. That said, this model will always guarantee resources to the org vDC even if other tenants or org vDCs in the provider vDC are consuming all their resources.

  This guarantee is calculated using the vCPU speed defined by the CPU allocation. For example, a vCPU speed of .5GHZ and a 10% reservation results in a 50MHz reservation on the org vDC resource pool.

- **vCPU Speed**—Also unlike the vCPU speed in the PAYG model, the vCPU speed for an Allocation Pool org vDC defines a value used to calculate the amount of resources to reserve. This does not place a limit on the VM or the resource pool. The vCPU speed is used only to calculate the reservation that should be placed on the org vDC resource pool.

- **Memory Allocation**—Much like the PAYG model, this defines the maximum amount of RAM that can be allocated to VMs. Even if a VM is using only 1GB of RAM, if it is configured with 100GB of RAM, the VM will consume 100GB of RAM out of the Allocation Pool.

- **Memory Resources Guaranteed**—Like the CPU resources guaranteed, this value is used to calculate how much RAM is reserved for the VM. Unlike the PAYG model, this reservation is not placed on the VM itself, but on the org vDC's resource pool in vCenter Server.

- **Maximum Number of VMs**—This field is the same as PAYG. Any VM that is defined, including catalog items, powered-off VMs, and powered-on VMs, are included in this value.

To bring all the concepts together for an Allocation Pool model org vDC, consider the following example. Assume you have an Allocation Pool org vDC defined with an allocation of 100GHz, vCPU speed of 2GHz, and a CPU guarantee of 50%. For each 2vCPU VM that is powered on in the org vDC, vCloud Director will reserve 2GHz of compute power for that VM.

The same applies to the memory allocation. Let's say the Allocation Pool org vDC is configured with 200GB of memory allocation and 50% guaranteed. A VM with a memory allocation of 50GB will receive an allocation from vCloud Director of 50GB from the 200GB available to the org vDC and set a reservation on the vCenter Server resource pool of 25GB.

The Allocation Pool model allows for more predictable billing for customers of service providers. It also enables a service provider's charge in an overage billing model, much like a 95th percentile-billing model.

A benefit of the Allocation Pool and PAYG allocation models is that they are dynamic. For each VM that is powered on, vCloud Director calculates the settings for the resource pool and reapplies the proper settings. This is different from the process used by the final allocation model, the Reservation Pool model, which we discuss next.

Reservation Pool Model

A Reservation Pool model is the easiest to define in terms of physical hardware. It is also the easiest to explain to someone new to virtualization or to the overcommitment of hardware.

A Reservation Pool allocation model is exactly what it sounds like, reserved capacity for the org vDC. This model enables a tenant to pay for 10GHz and 100GB of compute power, and that is exactly what they get—no more and no less. The tenant can then control which VMs get access to those resources through shares and limits on the individual VMs.

Although this enables easier accounting to the provider on resources (because there is no sharing of resources between tenants), it does present the possibility of wasted resources because an idle tenant's resources cannot be shared with other tenants that might need them.

An org vDC configured with the Reservation Pool model cannot be used with elastic provider vDCs. If the org vDC is assigned to a provider vDC with multiple resource pools, the org vDC will consume the first resource pool listed and will not expand or move to other resource pools listed. Figure 8-28 shows the Reservation Pool model org vDC properties.

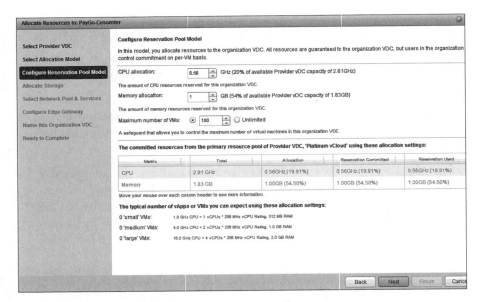

Figure 8-28   Reservation Model Org vDC Properties

When configuring a Reservation Pool org vDC, you will define the following:

- **CPU Allocation**—The allocation number that is defined here becomes the limit and the reservation of CPU resources in the vCenter Server Resource Pool.

- **Memory Allocation**—Like the CPU allocation, the allocation provided here becomes the limit and reservation for memory resources in the vCenter Server Resource Pool.

- **Maximum Number of VMs**—In the Allocation Pool model and PAYG model, this is the maximum number of VMs that can belong to the org vDC. Running VMs, catalog items, and VMs deployed but not powered on all count.

NOTE   Unlike the Allocation Pool and PAYG models, the Reservation Pool model reserves all its resources at creation, even if there are no powered-on VMs. Use caution when specifying numbers because you can reserve all resources in a vCenter Server resource pool, potentially starving other org vDCs of their resources.

For billing purposes when using vCenter Chargeback, the tenant's bill will be the same every month. With the Reservation Pool allocation model, the resources are reserved for the tenant whether they use them or not.

Select the Right Allocation Model

There is no perfect allocation model for every use case. In fact, most use cases fit well into more than one possible allocation model.

PAYG is traditionally used for transient work or VMs that have short life expectancies. In a hosting environment, the PAYG allocation model can cause variable billing. The Allocation Pool model is also commonly used in environments in which workloads come and go, but it also works well for environments in which the tenant is unsure of his true demand.

The Reservation Pool model is typically used as a premium service because there is no sharing of resources. Compute power assigned to a Reservation Pool org vDC is reserved for the tenant even if he does not use it. The Reservation Pool model can be considered the same as dedicating hardware to a tenant.

Create an Organization vDC

Now that we have discussed the allocation models in vCloud Director and their intended uses, we use the information you gathered previously to create an org vDC.

Activity 8-7: Creating an Org vDC

1. Log in to vCloud Director as a system administrator.

NOTE   When configuring the consumption of compute and storage resources, you must be logged in as a system administrator. Organization users do not have the permissions to create or alter these settings.

2. Select the organization for the new org vDC. In this example, OrgA has been selected, as shown in Figure 8-29.

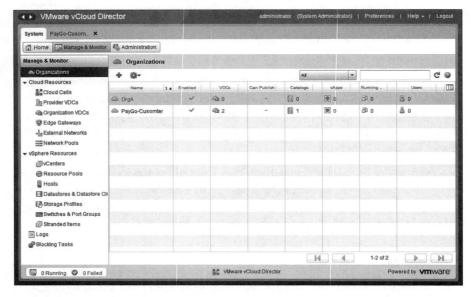

Figure 8-29 Organization Selection

3. Select the **Administration** tab for the organization, as shown in Figure 8-30.

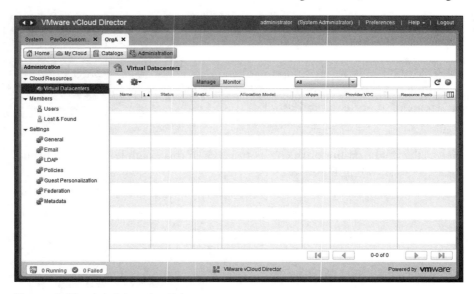

Figure 8-30 Administration Tab

4. Click the green + symbol highlighted in Figure 8-31. This starts the Add Resources Wizard.

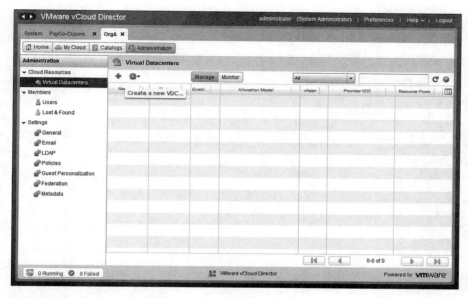

Figure 8-31   Starting the Add Resources Wizard

5. Select the provider vDC in which this org vDC will be created. Figure 8-32 shows the Platinum provider vDC being selected.

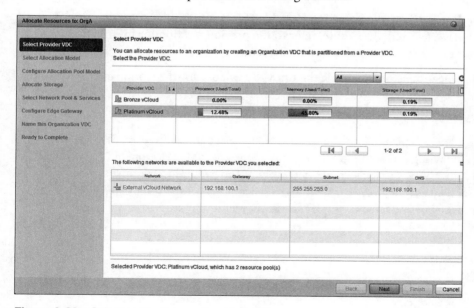

Figure 8-32   Selecting the Source Provider vDC

6. Select the allocation model you have chosen for this org vDC, as shown in Figure 8-33.

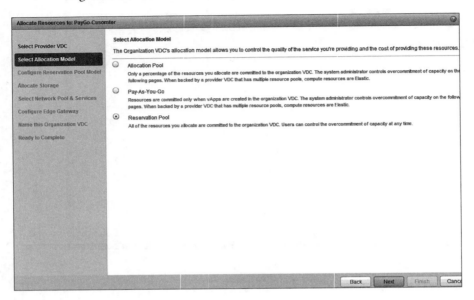

Figure 8-33   Org vDC Type Selection

7. Populate the allocation model fields as required for the allocation model you have selected. As a guide, refer to the previous section for information on each of the org vDC models and their required fields.

8. Select the storage profile the org vDC will use for the workloads.

NOTE   The Any profile in vCenter Server will select any storage available on the cluster, including local storage. If local storage is selected, vMotion and HA will not function for those VMs placed on local storage. To avoid this, simply create a storage profile and assign the proper datastores to the storage profile. Figure 8-34 shows the Any profile being selected.

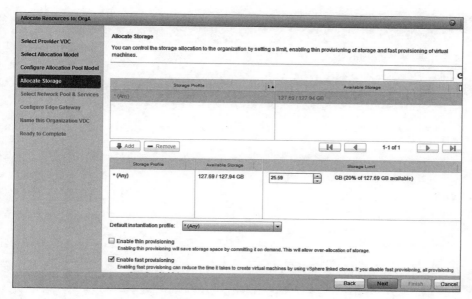

Figure 8-34   Storage Profile Selection

After you have created the compute resources for the org vDC, the next step is to configure the networking options for the org vDC. These options were covered in Chapter 7, "Configure and Administer vCloud Organizations." For configuration information on org vDCs, refer to that chapter.

After the networking options have been configured, specify a name for the org vDC. You have now completed the configuration of an org vDC. We next cover how to remove an org vDC from vCloud Director.

Delete an Organization vDC

Deleting an org vDC is similar to the deletion of a provider vDC. All contents of the org vDC must be removed before it can be deleted. Contents can include catalog items (media and vApp templates), vApps, networks, and edge gateways.

Here are the steps to check whether items still exist in an org vDC.

Activity 8-8: Preparing to Remove an Organization Virtual Datacenter

1. Log in to vCloud Director as a system administrator.

2. Select the org vDC that will be removed. The **Allocation** Org vDC has been selected in Figure 8-35.

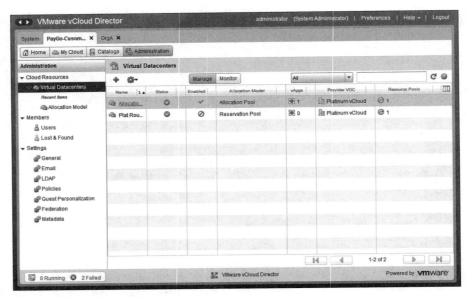

Figure 8-35   Organization vDC Removal

3. Verify that all vApps have been migrated off or deleted from the org vDC. Figure 8-36 shows an Organization vDC with 1 remaining vApp.

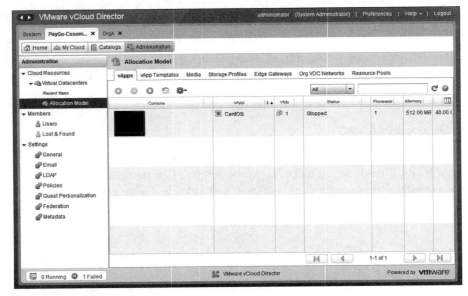

Figure 8-36   Org vDC vApps

4. Verify that all vApp templates, also referred to as Catalog Items, are removed from the org vDC. Figure 8-37 shows one remaining vApp template.

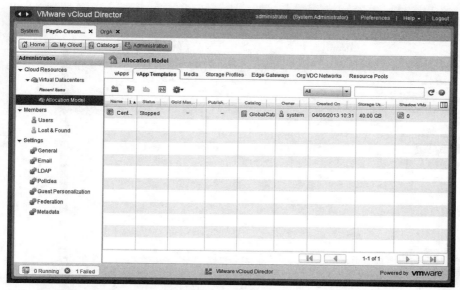

Figure 8-37 Org vDC vApp Templates

5. Verify that all media (ISO and FLP) files are removed from the org vDC.

6. Verify that the organization networks have been removed. These must be removed before removing the edge gateway that provides gateway or firewall services for the organization network. Figure 8-38 shows all org networks have been removed.

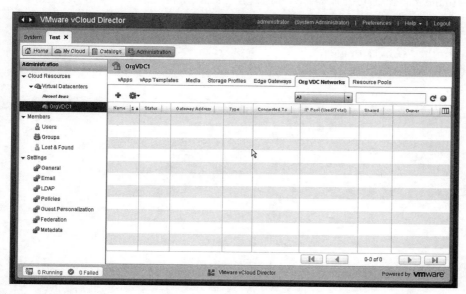

Figure 8-38 Org vDC Networks

7. Verify that all edge gateways have been removed from the org vDC, as shown in Figure 8-39.

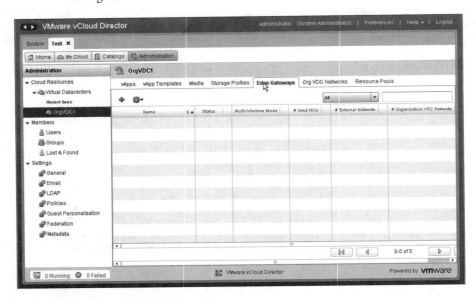

Figure 8-39   Org vDC Edge Gateways

8. Verify that all storage profiles have been removed from the organization virtual datacenter. vApps, vApp templates, and media need to be removed from the storage profile before it can be removed from the org vDC. Figure 8-40 shows that all storage profiles have been removed from the org vDC, except for the * (Any) storage profile.

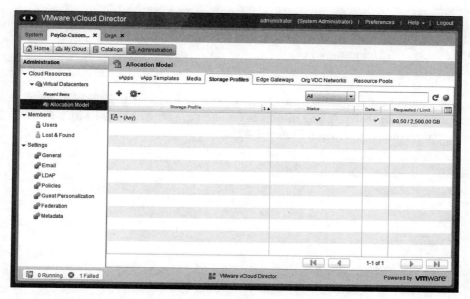

Figure 8-40   Org vDC Storage Profiles

9. Disable the org vDC, as shown in Figure 8-41.

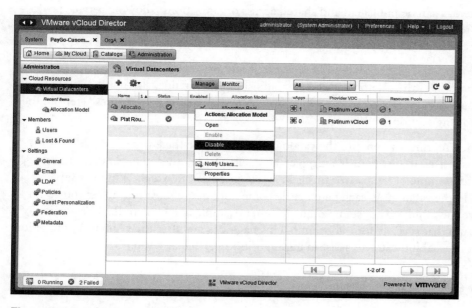

Figure 8-41   Disabling an Org vDC

> **NOTE** Disabling the org vDC will not power off vApps or delete any items from the datacenter. Disabling the org vDC will stop new items from being created and will prevent items from being powered on.

You now should be able to select the Delete option and remove the org vDC from the organization. If there are any resources remaining, you are alerted with a message similar to the one shown in Figure 8-42.

Figure 8-42 Org vDC Deletion Error

Catalog Management

Catalogs are a part of vCloud Director that enable tenants to easily create VMs. Catalogs can be published and shared across organizations, allowing service providers to provide a base template for tenants or for enterprises to publish prebuilt templates of operating systems.

Creating a catalog in vCloud Director is straightforward. The details are in the configuration of the catalog and include publishing the catalog, sharing the catalog, and populating the catalog with vApp templates and media. We cover these steps in the following sections.

When placing a vApp into the catalog, you can define the entry as a Gold Master. This is used to distinguish a vApp catalog entry from other items in the catalog. A good example of the use for this is in an environment in which Windows servers are in the catalog. As each patch cycle comes along, the most recent version could have the Gold Master stamp on it. Another example would be to flag the version of a vApp that is ready for publishing. This flag does not alter the vApp in any way; it is just a visual indicator to assist in highlighting a particular vApp.

Activity 8-9: Creating a Catalog

1. Sign in to the organization where you want to create the catalog.

2. Select the **Catalogs** tab, as shown in Figure 8-43.

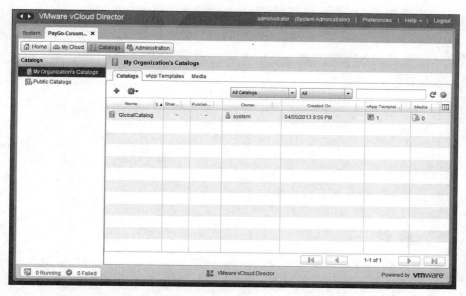

Figure 8-43   Organization Catalogs

3. Click the green **+** sign to create a new catalog, as shown in Figure 8-44.

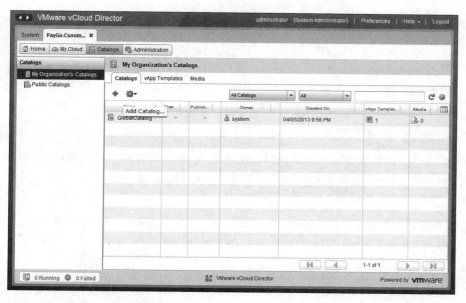

Figure 8-44   Add a Catalog Selection

4. Type in a name and description for the catalog to be created similar to the name and description shown in Figure 8-45.

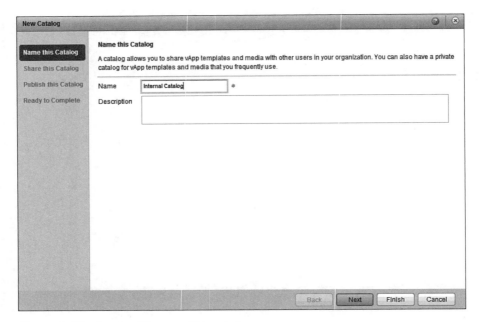

Figure 8-45   Catalog Name and Description

5. If items in this catalog need to be accessed by more than just the original cre-
ator of the catalog, they need to be shared to those users. For simplicity, an
item can be shared to all users in an organization by selecting the **Everyone in
the Organization** option, as shown in Figure 8-46. Conversely, you can select
individual users or groups that have been defined in the organization.

NOTE   You cannot share across organizations. If you require the ability for other organizations to access this catalog, it must be published. After a catalog is published, all
organizations can read it.

6. The Publishing the Catalog screen appears if the organization where the catalog is being created has permission to publish a catalog. Publishing a catalog
enables all organizations in the vCloud Director instance to access it. The
access is read only, meaning other organizations can deploy items from the
catalog but cannot add or remove items from the catalog. Figure 8-47 shows a
catalog being created that will be shared to other organizations.

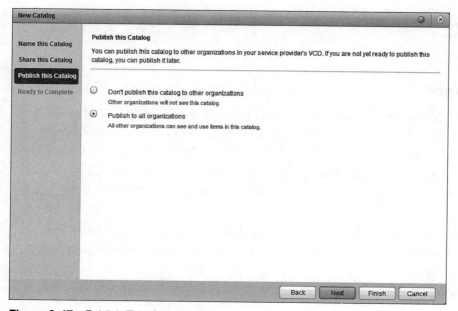

Figure 8-46   Catalog Sharing

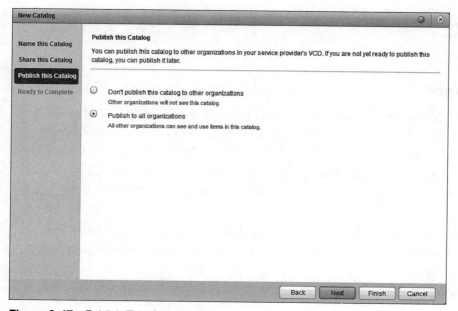

Figure 8-47   Publish This Catalog

NOTE   You can restrict an individual user from being able to access published catalogs. This is defined in the Roles section of the System Administration section. How to create the roles and use them was covered in Chapter 3, "Administer vCloud Users, Roles, and Privileges."

Now that you have created a catalog, it is time to populate (or add items to) the catalog.

Populate Catalogs

vCloud Director provides two ways to populate vApp templates to the catalog. The first is to import an existing VM from a vCenter Server that is attached to vCloud Director. The other option is to upload a VM(s) in OVF format.

Importing an existing VM from vCenter Server requires the system administrator role. Uploading an OVF can be done by a catalog author. The uploading of an OVF can be time consuming if there are bandwidth constraints, and there is no resume feature for failed uploads.

Media can also be uploaded much in the same way that vApps can be uploaded. If importing media from vCenter Server, the datastore name and the path to the media must be known. There is no browse feature or capability in vCloud Director.

NOTE   Media cannot be shared or published across organizations in vCloud Director 5.1.

Summary

In this chapter, we discussed how vCloud Director uses a provider vDC to create a pool of resources for organizations to consume. This pool can be static in size (single resource pool) or elastic (multiple resource pools).

We also discussed the models that vCloud Director allows for provider vDCs to be provisioned to organizations, as well as the removal of these resources from organizations.

Finally, we discussed the use of catalogs and the sharing of catalog entries between users of the same organization as well as sharing a catalog between organizations.

Exam Preparation Tasks

Review All Key Topics

Review the most important topics in the chapter, noted with the Key Topic icon in the outer margin of the page. Table 8-2 lists a reference to these key topics and the page numbers on which each is found.

Table 8-2   Key Topics

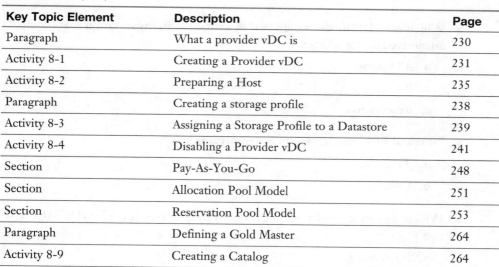

Key Topic Element	Description	Page
Paragraph	What a provider vDC is	230
Activity 8-1	Creating a Provider vDC	231
Activity 8-2	Preparing a Host	235
Paragraph	Creating a storage profile	238
Activity 8-3	Assigning a Storage Profile to a Datastore	239
Activity 8-4	Disabling a Provider vDC	241
Section	Pay-As-You-Go	248
Section	Allocation Pool Model	251
Section	Reservation Pool Model	253
Paragraph	Defining a Gold Master	264
Activity 8-9	Creating a Catalog	264

Definitions of Key Terms

Define the following key terms from this chapter, and check your answers in the glossary:

provider virtual datacenter (provider vDC), organization virtual datacenter (org vDC), catalog, storage profile, OVF, Pay-As-You-Go, Allocation Pool, Reservation Pool

Review Questions

The answers to these review questions are in Appendix A.

1. The vCPU speed in an allocation model is the limit of the vCPUs in the org vDC.

   a. True

   b. False

2. The CPU quota in a Pay-as-You-Go allocation model is elastic and can be exceeded for bursts.

   a. True

   b. False

3. Which org vDC model would best be suited for an organization that requires guaranteed performance?

   a. Allocation

   b. PAYG

   c. Reservation

4. ISOs and FLPs can be shared across organizations.

   a. True

   b. False

5. Which allocation models can be serviced by an elastic provider vDC? (Choose two.)

   a. Reservation

   b. Allocation

   c. PAYG

6. Before removing an org vDC, which two items must be removed or moved to another org vDC? (Choose two.)

   a. Catalogs

   b. vApps

   c. vApp templates

   d. Users

7. When creating a provider vDC, it is possible to assign a vCenter Server resource pool to multiple provider vDCs.

   a. True

   b. False

8. With an Allocation Pool org vDC, it is possible to exceed the memory allocation by using ballooning and other vSphere memory management technologies.

   a. True

   b. False

9. Where in an Allocation Pool model is the memory resource guarantee placed?

   a. VM

   b. Resource pool

   c. Cluster

   d. None of the above

10. Where in a PAYG model is the CPU limitation placed when VMs are deployed?

    a. VM

    b. Resource pool

    c. Cluster

    d. None of the above

11. When does a Reservation Pool org vDC reserve the capacity for the organization?

    a. At creation

    b. When a virtual machine is deployed

    c. Increased as each VM is deployed

    d. When a virtual machine is powered on

This chapter covers the following subjects:

- **Monitoring vCloud Director**—This section covers the monitoring of vCloud Director.

- **Monitoring Provider vDC Resources**—This section covers the monitoring of vCloud Provider Virtual Datacenter resources.

- **Monitoring Org vDC Resources**—This section covers the monitoring of Organization Virtual Datacenter resources.

- **Monitoring Network Resources**—This section covers the monitoring of network resources created by vShield Manager and vCloud Network Security.

- **Troubleshooting vCenter Chargeback Manager**—This section covers troubleshooting common problems with vCenter Chargeback Manager.

This chapter covers a portion of the VCP-Cloud Objective 15.1 and VCP-IaaS Objective 8.1.

CHAPTER 9

Monitor a vCloud Implementation

So far, we have discussed the installation of vCloud Director and the configuration and consumption of cloud resources. We are now going to cover how to monitor vCloud Director, where to gather logs, and how to monitor utilization of cloud resources.

"Do I Know This Already?" Quiz

The "Do I Know This Already?" quiz enables you to assess whether you should read this entire chapter or simply jump to the "Exam Preparation Tasks" section for review. If you are in doubt, read the entire chapter. Table 9-1 outlines the major headings in this chapter and the corresponding "Do I Know This Already?" quiz questions. You can find the answers in Appendix A, "Answers to the 'Do I Know This Already?' Quizzes and Review Questions."

Table 9-1 "Do I Know This Already?" Foundation Topics Section-to-Question Mapping

Foundations Topics Section	Questions Covered in This Section
Monitoring vCloud Director	1, 2
Monitoring Provider Resources	3–5
Monitoring Organization Resources	7
Monitoring Network Resources	6
Troubleshooting vCenter Chargeback Manager	8–9

1. When a user triggers the deployment of a vApp, which two vCloud Director logs record this action? (Choose two.)

   a. Provider tasks

   b. Provider events

   c. User's organization tasks

   d. User's organization events

2. In a default installation, where can you view vCloud Director tasks from 45 days ago?

   a. System event view

   b. API queries

   c. Organization event view

   d. Cell management tool

3. When configuring the Syslog server setting for vCloud through the UI, which two log actions are forwarded to the syslog server? (Choose two.)

   a. vShield tasks

   b. vCloud tasks

   c. vCloud events

   d. vShield events

4. The vShield Manager Audit Log contains which types of events?

   a. vShield Manager system events

   b. vShield Manager user actions

   c. vShield Edge device events

   d. vShield Edge deployment actions

5. When viewing the resource usage of a provider vDC, which two components are accounted for in the processor allocation metric? (Choose two.)

   a. An Allocation Model Org vDC's allocation

   b. A Reservation Model Org vDC's reservation

   c. A Pay-as-You-Go Model Org vDC's quota

   d. A Reservation Model provider vDC's reservation

6. Which two network types require an object from a network pool? (Choose two.)

   a. Direct connect organization networks

   b. Routed vApp network

   c. Non-routable vApp networks

   d. Routed organization networks

7. When viewing the CPU usage in an org vDC, what is actually reported?

    a. Actual CPU usage from vCenter

    b. The allocated CPU usage

    c. The CPU overhead

    d. The reserved CPU amount

8. What are the two main tools for troubleshooting vCenter Chargeback Manager? (Choose two.)

    a. The vCenter Chargeback Manager troubleshooting utility

    b. The vCloud Director troubleshooting utility

    c. The Windows Event Logs

    d. The vCenter Chargeback Manager–specific logs

9. The vCenterCB.log file includes information about what?

    a. The errors detected with the Chargeback application

    b. General Information on the Chargeback Manager application

    c. General Chargeback Manager application information along with authentication information

    d. General Chargeback Manager application information along with information about the load balancer

Foundation Topics

Monitoring vCloud

In this section, we focus on how to use tools provided with vCloud Director to gather troubleshooting data and monitor resource utilization. These tools include

- vCloud Director
- Syslog
- Performance charts
- vShield charts

We cover how to gather relevant data from these tools for a vCloud deployment. After the data has been gathered, we review how to analyze it to identify hot spots and problems.

View Events in vCloud

vCloud tasks and events are filtered much like the events in vCenter are, with the primary difference being how this data is handled in a multitenant environment. When viewing tasks and events for an organization, the view is filtered to show only the tasks and events relevant to that organization. vCloud Director events represent one-time events, typically a state change or similar event. vCloud Director tasks are considered long-running operations that change status as they progress. Logs for vCloud Director can be found on the System tab, as shown in Figure 9-1, and logs specific to a given organization can be viewed by logging in to that organization, as shown in Figure 9-2.

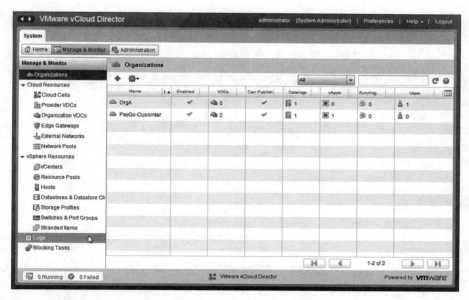

Figure 9-1 vCloud System Logs

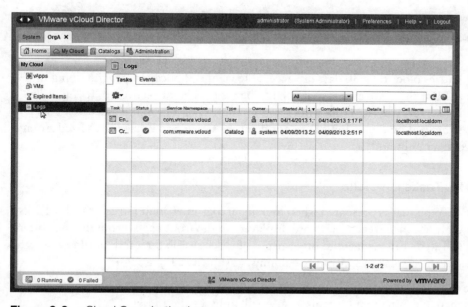

Figure 9-2 vCloud Organization Logs

Although vCloud Director maintains 90 days of tasks and events in the database by default, only the last 30 days of tasks and events are visible, again by default. These settings can be modified and are shown in Figure 9-3.

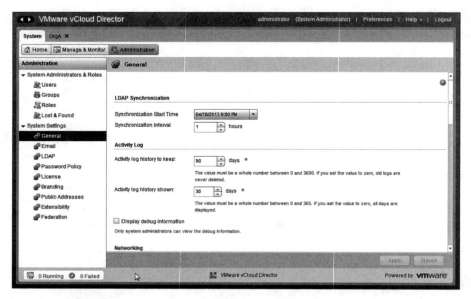

Figure 9-3   Activity Log Retention Settings

Log entries older than 30 days are accessible via the application programming interface (API) if there are events that need to be researched or recovered. If you utilize a syslog server, you can reduce the retention period of logs in the database. This reduces the load on the vCloud Director database server and keeps the utilized storage space to a minimum.

Search for Tasks in vCloud

The first tab that is presented when looking at logs in vCloud Director is the Tasks tab. Only the most recent tasks are displayed on the front page. From the user interface (UI), you can navigate to other pages of tasks, search for a task or filter a search, and sort the display by any of the columns, as shown in Figure 9-4.

The tasks logs interface filters tasks based on the organization in which it was launched, meaning that Organization A will only see their tasks.

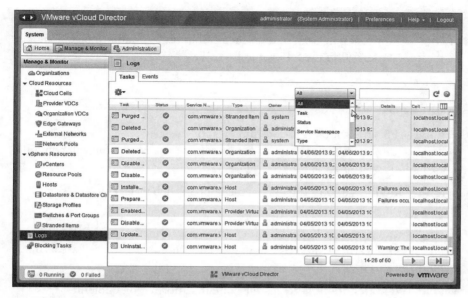

Figure 9-4   Tasks Logs Interface

The Events tab displays events in much the same way the Tasks tab displays tasks. Searching, filtering, and sorting are all available and work the same way, as shown in Figure 9-5.

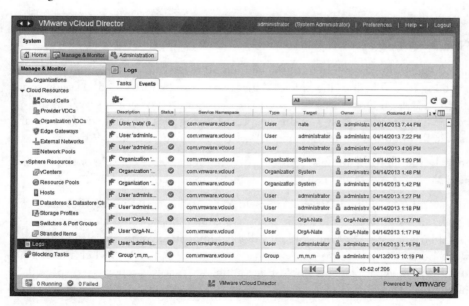

Figure 9-5   Events Logs Interface

vCloud Director Log File Locations

vCloud Director stores log information on each cell in the vCloud instance. These logs are located on the cell in the following directory:

```
/opt/vmware/vcloud-director/logs
```

The files are named

- **cell.log**—This file contains the startup logs for the specific cell server. If vCloud is not starting or appears to not be serving pages, this file will contain information regarding the related event.

- **vcloud-container-debug.log**—This file contains debug-level log messages from the cell.

- **vcloud-container-info.log**—This file contains informational log messages from the cell. Warning and error messages encountered by the cell are also included in this file.

- **vcloud-vcd-watchdog.log**—This file contains informational log messages from the watchdog process. The watchdog restarts the cell services if they fail and logs its actions to this file.

Each cell contains its own copy of the logs. When troubleshooting an event, you might need to examine each cell's log files to determine which cell encountered the problem.

vShield Manager Logs

vShield Manager is a component of the vCloud Suite package and maintains its own logs and log files. The logs in vShield Manager can also be forwarded to syslog servers, such as vCloud Director. We discuss the configuration of syslog server in the section "Syslog Settings," later in this chapter. The log files for vShield Manager are accessible through the vShield Manager WebUI, as shown in Figure 9-6.

If more detailed information is required, you can log in to the console or SSH to the vShield Manager server and issue the show tech-support command.

Unlike vCenter or vCloud Director, vShield Manager separates its log files into two categories: System Events and Audit Logs. System Events contains all events related to vShield Manager operation, vShield Edge deployments, communication faults between Edge devices, and so on. As shown in Figure 9-7, the AESNI crypto engine is up. This is an event from a vShield Edge appliance that was reported to vShield Manager.

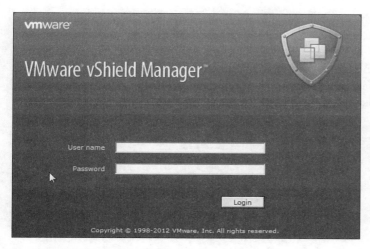

Figure 9-6   vShield Manager WebUI Logs

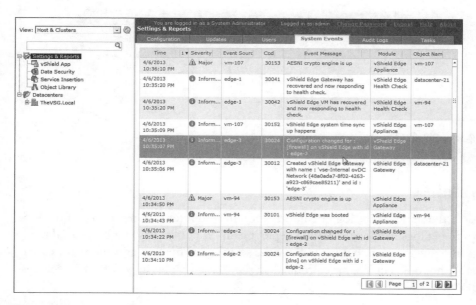

Figure 9-7   vShield System Events UI

Notice that there is no NetFlow data or network traffic data in this display. To receive logging data from vShield Edge devices, you need to configure the syslog server settings on the edge device or log in to the console of the edge appliance. NetFlow is a network technology that collects network traffic Internet Protocol (IP) information for use in debugging and analyzing networks and their performance.

The final log to view through the vShield WebUI is available on the Audit Logs tab and contains events that users have initiated. This includes the type of information you would expect a typical audit log to contain: the who, what, when, and where. Log entries include who performed the action, what was changed, when the change was made, and which resource the change affected. The example shown in Figure 9-8 shows that the admin user modified the vShield Edge firewall named vse-Linux Gateway.

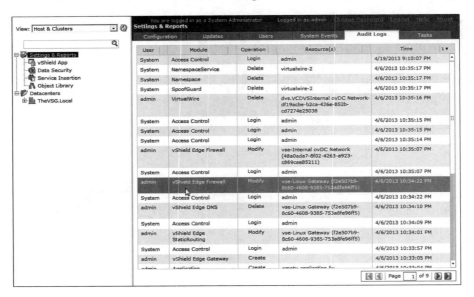

Figure 9-8   vShield Manager Audit Logs

Syslog Settings

Syslog, the standard for logging information in computer systems, is one of the best ways to get logs from your vCloud deployment. Not only does it aggregate all the logs into one location, but it also provides security for the logs and allows for easier troubleshooting. All VMware products in the vCloud Suite support logging to a syslog server.

The following list explains how to configure vCloud Director and vShield Manager to log to a syslog server:

- **vCloud Director**—To configure vCloud Director to log to a syslog server, log in as a system administrator. Select the **Administration** tab, and then select **General**. Part of the way down the page are syslog server settings, as shown in Figure 9-9.

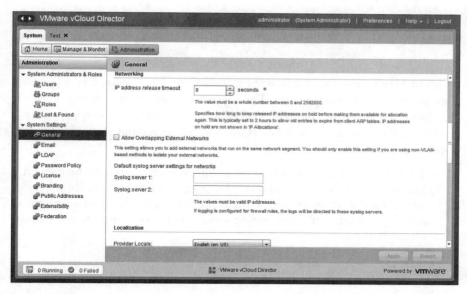

Figure 9-9 vCloud Syslog Settings

Settings configured here will be used for all vShield Edge gateways, synchronized through the vCloud Director installation. If you ever change the syslog settings for vCloud Director, you need to resynchronize the syslog settings through the Edge Gateway configuration page, as shown in Figure 9-10.

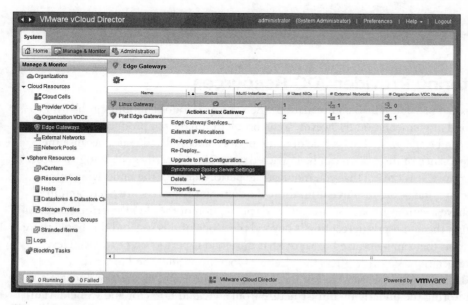

Figure 9-10 Synchronize Syslog Server Settings

> **NOTE**   For configuration of logging vCloud Director jmx server and cell.log files to syslog, refer to Chapter 2, "Install and Configure vCloud."

- **vShield Manager**—You can forward vShield events to a syslog server by configuring settings in two locations. For logging system events and audit events, configure syslog settings in the vShield Manager WebUI. For logging traffic and firewall rule actions, configure syslog settings in vCloud Director. These settings are discussed in Chapter 2:

  - To configure the syslog settings for vShield event, log in to the vShield Manager WebUI as an administrator, select the **Settings & Reports** option on the left pane, and scroll to the bottom of the Configuration tab. Select **Edit** next to the Syslog server field at the bottom, as shown in Figure 9-11.

Figure 9-11   vShield Manager Syslog Server Information

Monitoring Provider vDC Resources

Logs can provide valuable information when you are troubleshooting problems in a vCloud implementation. However, some problems might not produce a log output that can be analyzed. This is true of many performance-related issues because the performance of the system can be impacted without necessarily generating an error. Therefore, it is critical that you monitor the performance of the underlying infrastructure, including resource utilization. The amount resources are overcommitted can have a serious impact on an end user's perception of the cloud's performance. Although the end user's perception is beyond the scope of this test and this book, there are tools that can be utilized to verify that the cloud is performing to a given level of expectation. VMware offers the vCenter Operations Suite, and other third-party products are available as well. For the purposes of the exam, this section focuses on monitoring the underlying infrastructure from a vCloud Director and vShield Manager perspective, as well as monitoring the overcommitment of resources.

CPU

Although CPU resources are not overcommitted as often as memory resources are, when insufficient CPU resources exist to satisfy the current requirements, the impact can be severe. This is because CPU cycles are used for some network operations, especially for storage operations traversing the network. To keep an eye on CPU utilization, vCloud Director enables the monitoring of several CPU metrics, as detailed next.

From vCloud Director, navigate to the Manage & Monitor tab, select **Provider VDCs** from the left pane, and select the **Monitor** option, as shown in Figure 9-12.

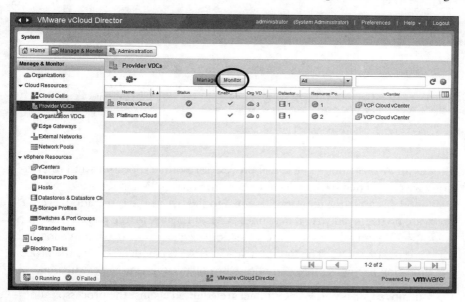

Figure 9-12   Provider vDC Monitor Tab

The metrics that are important for CPU performance are

- **Processor Used**—This is the actual processor usage as reported by vCenter for the resource pools associated with the provider virtual datacenter (vDC). Because a provider vDC can have more than one resource pool or cluster associated with it, the available processor resources are a combined total of all available CPUs. By hovering over the bar of the Processor Used column, a box like the one in Figure 9-13 appears giving the total consumed and total available processor in GHz.

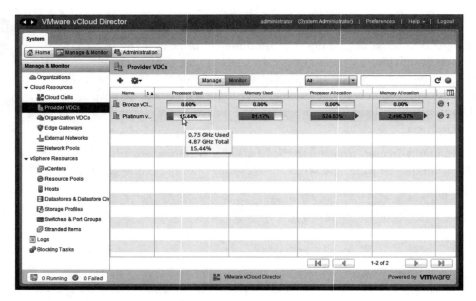

Figure 9-13 Used and Total Processor Used

- **Processor Allocation**—The actual processor resource allocations and reservations are closely tied to the selected Allocation model. When the Reservation Pool model is used, the allocation is equal to the size of the reservation, even if there are no deployed virtual machines (VMs) in that resource pool. When the Allocation Pool model is used, the allocation is equal to the maximum allocated CPU for the org vDC. The Pay-as-You-Go (PAYG) model is where the processor allocation becomes more complicated from a resource usage calculation.

  Only deployed VMs in a PAYG model are counted against the processor allocation. This enables the overcommitment of physical processor resources. After the overcommitment becomes large enough, VM performance starts to suffer.

- **Processor Overhead**—This value represents the amount of overhead or management that the vSphere hosts incur to run the virtualized workloads.

Memory

After running several lab manager environments and vCloud environments and designing more vSphere environments than we can count, we have come to realize that more often than not memory (RAM) is the limiting factor in a virtualized environment. There are rare use cases of course where the CPU is in demand without much RAM being required, but those are just that: rare use cases.

The following metrics are important for memory performance:

- **Memory usage**—Similar to the CPU usage numbers, the memory usage indicates the utilized memory in the provider vDC.

> **NOTE**   When specifying a reservation for memory, the amount of memory reserved cannot be shared, swapped, or compressed. This means that reserved memory resources cannot take advantage of all the vSphere memory sharing features, including transparent page sharing, compression, and so on.

- **Memory allocation**—The memory allocation metric should be closely monitored to avoid worst-case scenarios for memory usage, in which memory use could reach 100% saturation. As an experienced VMware administrator, you know that it is common to configure some degree of memory overallocation in a virtualized environment. However, there comes a point when the overallocation of RAM reaches a high enough level that performance problems in VMs are unavoidable. Figure 9-14 shows that the provider vDC is overallocated by 108%.

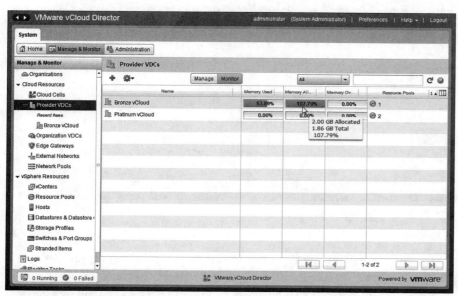

Figure 9-14   Memory Overallocation

When used with an Allocation Pool model or Reservation Pool model, the amount of RAM allocated to those org vDCs is considered allocated at the creation of the org vDC. With a PAYG allocation model, memory is allocated only when a VM is deployed to the org vDC.

■ **Memory overhead**—Similar to CPU overhead calculations, there is a management overhead to running a VM. The more resources the VM needs, the larger the overhead. This metric shows how much RAM is being used to manage the current running workloads.

Storage

A provider vDC can have multiple storage profiles attached to it. Conversely, a storage profile can be attached to multiple provider vDCs. This makes monitoring storage usage difficult from the provider vDC Monitor view. To view the usage of a storage profile, log in to vCloud Director. Next, click the **Manage & Monitor** tab and select **Storage Profiles** in the left pane. Your view should now look similar to what is in Figure 9-15.

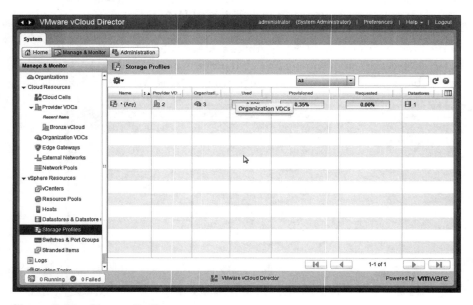

Figure 9-15 Storage Profiles

From this view, you will see the aggregate information for the storage profiles that vCloud Director has discovered from the attached vCenter Servers. This is particularly useful when you consider that a storage profile can have more than one datastore associated to it. The Storage Profile view contains the following information:

■ **Provider VDC**—The number of provider vDCs that have been defined to access the storage profile. Even if a storage profile is disabled in a provider vDC, it still appears in this count.

- **Organization VDC**—The number of org vDCs that are consuming the storage profile. Similar to the provider vDC count, even if an org vDC is disabled or the storage profile is disabled in an org vDC, this count will still reflect those objects.

- **Used**—An aggregate of the actual storage space used across all LUNs or datastores associated with the storage profile. When utilizing fast-provisioning and thin-provisioning, this number is the actual on disk storage usage, even though the virtual disks may be much larger.

- **Provisioned**—With the use of fast-provisioning and thin-provisioning, the disk utilized is often less than the disk space allocated or provisioned.

  Imagine an R&D scenario in which someone needs to test what happens when a 2TB disk is attached to the software they are developing. 2TB of storage area network (SAN) attached disk for a VM can be expensive to provide for a testing scenario. With a vCloud implementation, you can present a virtual 2TB disk to the guest while consuming only a small amount of space on the storage array. The number reported here is the total disk space provisioned to all VMs in the storage profile. It is not uncommon to see 300%–600% storage overcommitment depending on the use of the storage profile. Production environments tend to use overcommitment conservatively and are generally in the 75%–150% range.

- **Requested**—Similar to the provisioned storage number, this number reflects the storage requested by vCloud Director workloads. The difference is that this number reports only the disk usage for vCloud-managed objects. If a LUN is shared with a management stack, or other services, it is excluded from the calculations of this number.

- **Datastores**—How many datastores are associated with the storage profile? That is what this number represents. Even if the datastore is disabled, it is still counted here.

A more granular view of storage usage is through the Datastores view under the Manage & Monitor tab, as shown in Figure 9-16.

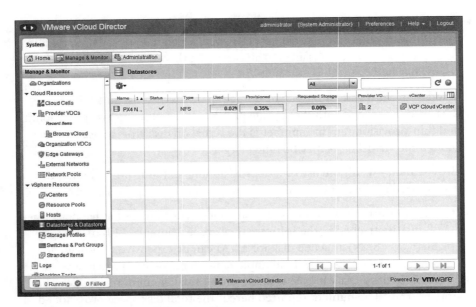

Figure 9-16   Datastores & Datastore Clusters

Through this view, you are able to see individual usage of a datastore or datastore cluster. With vCloud Director 5.1, the ability to use storage clusters from vCenter was introduced. This enables vCloud to consume the Storage Distributed Resources Scheduler (SDRS) clusters that are presented by vCenter. If you have a storage cluster, the number presented in this view will present as a single datastore, meaning all numbers reported will be the total of all LUNs in the storage cluster. Storage clusters are represented by a different icon, as shown in Figure 9-17.

The fields presented here are similar to the Storage Profile section, with the exception of the vCenter column. Datastores are unique between vCenter Servers, so when a datastore is presented to multiple vCenters, multiple reference IDs are generated. As a result, a LUN presented to multiple vCenter Servers will have a unique ID presented by vCloud Director for each vCenter Server to which it is presented.

The metrics used to monitor a provider vDC can give you a high-level view of how the cloud as a whole is performing. The next step is to drill down to the individual org vDCs. The metrics used at this level and the differences between metrics provided at the provider and org vDCs are outlined in the next section.

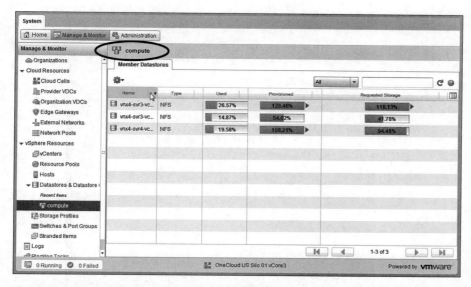

Figure 9-17   Storage Cluster Icon in vCloud Director

Monitoring Org vDC Resources

More often than not, the first place for an administrator to look when dealing with performance issues is at the org vDC allocations and their usage. If an allocation model is configured improperly or insufficient resources have been allocated to the org vDC, VMs in the vDC will be impacted, regardless of the available resources at the provider vDC level. Only after you have determined that the resource issue is not restricted to the org vDC in question should you look at provider vDC utilization. If you do determine the problem lies at the provider vDC level, refer to the section "Monitor Provider vDC Resources."

CPU

Unlike the provider vDC monitor screen, the org vDC screen is available to organization administrators to view how, what, and where they are consuming resources. This view can be accessed in a variety of ways; the method we focus on for the purposes of the exam is access through the organization from the System view by selecting the organization VDCs on the left menu of the Manage & Monitor tab.

Log in to vCloud Director as an organization user with sufficient privileges or as the system administrator; then select the target organization. Next, select the **Administration** tab, and select **Monitor** in the Virtual Datacenters view, shown in Figure 9-18.

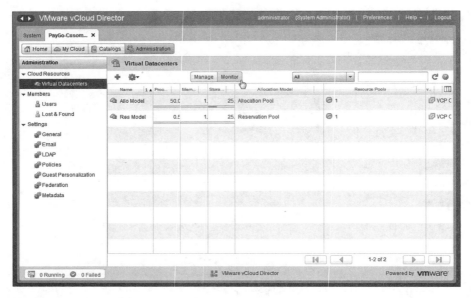

Figure 9-18   Org vDC Monitor View

The processor usage listed represents different things based on the type of allocation model around which the org vDC is created:

- **Pay-As-You-Go**—When using a PAYG model, the processor usage shows the % usage of the org vDC's quota. This percentage is calculated using the following formula:

```
(vCPU Speed * # of vCPUs * % guaranteed) / (Org vDC quota)
```

NOTE   The vCPU speed in a PAYG model becomes the limit of the vCPU speed for VMs provisioned in the vDC. The VMs cannot exceed this limit. For example, a VM deployed with two vCPUs in a vDC with a PAYG model with a vCPU speed of 2GHz will have a 4GHz limit.

- **Allocation model**—An Allocation model org vDC is similar to the PAYG model for calculating usage. The difference lies in the way the allocated usage is calculated. Because an Allocation model does not set limits on the individual VM, VMs can be allocated more CPU than is actually available. A vDC configured to use the Allocation model uses the following formula for calculating CPU allocation usage:

```
(vCPU Speed * # of vCPU * % guaranteed) / (Allocation of CPU)
```

NOTE   The vCPU speed in an Allocation model is used to calculate the number of reserved CPU cycles on the org vDC. There is no limit placed on a VM in an Allocation model.

- **Reservation model**—An org vDC created with a Reservation model is the only type of vDC where it is impossible to oversubscribe resources. As a result, the calculation for resource usage is much closer to the actual usage. The usage number for CPU consumption comes directly from vCenter. There is no formula for the calculation of usage because there is no overcommitment of resources.

Memory

The most likely reason for bottlenecks and performance issues in a vCloud implementation results from consumption of memory in an org vDC. It is not uncommon to have a new vApp author overallocate memory resources to a single VM. This can cause the org vDC's allocation or memory quota to become exhausted. This makes understanding memory allocation and monitoring memory consumption one of the most critical tasks an administrator has.

Similar to the way CPU usage is calculated, memory consumption calculations are different for each allocation model:

- **Pay-As-You-Go**—Memory allocation for a vDC configured with the PAYG model in vCloud Director 5.1 works the same as it does with CPU allocation. The formula for calculating the usage is

```
(Memory Allocated to VMs * % Guaranteed) / Memory Quota
```

NOTE   Unlike CPU allocation, there is no per-unit calculation for memory reservation. This is defined by the vApp author, who is creating the VM, and is where an unknowing vApp author can misconfigure a VM with too much memory, consuming all the available quota for that org vDC.

- **Allocation model**—An org vDC that is configured to use the Allocation model calculates its memory usage based on the following formula:

```
(Memory Allocated to VMs * % Guaranteed) / Memory Allocation
```

If you hover over the memory usage bar, you are presented with a breakdown of how the memory allocation is spread out.

- **Reservation model**—As with CPU consumption in an org vDC configured to use the Reservation model, this metric reflects the real memory configuration of the VMs. Also as mentioned before, there is no overcommitment of resources in a Reservation Pool; everything is guaranteed.

Storage

When an org vDC has fast-provisioning and/or thin-provisioning enabled, the number reflected here is larger than the actual on-disk usage. This is because the org vDC allocation does not account for space savings; it assumes that a VM configured for 100GB uses 100GB of disk space. If fast-provisioning and/or thin-provisioning is disabled, then the number reported here is the actual on-disk usage. This number also does not calculate any storage array space-saving technologies, such as de-duplication, compression, or other methods of reducing disk space usage.

NOTE As a tenant, the only way to determine how much disk usage an org vDC is consuming is to refer to vCenter for the disk space usage of the VMs associated with the org vDC. If the tenant is the only tenant of the storage profile, the provider vDC view of storage usage equals the amount of actual on-disk usage.

Monitoring Network Resources

Monitoring network consumption in a vCloud environment requires both the vShield Manager interface as well as the vCloud Director interface. From vCloud Director, we can determine how many networks are still unassigned in the network pool. From vShield Manager, we can determine transfer rates, types of packets, and other items from the vShield Edge configuration pages. This section covers where this information is accessed and what it means.

External Networks

External networks in vCloud Director refer to networks outside the vCloud environment. These can consist of a network on the Internet, on an intranet, or just something outside the cloud. Monitoring these networks requires access to vSphere for traffic flows. For something more granular, switch-level access might be required because, for this type of network, there is no vShield Edge or similarly managed vCloud device.

Organization Networks

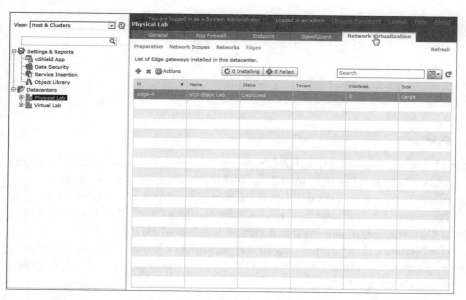

Organization networks can be isolated, routed, or direct-connected to an external network. If the organization network is connected to an external network directly, there will be no vShield Edge device and no network pool object to monitor from within vCloud Director. In this case, monitoring must be performed in the same way as it is for external networks.

If the organization network is routed or isolated, the organization network will consume an object from the Network Pool. In this case, there are items that can be monitored in vCloud Director or vShield Manager. The first place to monitor these types of organization networks is through vShield Manager and the vShield Edge bandwidth monitoring page.

Log in to vShield Manager and select the datacenter where the vShield Edge devices are deployed; this is the same datacenter in which the provider vDC is defined. Select the **Network Virtualization** tab as shown in Figure 9-19. Then select the proper vShield Edge device.

Figure 9-19   vShield Manager Network Virtualization Tab

NOTE   Making changes to a vShield Edge device from vShield Manager is not supported if the vShield Edge device was deployed from vCloud Director. Any changes made through vShield Manager are lost when the edge is re-deployed by vCloud Director.

Click the **Statistics** menu tab. This brings up two graphs displaying throughput and concurrent connections, as shown in Figure 9-20. Both graphs have a modifiable range for the data shown.

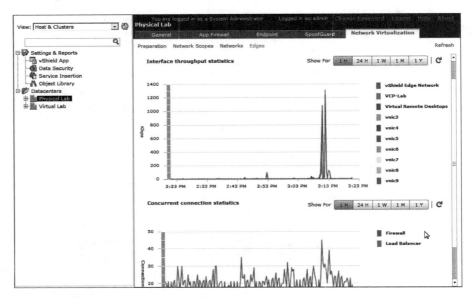

Figure 9-20   vShield Edge Statistics

Network Pools

vCloud Network pools, discussed in Chapter 6, "Configure and Administer vCloud Networking," are another item in vCloud that must be monitored for capacity. Remember that a network pool object is consumed each time a routed or nonconnected network is created and deployed. Under the Manage & Monitor tab in the vCloud Director system administrator view, select **Network Pools** on the left side. The Network Pools option lists all the network pools that are defined for the vCloud instance, including VXLAN, vCD-NI, Port Group, and VLAN pool types, as shown in Figure 9-21.

If you are running out of pool objects in your network pools, you can expand the VXLAN and vCD-NI network pool types. In the event you have a VLAN or port-group backed network pool, you need to create new port group objects or provision new VLANs in vCenter and then add them to the network pool in vCloud Director. For guidance on how to add items to network pools, refer to Chapter 6.

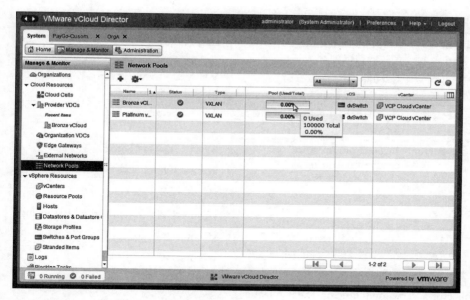

Figure 9-21   vCloud Network Pool Display

vShield Manager Log File Gathering

In the event of a vShield problem or when troubleshooting a vShield problem, you might need to gather logs from vShield Manager. These log files can be retrieved by following this KB article from Vmware: http://kb.vmware.com/kb/2012760.

Troubleshooting vCenter Chargeback Manager

vCenter Chargeback Manager has two main tools for troubleshooting, and they are separate from the tools used to monitor and troubleshoot vCloud Director. The tools used to troubleshoot vCenter Chargeback Manager are log files and the troubleshooting utility.

Log Files

There are many log files and log file locations in vCenter Chargeback Manager 2.5. Log files are your main tools when troubleshooting Chargeback Manager.

Table 9-2 outlines the various log files and their locations.

Table 9-2   vCenter Chargeback Manager Log Files

Chargeback Component	Log File Location	Log File(s)
Installer	InstallationDirectory/	VMware_vCenter_Chargeback_InstallLog.log
Load Balancer	InstallationDirectory/Apache2.2/logs	Apache Server log files
Chargeback Server	InstallationDirectory/apache-tomcat/logs	Apache Tomcat logs vCenterCB.log vCenterCB_Errors.log vCenterCB_Authentication_Errors.log
vCenter Data Collector	InstallationDirectory/DataCollector-Embedded/logs	vCenterDC.log vCenterDC_Errors.log
vCloud Director Data Collector	InstallationDirectory/CloudDirector_DataCollector_Name/logs	vCloud-DC.log vCloud-DC_Errors.log
vCNS (vShield) Manager	InstallationDirectory/vShieldManager_DataCollector_Name/logs	VSM-DC.log VSM-DC_Errors.log

InstallationDirectory in Table 9-2 refers to the root directory where vCenter Chargeback Manager was installed. By default, the installation directory is

C:\Program Files (x86)\VMware\VMware vCenter Chargeback

Each log file is explained here:

- **VMware_vCenter_Chargeback_InstallLog.log**—This file contains information about the tasks that took place during installation.

- **Load Balancer logs**—These are simply standard Apache web server log files.

- **Apache Tomcat logs (Chargeback Server)**—These are standard Apache Tomcat application logs.

- **vCenterCB.log**—This log contains information on the core Chargeback Server application. The log detail is dependent on the level of logging set in the application.

- **vCenterCB_Errors.log**—This log includes information about all errors related to the core Chargeback Manager application *except* authentication errors.

- **vCenterCB_Authentication_Errors.log**—This log contains information about authentication errors for the core Chargeback Manager application.

- **vCenterDC.log**—This is log information specific to the vCenter Server(s) that vCenter Chargeback Manager is connected to and the log level set for the connection.

- **vCenterDC_Errors.log**—This log contains information about errors occurring with the vCenter Server data collector.

- **vCloud-DC.log**—This contains information related to the vCloud Director data collector(s) to which vCenter Chargeback Manager is connected and the log level set for the connection.

- **vCloud-DC_Errors.log**—This log includes information about errors occurring with the vCloud Director data collector.

- **VSM-DC.log**—This contains log information related to the vShield Manager (vCNS Manager) data collector(s) to which vCenter Chargeback Manager is connected and the log level set for the connection.

- **VSM-DC_Errors.log**—This log includes information about errors occurring with the vShield Manager/vCNS Manager data collector.

Troubleshooting Utility

The troubleshooting utility in vCenter Chargeback Manager collects the log files from the various directories listed previously, in addition to configuration files, the Windows Application and System logs, and some other information, and writes that information to a single .ZIP file. Run the troubleshooting utility by executing the following command:

InstallationDirectory/vCenter-CB-Tools/troubleshooting/bin/vCenterCB-support.bat

The utility can also be run from the Windows Start Menu.

The .ZIP file is stored in

InstallationDirectory/vCenter-CB-Tools/troubleshooting/collected_logs

Summary

In this chapter, we briefly covered how to monitor utilization and performance in a vCloud implementation and how to use this information along with log data to troubleshoot common problems that occur within the environment:

- We covered how to view events and retrieve logs for vCloud Director and vShield Manager.

- We covered how to monitor utilization of provider vDCs and how to interpret resource metrics.

- We discussed how to monitor utilization of org vDCs and how to interpret resource metrics. We also compared differences between these metrics and those for provider vDCs.

- We covered how to monitor network resources for the various network types and where to locate this information.

- Finally, we discussed where to locate log information for vCenter Chargeback Manager and how to use the troubleshooting utility to compile this information.

Exam Preparation Tasks

Review All the Key Topics

Review the most important topics in the chapter, noted with the Key Topic icons in the outer margin of the page. Table 9-3 lists a reference to these key topics and the page numbers on which each is found.

Table 9-3 Key Topics

Key Topic Element	Description	Page
Paragraph	vCloud Director log retention	278
Bulleted list	Syslog settings	282
Section	Provider vDC CPU metrics	285
Section	Provider vDC memory metrics	286
Section	Provider vDC storage metrics	288
Section	Org vDC CPU metrics	291
Section	Org vDC memory metrics	293
Section	Org vDC storage metrics	294
Section	Organization networks	295
Table 9-2 and following discussion	vCenter Chargeback Manager Log files	298

Definitions of Key Terms

Define the following key terms from this chapter, and check your answers in the glossary:

vCloud task, vCloud events, vShield events, vShield audit logs, Syslog, overhead, provisioned storage, requested storage

Review Questions

1. When using an Allocation model, what is the vCPU speed related to?

   a. The limit of vCPU resources

   b. The number of reserved vCPU cycles

   c. The reserved amount of vCPU resources

   d. The percentage of reserved vCPU cycles

2. What is the proper way to set the Syslog server setting for vCloud Director to log system events?

   a. Through the configure script

   b. Through the System Administrator page

   c. Through vCenter

   d. Through vShield Manager

3. When utilizing vShield Edge devices, where can a system administrator set the syslog setting for logging firewall events?

   a. vCloud Director Org vDC Settings page

   b. vCloud Director Provider vDC Settings page

   c. vCloud Director System Administrator page

   d. vShield Manager Syslog page

4. The vShield Manager Audit Log contains which types of events?

   a. vShield Manager system events

   b. vShield Manager user actions

   c. vShield Edge device events

   d. vShield Edge deployment actions

5. When monitoring the provider vDC usage, the memory allocation includes what information?

   a. Pay-as-You-Go quotas

   b. Allocation models, allocations

   c. Powered on VM usage from Reservation models

   d. Reservation model overcommitment

6. Which information is included in storage profiles' requested usage?

   a. Storage requested by vCloud Director managed workloads

   b. Storage requested by vCloud Director and vCenter managed workloads

   c. Storage requested by vCenter managed workloads

   d. Storage requested by vCloud Director workloads and management services

7. When viewing a storage profile when fast-provisioning is enabled, which usage is reported?

   a. Actual disk usage

   b. Provisioned usage

   c. Requested storage

   d. Average disk usage

8. Which vCenter Chargeback Manager log file contains information about the installation of vCenter Chargeback Manager?

   a. vCCBM_log.log

   b. VMware_vCenter_Chargeback_InstallLog.log

   c. vCenterCB_Install.log

   d. installer.log

9. What does the vCenter Chargeback Manager troubleshooting utility do?

   a. Helps you determine why users cannot run reports

   b. Collects log information into a .ZIP file

   c. Runs a wizard to help you determine what is wrong with the installation

   d. Finds and fixes problems with your vCenter Chargeback Manager installation

This chapter covers the following subjects:

- **Download the Exam Blueprint**—The exam blueprint contains all the information necessary to pass the exam.

- **Gain Hands-On Experience**—Hands-on experience is necessary for a successful exam experience.

- **Complete the Practice Exams**—There are review and practice questions in this book and on the DVD.

- **Exam Registration**—We walk you through registering for the exam.

- **Exam Day**—What to expect on exam day.

This chapter does not cover any specific exam objectives. Instead, we give you advice and instruction on preparing for, scheduling, and taking the exam.

CHAPTER 10

What Do I Do Now?

Now that you've finished reading the book, what should you do next? Well, if you've taken VMware exams (or any IT certification exam, really) before, then you likely know the drill. For those of you who are new to the IT certification game or just new to VMware exams, this chapter helps you prepare. Between the two of us, we've probably taken between 20 and 30 VMware exams and at least that many exams for other IT certifications.

In our experience, the first two things that you should do are (1) download the exam blueprint and (2) schedule the exam. The exam blueprint provides an outline of the knowledge necessary to pass the exam. Scheduling the exam gives you a target date to work toward, and we find it motivates us to study if we have a deadline. This chapter details both of these processes as well as provides some additional exam-related information, all in an effort to help you prepare for and pass the VCP-IaaS exam and achieve VCP-Cloud certification.

NOTE As mentioned in Chapter 1, "Introduction to the vCloud Suite Certifications," this book covers only material that maps to the objectives on the VCP-IaaS exam blueprint. If you plan to take the VCP-Cloud combined exam, you will need to supplement the information in this book with *The Official VCP5 Certification Guide* by Bill Ferguson. Aside from the blueprint differences, this chapter applies to both the VCP-IaaS and VCP-Cloud exams.

Foundation Topics

Download the Exam Blueprint

VMware publishes an exam blueprint for each exam, so downloading the exam blueprint should be your first step toward any VMware certification. The exam blueprint is the official answer to the question "what's on the exam?" It provides two very important pieces of information—the exam logistics (number of questions, passing score, time limit, and so on) and the exam objectives with supporting documentation. The exam blueprint provides the exact information you need to study to pass the exam. It can be found on the VMware website at www.vmware.com/certification.

We wrote this book to map directly to the objectives in the VCP-IaaS exam blueprint, and each chapter overview provides the blueprint objective numbers that are covered in the chapter. Though we did not follow the blueprint linearly, all the objectives of the VCP-IaaS exam are covered in this book. Read through the blueprint and perform a gap analysis on your knowledge. Determine the areas where you feel you are weak, and use this book along with the recommended resources for each blueprint objective to enhance your knowledge.

CAUTION Exam blueprints are updated occasionally; make sure that you are working from the latest blueprint version.

NOTE You will need a VMware Training ("MyLearn") account to download an exam blueprint. When you click the link for the exam blueprint, you are redirected to a login page. If you already have an account, enter your credentials. The username is typically your email address. If you do not have an account, you can create one on the same page. This is a one-time registration and is necessary for VMware certifications.

Gain Hands-On Experience

Hands-on experience with the products covered on the exam is important to your success. It will be difficult to pass the VCP-IaaS or VCP-Cloud exam without direct experience installing and configuring vCenter, ESXi, vCloud Director, vCenter Chargeback, and vCloud Networking and Security (formerly vShield). Although the VCP exams are considered entry-level, they are not easy exams, especially if you don't have experience with the products.

If you do not work directly with these products as part of your job, consider installing the products in a lab environment. Informational materials and tutorials are available online for setting up a home lab either on dedicated hardware or by using a host-based virtualization solution with VMware Workstation or VMware Fusion. If you are considering pursuing any of the advanced certifications, a home lab of some sort is almost mandatory to get the exposure to the products that you will need. Being able to build up, tear down, rebuild, and break things in a home lab and then troubleshoot and fix them is well worth the investment in hardware.

VMware also offers a new product called VMware Lab Connect. This product is a cloud-based, on-demand, multiplatform lab environment that can be used to, among other things, prepare for VMware certifications. The product includes a complete virtual lab environment and the actual hands-on labs from several of our courses. To see whether this might be a useful option in your exam preparation, visit the website here: http://mylearn.vmware.com/mgrReg/plan.cfm?plan=34640&ui=www_edu.

However you choose to gain hands-on experience, go through the exam blueprint and product documentation and the examples in this book and perform the tasks. Make sure that you truly understand the basics and the concepts covered in the exam blueprint, instead of just being able to complete the tasks that are listed. Be able to explain—at a basic level—each of the items in the blueprint. VCP exams can be tricky if you don't know the material well, but if you have a good understanding of the objectives, you should do well on the exam.

Practice Exams and Preparation Material

Each of the chapters in this book (with the exception of the first and last chapters) contain "Do I Know This Already?" questions at the beginning and "Review Questions" at the end. Both types of questions check your knowledge and help you understand why an answer is right or wrong. If you are able to identify the correct answers and *why* those answers are correct, you will be well on your way to a successful exam. Be able to identify why incorrect answers are not the best choice. Don't just memorize facts—understand the concepts.

In addition to the pre- and post-chapter review questions, VMware provides practice exams for both the VCP-IaaS and VCP-Cloud exams. These are available at the same location as the exam blueprint and typically include 25 questions. You must log in using your MyLearn account to take the practice exam, just as you did when you downloaded the exam blueprint. These practice questions are a good representation of what you will see on the actual exam. Again, you should understand *why* an answer is the best choice. Following the practice exam, you will be shown the questions you answered incorrectly (along with an explanation in many cases) but will not be given the correct answer. If you answer all the questions correctly, you will not be allowed to take the practice exam again, so we recommend that you answer at least one question wrong.

Finally, some excellent instructional videos are available from VMware at http://vmwarelearning.com. These have been produced and released by VMware Education instructors and are valuable for both learning and reviewing the material prior to the exam. Similarly, there are also some great resources available on the YouTube VMware TV Channel at http://youtube.com/vmwaretv.

Register for the Exam

Register for the exam in advance to set a goal. We find it easier to motivate ourselves to study and practice for an exam when we have a looming deadline. The exam can be easily rescheduled if you find that you aren't ready, but having a goal date is a great motivator. Note that Pearson VUE requires you to reschedule or cancel an exam within 24 hours of the scheduled exam time to avoid forfeiting the exam fee.

Find a time of day that works best for your schedule. For some, this is first thing in the morning when the mind is fresh, while others prefer afternoons. Some testing centers are open on Saturdays and Sundays if you would like to schedule the exam for a weekend. Generally speaking, the mind is at its best in the mid-morning after a good night's sleep and a healthy breakfast.

The test is administered only through Pearson VUE. You can find a link to the exam registration in the same location you accessed the exam blueprint download and the practice exam. You will need to register for an account on the Pearson VUE site if you don't already have one, and you will also need to register for the VMware program if you haven't already done so. Follow the exam registration link from the VMware site; you will be walked through both registrations. The cost of the exam is USD $225, but be sure you check the VMware Certification site prior to scheduling your exam because discounts and promotions are frequently offered.

Exam Day

If you've taken IT certification exams through Pearson VUE before, you likely know what to expect. When you schedule the exam, you're asked to arrive 15 minutes early; however, we suggest that you allow about 30 minutes extra so that you aren't rushed. Your mind and body will already be stressed by the preparation and anxiety. So there's no need to add being late for the exam to your stress! Give yourself some extra time to arrive early, visit the restroom, and complete the check-in process without feeling like you are being rushed.

Speaking of the check-in process, prepare to be photographed and to read and acknowledge the testing center rules. Also, make sure that you bring two forms of ID for verification of your identity. You will be given a locker where you will be asked to place everything except your ID. Some testing centers ask you to turn out your pockets to prove that you aren't taking anything into the testing center. And some testing centers allow you to chew gum or bring in a water bottle, but others don't. You can count on being given a dry-erase sheet and marker and ear plugs if you request them and then being escorted to your testing station.

Before the actual exam begins, you will be asked to complete eight pre-exam survey questions about your experience and knowledge with the associated products. These questions have nothing to do with your score or the questions you receive—they're merely demographic questions for VMware. Answer them and move on. The actual exam begins as soon as the last survey question is completed and you submit your responses.

During the exam, be sure you read each question thoroughly and pay attention to what the question is asking, including the number of answers requested. Some questions will be true/false; others will be multiple choice/multiple answer. Remember that you are searching for the *best* answer and that some questions are asking for multiple answers.

You are allowed to mark questions for later review, and you can move back to a previous question if you feel you need to. We find that the best strategy is to read and attempt to answer each question in order. If you don't know or aren't certain of the answer, mark the question and return to it after all questions have been attempted. Don't get hung up on any individual question that you can't answer in less than a minute. If you are going to struggle determining the answer, mark it for review and return to it later. If you finish all questions with time to spare, review your answers for completeness and correctness. However, you should make changes only if you are sure you initially answered a question wrong. Studies have shown that your first answer is usually your best answer.

After reviewing all the questions (or when your time runs out), you will submit your answers. Following the submission, you will be presented with a screen letting you know your results: success or failure. You will exit the testing area and be given a printout of your results. After you've passed—congratulations! In the unfortunate event that you fail the exam, VMware provides you a report detailing each exam objective in which you missed half or more of that objective's questions. Use this information to return to the blueprint and target these areas for further study. Determine any other weak points and study those objectives. Reschedule the exam and repeat the process.

Best of luck—and thank you for reading!

—Tom and Nate

Answers to the "Do I Know This Already?" Quizzes and Review Questions

Chapter 2

"Do I Know This Already?"

1. C
2. A and B
3. B and C
4. A
5. B, C, and D
6. A and C
7. A
8. A

Review Questions

1. D
2. A and B
3. B
4. C and D
5. B, C, and D
6. A
7. C
8. B

Chapter 3

"Do I Know This Already?"

1. D
2. A, B, and D
3. A
4. B
5. A and C
6. D
7. C
8. B

Review Questions

1. B and D
2. C
3. C
4. A and D
5. D
6. A
7. B and C
8. B
9. A and D
10. D

Chapter 4

"Do I Know This Already?"

1. A and D
2. B
3. B
4. D
5. A and D
6. C and D
7. C and D
8. A and D
9. A, C, and D
10. A
11. D
12. C
13. B, C, and D
14. B and C

Review Questions

1. B and C
2. B and C
3. B and D
4. B
5. B and D
6. C
7. C
8. A, C, and D
9. D
10. C
11. D
12. C and D
13. A and C

14. D
15. A, C, and D
16. B
17. C
18. B, C, and D
19. C
20. C

Chapter 5

"Do I Know This Already?"

1. A and C
2. C
3. C
4. C
5. A and B
6. A
7. B

Review Questions

1. B
2. B
3. A and B
4. B
5. C
6. B

Chapter 6

"Do I Know This Already?"

1. B
2. C
3. A
4. A and B
5. B and D
6. C
7. A
8. B and C

Review Questions

1. C
2. A and D
3. C
4. B and C
5. C
6. B
7. B

Chapter 7

"Do I Know This Already?"

1. C
2. A
3. C
4. A
5. A and B
6. A
7. B
8. A and B

Review Questions

1. A
2. A
3. A
4. C
5. A and B
6. B, C, and D
7. B

Chapter 8

"Do I Know This Already?"

1. A
2. B
3. C
4. A, B, and D
5. B
6. A and D
7. A
8. D
9. A

Review Questions

1. B
2. B
3. C
4. B
5. B and C
6. B and C
7. B
8. B
9. B
10. A
11. A

Chapter 9

"Do I Know This Already?"

1. A and C
2. B
3. B and C
4. B
5. A and B
6. B and C
7. B
8. A and D
9. B

Review Questions

1. B
2. A
3. C
4. B
5. B
6. A
7. B
8. B
9. B

vCenter to vCloud Resource Table

vCloud Object Name	vCenter Resource	Description
Provider Virtual Datacenter (vDC)	User-defined resource pool	In vCenter, a cluster is considered to be a parent resource pool. Although a provider vDC can be attached to a child pool in vCenter, it is recommended that they be attached to the uppermost resource pool.
Organization vDC	vCloud Director–created resource pool	vCloud Director will create a child resource pool in vCenter for each organization vDC.
External Networks	Port group	vCloud Director will attach virtual machines connected to an external network to a user-created port group in vCenter.
Network Pools		VXLAN and vCD-NI do not create objects in vCenter until needed. Port group and VLAN backed objects must be created prior to vCloud consuming them.
vApp Networks	Port group	vApp networks require either a created port group from the network pool or a previously created port group.
vApps	Virtual machines	A vCloud Director vApp consists of one or more vCenter virtual machines. Although vCenter also uses a vApp construct, it is used for a completely different purpose and should not be confused with the vCloud Director construct.
Catalogs		Catalogs in vCloud are not reflected in vCenter.
vApp Templates	Virtual machines	Both vApps and vApp templates map to one or more virtual machines in vCenter. From a vCenter perspective, there is no difference.

This appendix covers the following subjects:

- **vSphere Licensing**—The licensing editions supported and recommended for vCloud Director

- **vCenter Server Configuration**—Considerations for vCenter Server configuration and architecture in a vCloud Director environment

- **vCenter Host and Cluster Resources**—Required and recommended configurations for hosts and clusters to support vCloud Director

- **Networking**—Networking considerations for vCenter Server when operating in a vCloud Director environment

- **Storage**—Requirements and recommendations for storage and storage profiles for vCloud Director

This appendix does not cover any specific exam objectives. Instead, we give you requirements and recommendations on configuring vSphere clusters, networking, and storage for use with vCloud Director.

Configuring vSphere for vCloud Director

If you're planning on taking the VCP5-IaaS exam, then you've likely gained a good deal of experience with the core vSphere product. That's good because vSphere is the foundation upon which vCloud Director is built. vSphere sits between physical resources and vCloud Director, providing networking, compute (processor and memory), and storage resources needed by vCloud Director.

As a general rule, you should ensure that vSphere best practices and design principles are followed when building a vCloud Director infrastructure. Remember, vSphere is the foundation for vCloud Director, and building the vCenter Server, hosts, clusters, networking, and storage to design best practices will help ensure your cloud operates optimally.

In this appendix, we briefly cover specific requirements and best practices for configuring vSphere for use with vCloud Director. This information should help you better prepare for the exam objective "Map vCloud Resources to vSphere Resources," which is found as Objective 8.2 on the VCP-IaaS exam and as Objective 15.2 on the VCP-Cloud exam.

vSphere Licensing

vSphere Enterprise licenses are required—at a minimum—to build a supported vCloud Director infrastructure. Enterprise licensing enables Distributed Resource Scheduler (DRS) functionality, which is a requirement for vCloud Director. Enterprise Plus licensing is strongly encouraged, however, so that the Distributed Virtual Switch (DVS) can be used. Although standard switches are supported, they introduce design and functionality constraints that DVS eliminates. The DVS enabled by Enterprise Plus licensing enables isolated networks and VLAN-backed network pools, two very important networking constructs in cloud infrastructures.

vCenter Server(s) Configuration

vCenter Server manages the operation and abstraction of a vSphere infrastructure and is a required component for a vCloud Director implementation. In fact, it is recommended that more than one vCenter Server be used: one for management infrastructure and one (or more) for cloud resources. Although your vCloud infrastructure can start with a single vCenter server providing the resources for cloud consumption, you might want or need to add more vCenter servers as your environment grows and scales. Adding more vCenter servers (up to a total of 25 in vCloud Director 5.1) to your cloud infrastructure and offering their additional resources to Cloud consumers is easy.

The management vCenter Server hosts the ESXi cluster running the virtual machines required for the day-to-day operation of the vCloud Director infrastructure. These include the resource vCenter Server, one or more database servers, the Red Hat virtual machines hosting vCloud Director cells, vCloud Network and Security (vCNS) manager, vCloud Connector components, and vCenter Chargeback Manager. Other management virtual machines such as vCenter Operations Manager (vC Ops) and vCenter Configuration Manager (vCM) also can be placed in the management cluster. In many environments, the management cluster is hosted in the vCenter Server infrastructure that provides general (non-cloud) virtualization infrastructure to the environment.

The resource vCenter Server(s) hosts one or more clusters of ESXi hosts dedicated to providing resources for the vCloud environment. It's a recommended best practice to dedicate all the resources in a cluster to vCloud Director by attaching the cell at the cluster level. Furthermore, don't add virtual machines to the cluster outside of those added by vCloud Director, and don't subdivide a cluster into resource pools and allocate only a single resource pool in that cluster to vCloud Director. This will ensure that vCloud Director is aware of all virtual machines in the environment and can accurately manage and report on resources.

vCenter Host and Cluster Resources

Provider virtual datacenters (vDCs) are composed of resources provided by the individual hosts, networks, and storage attached to each vCenter cluster. As mentioned previously, it is a recommended best practice to dedicate all the resources within a cluster to vCloud Director. DRS is a required component and should be set to automatically place and balance virtual machines within each cluster. High Availability (HA) is not technically required, but it should be enabled nonetheless. You don't want a failed host to cause an extended outage, do you? Furthermore, Admission Control should be enabled and properly configured to ensure that resources are reserved to provide host failover protection.

Networking

The DVS, which is enabled by Enterprise Plus licensing, gives you the most flexibility for defining networking within a vCloud. It also enables all the advanced networking functionality within vCloud Director. The Cisco Nexus 1000v switch imposes a constraint on vCloud Director. VLAN-backed network pools are not possible when using the Nexus 1000v switch; only port-group backed network pools can be configured. Keep this in mind if you are designing or deploying vCloud Director on Vblock or other infrastructure that includes the Cisco Nexus 1000v.

If you are using Enterprise licensing rather than Enterprise Plus for your vCenter resource hosts, you should consider upgrading to Enterprise Plus to enable DVS. If you can't upgrade to Enterprise Plus, you will have the same constraint as when using the Cisco Nexus 1000v switch—you will be able to configure only port-group backed network pools. VLAN-backed network pools can be configured only when the ESXi hosts within the cluster are using Enterprise Plus licensing.

Jumbo Frames must be configured on any physical and virtual switches that carry cloud isolated network traffic or that participate in VXLAN. The standard maximum transmission units (MTU) size on physical and virtual switches is 1,500 bytes. The additional encapsulation necessary for cloud-isolated networks and VXLAN networks would create packets larger than 1,500 bytes, resulting in fragmentation and performance loss. To avoid packet fragmentation, increase the MTU to at least 1,600 bytes on all physical and virtual switches that pass VXLAN or cloud-isolated network traffic.

Storage

vCloud Director requires shared storage (Fibre Channel, NFS, or iSCSI) within resource clusters. This is a recommended practice in vSphere but is required in vCloud Director. Every host within a resource cluster must have access to the same set of shared datastores for vCloud Director to function properly.

vSphere storage profiles might be a new concept to you because they were only recently introduced to vSphere. A storage profile is simply a set of capabilities into which datastores can be grouped. These groups can be defined by the administrator or can be created based on capabilities reported to vCenter when communicating with storage arrays that are compatible with vSphere Storage APIs for Storage Awareness (VASA).

After storage LUNs are grouped by capability into Storage Profiles, they can be presented to vCloud Director as pools of storage resources. Each Provider vDC must contain storage from at least one storage profile. You can, of course, add multiple storage profiles to a Provider vDC. For example, storage can be broken into Storage Profiles of gold/silver/bronze based on performance capabilities and then added to a single Provider vDC. That Provider vDC would then be able to offer storage and set pricing (through integration with vCenter Chargeback) based on performance capabilities.

Glossary

Allocation Pool   The Allocation Pool model defines resource settings at the org vDC or the Resource Pool. This enables all virtual machines in the org vDC to consume the pool of resources and not be limited by their individual settings.

base rate   A cost element, the base rate is the global rate that is charged for each individual unit of chargeable computing resource that is used, reserved, or allocated.

billing policy   A cost element, the billing policy is a collection of chargeable computing resources combined with the base rate, any rate factors, and any fixed costs.

catalog   An organization's collection of vApp templates and media, a catalog is sharable between other organizations by publishing the catalog. Sharing the catalog applies only to interorganization access to the catalog.

cost element   Cost elements are the basis for costing and billing.

cost template   A cost element, cost templates are made up of entity-specific cost configuration details.

data collector   A data collector enables integration of vCenter Chargeback Manager with vCenter Server, vCloud Director, and vCloud Networking and Security Manager.

direct network   A network connection without a vShield Edge device, that is, a direct connection.

external network   Any network outside the vCloud instance. This can be an internal company network or the Internet. As long as it is outside the cloud, it is an external network

federation   The ability to define a user across multiple systems while using an identity management solution.

fixed cost   A cost element, fixed costs are costs that do not vary.

global.properties file The configuration file that is created during the first vCloud installation. This file should be copied between cells and used with additional cells to ensure uniform installations.

IDP An identity provider provides the identity of users and their authentication in a federated configuration.

intensive tasks Certain tasks in vCloud Director are considered resource intensive—for example, copy and move tasks are more intensive than others.

internal network A network inside an organization that has no connectivity to an external network.

IP allocations A range of IP addresses that are assigned either manually or automatically to machines or appliances connected to the network.

keytool The Java application that creates and manages the certificate store for vCloud Director. Although this is upgradable to newer versions, the one that ships with vCloud Director is the supported version.

LDAP Lightweight Directory Access Protocol. A protocol for accessing directory information over IP networks.

load balancer A network appliance that balances webpage requests between all available cells. To work with vCloud Director, the load balancer must support SSL sticky sessions or SSL persistent sessions.

lossless export vCloud Director 5.1 introduced a feature of lossless export, which includes all VM identity information, NIC information, and the PCI device ordering. Without lossless export, virtual machines generally require reactivation or relicensing, reconfiguration of the network interfaces, and redetection of the virtual hardware.

metadata Defines data about data; in vCloud Director metadata enables additional descriptive attributes to be applied to objects in vCloud Director.

NFS transfer share When using vCloud Director in a multicell environment, the NFS transfer share is a mounted network share between all the cells. This share facilitates the export and import of vApps and the migration of vApps between vCenters.

organization A logical grouping of users that require access to similar compute resources.

organization virtual data center (org vDC) Contains an organization's defined resources. These can be reserved resources and first come first served resources. The definition of the resources and their allocation is based on the allocation model chosen.

Overhead The resources (CPU/Memory) required to run a virtual machine.

OVF   The Open Virtualization Format is an open standard for packaging and distributing virtual machines. This can be a single virtual machine or multiple virtual machines. The OVF file itself is an XML file containing the settings and configurations of the VMs associated.

Pay-as-You-Go   The PAYG allocation model enables individual virtual machine limits and reservations of resources.

port-group backed   A vCloud Director network pool that uses predefined port groups in vCenter.

pricing model   A cost element, the pricing model defines the currency to be used, the billing policy in effect, and the base rates for the chargeable computing resources that will be used.

privileges   Privileges are also called rights; they specify which actions a user can and cannot perform.

provider virtual data center (provider vDC)   Contains the physical resources presented from vCenter Server. It is recommended that the provider vDC be defined at a top-level resource pool in vCenter Server such as a cluster.

Provisioned Storage   Storage that is provisioned to virtual machines either through vCenter Server or vCloud Director. In a thin- or fast-provisioned environment, this number is commonly well above 100%.

Proxy Console Service   Provides access to the console of a running VM in vCloud Director.

quota   Defines how many VMs can be stored or running in the organization; this is also a per-user setting. The setting at the organization level is defined for the total VMs in the organization, running or stored.

rate factor   A cost element, the rate factor is a multiplier used with the base rate to charge more or less for a resource.

Requested Storage   Storage that is provisioned to virtual machines that are managed via vCloud Director.

Reservation Pool   A Reservation Pool model guarantees a set amount of resources for an org vDC. These resources are not shared with other tenants.

rights   See *privileges*.

role   Roles are collections of privileges that map to job functions.

routed network   A network that has a vShield Edge device deployed between it and the network to which it is connected.

runtime lease   Defines how long a vApp can run without being extended. A deployed VM will use this lease for its runtime.

SAML   Security Assertion Markup Language is an XML-based open standard for exchanging authentication and authorization data between service providers and identity providers.

SMTP server   Mail server for sending outbound email, typically it runs on port 25.

storage lease   Defines how long a vApp or vApp template will be stored in the vCloud Director instance. The storage lease is in effect only for powered-off vApps; if a vApp is powered on, it will restart the storage lease when the vApp is powered back off.

storage profile   A storage profile is a collection of one or more vCenter Server datastores with like capabilities that are presented to vCloud Director org vDCs for consumption.

Syslog   A protocol for logging events over a network to a centralized log collector; the default port and protocol is 514/UDP.

vApp network   A network that connects VMs belonging to a vApp. The connection can be a direct connect to an external network or a connection through a routed network.

vCD-NI   vCloud Director – Network Isolation is a legacy segmentation technology deprecated in vCloud 5.1. vCD-NI segments traffic on a Layer 3 network by using a proprietary MAC-in-MAC encapsulation.

vCenter Proxy   The vCenter proxy service that issues all commands for the vCenter it is connected to at the time. This service rotates between vCloud cells as they are restarted. It is a recommendation that there is one cell per vCenter, plus an extra in the event of a cell outage or maintenance.

vCloud Connector Node   The worker of a vCloud Connector deployment. Content, deployment commands, and tasks are executed by the node servers.

vCloud Connector Server   The control server of a vCloud Connector deployment, all commands will originate through this server.

vCloud Director Cell   A vCloud Director cell is a part of the vCloud instance, containing the HTTP UI and the consoleproxy service.

vCloud events   A system-initiated operation. vCloud events and information related to the event are reported to vCloud Director and can be viewed on the Events tab. Events can generate alerts or maintain the system state—for example, purging deleted items or expiring items when a lease expires.

vCloud System ID   The installation ID of a vCloud installation, this must be unique in each datacenter. This value also affects the MAC address generated by vCloud Director for VMs.

vCloud task   A user-initiated operation. vCloud tasks and the status of those tasks are reported to vCloud Director and can be viewed on the Tasks tab.

VLAN backed   A vCloud Director network pool that uses a range of VLAN IDs for network segmentation.

vShield audit logs   A listing of auditable events in vShield, including user login, rules changes, and other events that a user initiates.

vShield Edge   A virtual appliance that offers many networking services such as DHCP, NAT, Firewall, Load Balancer, DNS Relay, VPN endpoint, and so on.

vShield events   An event that modifies or changes system settings for vShield Manger, vShield App, vShield Edge, or other vShield modules.

VXLAN   Virtual eXtensible local area network, a Layer 3 segmentation technology that allows multiple Layer 2 networks on a single Layer 3 network.

Web UI   The web interface that users access.

Index

A

access

direct console, restricting, 54

RBAC (role-based access control), 48

vCloud Connector UIs, 128

access control lists. *See* **ACLs**

accounts

Chargeback Manager (vCenter), 93

MyLearn, 307

VMware exams, registering, 306

ACLs (access control lists), vShield Manager, 31

actions, LDAP (Lightweight Directory Access Protocol), 72-74

Active Directory. *See* **AD**

activity log retention, configuring, 278

Activity Log setting (vCloud Director), 36

AD (Active Directory), 45, 64

Add Resources Wizard, 256

Add Subnet Wizard, 159

adding

catalog selections, 265

Edge gateways, 167

external networks, 156-161

LDAP (Lightweight Directory Access Protocol) users, 210

local users, 204

NFS mount to fstab, 17

port groups, 181

provider NDCs, 231

roles, 54

servers, 320

System Administrator role, 58

users to Chargeback Manager (vCenter), 102

addresses

DNAT (Destination Network Address Translation), 187, 191

IP (Internet Protocol)

pools, 169

selecting, 23

NAT (Network Address Translation), 163

public (vCloud Director), 39

SNAT (Source Network Address Translation), 187, 191

administration. *See also* **managing**

Chargeback Manager (vCenter), 83

privileges. *See* privileges

roles. *See* roles

VCAP-CIA (Cloud Infrastructure Administration), 7

Admission Control, 321

Advanced (vCloud Connector), 127

allocation

memory, 287

W

X

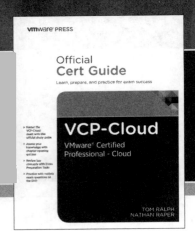